BELOVED
EXECUTIONER

Books by Kate Thomas

SIGNALS FROM ETERNITY Volume 1 of a Trilogy

Part 1 *Intimations*
Part 2 *Framework for Tuition*
Part 3 *Approach to the Teacher*

BELOVED EXECUTIONER Volume II

Part 1 *The Teacher*
     (Life in the midst of death)
Part 2 *The Test*
     (Death in the midst of life)
Appendix

A CHARTED DESTINY Volume III

Part 1 *Route of return*
Part 2 *Subterranean descent*
Part 3 *Gateway to Eternity*

BELOVED

EXECUTIONER

An account of training
for Seership

KATE THOMAS

 ROSEKING PUBLICATIONS

Cover: Jill Wood

Photoset in England by The Granta Press, Cambridge.

Published by ROSEKING PUBLICATIONS,

P.O. Box 13. CAMBRIDGE CB4 1EZ ENGLAND.

Printed and bound in Great Britain by
Redwood Burn Limited, Trowbridge, Wiltshire

CONTENTS

Acknowledgement

My grateful thanks to the students of the Cambridge Research Centre for Metaphysical & Evolutionary Studies who corrected the proofs of this book.

Author's Note

Readers may observe that each book in this autobiographical series is written in a different style. This was not intentional and is simply the result of reliving in retrospect events and experiences of long ago, and recounting them in accord with situations and viewpoints then current; plus the incorporation of existing notes from the appropriate period. For this reason the entire record has been separated into three sections, reflecting as adequately as possible the changes that occurred as the link between spirit and personality grew stronger.

K.W.T.

FOREWORD

Some readers of this book may object to the use of the word Master or the capitalised 'Teacher', equating it associatively with various cultish forms of devotionalism. But these terms are merely labels used to delineate certain functions, and in our present communication system we still need to use labels.

This whole issue has been sadly obscured by the outright misuse of such terms by those who have no real understanding of the structures behind them. There exists an entire hierarchy of highly developed beings of which most of us are completely unaware; the product of a universal training process quite outside our normal scope of comprehension. Our planet has its own 'growth' system, and the teaching frames used by genuine Teachers of the past — the priests and prophets of another age, mapped methods of individual development that culminated in states of enlightenment, later designated nirvana, liberation, God-realisation etc. — terms limited by the understanding of the taught.

Yet within each one of us lies the potential to overcome these limitations. The universal process is without limit, and beyond the developmental scheme applicable to the earth are others, which cannot usefully be described as they remain forever beyond our comprehension *as man*. Remember Jacob's ladder, and "In my Father's house are many mansions"? Man is an evolving organism — an unfinished product. The spark of spirit within him is sullied by unconsciousness, and his lifespan is often wasted through the errors that arise from unawareness.

Whatever dogmatic stance we may take, or belief structure we adhere to, does not alter the existent, orderly gradation of spiritual evolution; and the forerunners of all ages and all races who have developed the true seeing eye (the power of seership, or organ of perception) have tried to communicate to us this fact.

The side-effects of such evolutionary development take

i

many forms and invariably cause offence to those not currently involved. Elements of fanaticism are obviously undesirable, but equally offensive are the emotional blindnesses of devoteeism, the self-centred distortions of psychism, the pious rigidities of monasticism: plus the unbalancing effects of an excess of mystical visions, ecstatic raptures and other manifestations. But *they are only* effects, the *side-effects* of a partial spiritual growth, blurred and marred by the human personality that cannot, of its own nature and function, integrate and absorb the forces that play upon it; at least without time and proper training.

The human body is the crucible and essential ground of this process, along with its intellect and emotions. And when body, psyche and spirit are correctly aligned and freed from the conditioned distortions of an obstructive ego, we will have 'fire without smoke' — a state of perpetual inner consciousness of an inconceivably high order, cloaked in a normal human organism and capable of sustaining a normal everyday life, without displaying any side-effects whatever *unless so chosen* for specific teaching or demonstration purposes.

It is only *after* the completion of such training when, tried and tested in many traditional ways, a mandate to teach is given. These authorisations are *not* conveyed orally or on paper (though they can be substantiated in this way). Nor are they given in trance, or via an elevated spiritual experience in which one is told what to do. An authentic mandate signifies a spiritually ascertained ability, of the highest integrity and responsibility, and includes the *power to awaken,* lawfully, safely, and with specific evolutionary aims in view.

By what means can we therefore recognise such development — the true Teachers amongst us, *for only these* are capable of providing a properly adjusted training for mankind. If we use our own perception, our psychic sensing and seeing, we will perceive only according to our capacity, and may thus label as teachers those who are still struggling like ourselves. And these may in all sincerity accept such status, setting up Centres and enrolling students for legitimate and useful workshops and courses . . . or they may, conversely, chase the moonbeams of easy money, fame or egotism. Either way, they can only teach us elementary lessons, usually cautionary (needful, of course).

Discernment lies the other way round. The genuine Teacher is sent to dwell amongst us and share our lives (and there is always one, at any time, in any place, available to the *bona fide* aspirant, whom he may recognise or not, depending on his stage of development). He acts as leaven and quickens those in his radius — which can be large or small according to his hierarchical abilities . . . imparting where necessary the awareness of his identity by a direct stimulus accelerating previous growth. By a tempered use of that same stimulus, he affects more generally the mechanical processes of large numbers of our slumbering egos, and in this way, and *this way alone,* en masse and as individuals, we stir and waken.

This book is sent out to record one such awakening, and includes in detail some of the inevitable preliminary discords and miasmas — to further signal this process, and to firmly signpost this way.

This is the second book of a trilogy. In the first was described my early life, and the progressively developing spiritual experience that led to the bringing together of a group of similarly oriented people.

Apart from myself, aged thirtyfour when Book II begins, the record, with one exception, revolves around the same persons found in 'Signals from Eternity', principally:

Alison, now fortyone; forthright, intelligent, plump and comely; a Theosophist.

Rose, thirtyeight; intuitive, clever; slim and vivacious; a spiritualist medium.

Joan, thirtyfour; attractive, sympathetic, sincere, motherly. An Anglican.

Betty, fortyone; petite and plumpish; warm, aspirational, humourous. A spiritualist medium.

Lois, sixty; calm, friendly, studious — a spiritualist with Buddhist sympathies.

Margaret, fiftyone; loving, dedicated, ever helpful. A practising Christian.

Nell, seventy; alert, lively, argumentative, devotional. A lifelong Theosophist.

and our husbands, children, relations and friends.

Names and several placenames have been altered and some relevant incidents omitted, but the latter do not affect the main theme of this account.

My sincere apologies to those of the group whom I may unwillingly offend in presenting this material for publication, and heartfelt thanks to friends courageous enough to consent to making these facts available. They may thus in time add to the growing body of research data positing the existence of latent evolutionary possibilities in the human brain: their purpose and function, and the effects of meaningful activation.

Kate Thomas

To Inder Sain

In grateful tribute

How could the love between Thee and me sever?
As the leaf of the lotus abides on the water: so
Thou art my Lord, and I am Thy servant.
As the night-bird Chakor gazes all night at the
moon: so Thou art my Lord and I am Thy servant.
From the beginning until the ending of time, there
is love between Thee and me; and how shall such
love be extinguished?
Kabir says: 'As the river enters into the ocean, so
my heart touches Thee.'

*Poem 34. One Hundred Poems of Kabir. Translated by
Rabindranath Tagore. Macmillan & Co. Ltd.
London. 1961.*

PART I

THE TEACHER

Life in the midst of death

Before me as I write these words is the lengthy manuscript containing the record of my personal contact with Inder Sain and the Sufi Master, Meher Baba. It involved, in the main, immense suffering — in fact the script reads rather like a long dirge. It is meticulously detailed, and so painstakingly precise I fear no budget-conscious publisher would wish to consider it. I am therefore about to pare it drastically and insert comments in retrospect which will hopefully prove more enlightening than the original account; as in 1964 when it was written (concurrent with the latter events described) I had no real understanding of what this all-consuming episode in my life was for. That it was by design I could not doubt, but the awareness of a progressive and deliberate process of annihilation applied to one's own precious ego produces shock to the system and clouds the ability to comprehend — and to this process I was submitted, with neither promises, explanations or guarantees as to the outcome.

Prior to Baba's bodily death in 1969, he severed me seemingly irrevocably from the movement that bears his name, and in certain ways ensured my connection with the current Sufi Exemplar, Idries Shah, whose methods are somewhat different and more closely oriented to our Western psychology.

Throughout the event-packed years that followed, I remained in ignorance of the basic reason for the ultra-harsh treatment meted out to me — and only in March 1977 was revelation vouchsafed, and everything made clear.

There is little I can do now to alter the overtly emotional nature and the Indian devotee 'flavour' with which the following material is coloured, for this is how it really was — the way the Teacher presented myself and others with what he wished us to learn.

It should also be remembered that the things Inder said and

1

did were likewise, of necessity, shaped by our ignorance and by the lack of preparation dictated by our culture. With myself, for instance, who saw his instrumentality and function with consistent clarity, he was yet obliged to use the terminology, however unsuitable, with which I was familiar; and to feed me with the minute portions of truth that were all I could then take without dislodging disastrously my mundane consciousness of daily life. To outside observers this appeared the extent of his ability and he was judged accordingly — but he Knew. His knowledge was the Totality of the Perfected man, and by the radiation of his spirit were we all quickened and compelled to grow.

As I look back on the humility, and humiliation, of his work with us, I am aware now, in part, of what it must have brought him in terms of suffering. For when we come into the presence of the truly great, we do not see them as they are — we are too small to encompass them. They stoop to our level, and conceal from us by the brilliantly simulated anger and severity, aloofness and displeasure required at certain stages of our training, the cost to themselves in rendering us suitable candidates for spiritual enlightenment.

Therefore Inder was not as I have depicted him, and should not be assessed by the rational mind through the way he was obliged to present himself. His attitudes and actions were tailored, in their entirety, to the limited capacities of those he worked with — to whom, in love and service (well-hidden) he gave of his substance.

To begin at the beginning:

September 1962

Feeling tired, bored, unhappy and utterly useless — on impulse one afternoon I telephoned Alison and asked her if there would be a meeting of the Theosophical Society that evening. She said yes, the long holiday recess was now over, in fact the group had met last Thursday while she was still away.

I had ventured to the Lodge for the concluding session of the term at the end of July — our own group having permanently disbanded the previous week — and had found it as disappointing as ever, save for one woman (a newcomer) who recounted a 'memory' from a former incarnation. This was of a house that was later confirmed as having existed, and its

2

authentic nature had caused quite a stir. I hoped she would be there again.

Without any real enthusiasm I went. The date was September 13th, and I had reached my lowest physical and spiritual ebb for a very long time. The elderly couple who were the backbone of the Society were already present, Alison also. She smiled as I entered and settled myself down, and commented that she must introduce me to the Indian gentleman who was likewise a visitor to the Lodge this evening. I noticed then a dark-haired young man sitting behind the still-open door. He was short, cheerful and smiling — giving a vague impression of all-over light brown, for his skin was fair for an Indian's, and his suit of a brownish material. He rose to his feet and beamed at me, proffering his outstretched hand — his beautiful brown eyes shining with amusement and friendliness. His name, he said, was Inder Sain, but please to call him Inder . . .

I re-seated myself, feeling rather disappointed not to see Mrs G., who apparently did not intend to be present. I had no inkling of the significance of the newly made introduction; or that in this inconspicuous manner I had kept an appointment with my destiny.

Nell Dunstan rolled her eyes at me as if he were a great trial, and I soon realised what she meant, for he began to talk and was obviously well-equipped to continue all night. But I did not find him a trial. On the contrary, my interest was immediately caught and sustained, for he spoke of the age-old relationship of pupil and Teaching Master, and all that this implied; and of the necessary establishment of trust and rapport between them that would enable the pupil to prepare for the more stringent shaping preceding certain specific experiences. As the evening passed I had the curious and repeated sensation that I knew him, indeed, had sat at his feet long, long ago, listening as I did now. When it was time to leave, he asked Alison and myself if we would be present next week, and we said yes, though I explained that I was not a member of the Theosophical Society and did not usually attend their meetings. I went home feeling unexpectedly and joyously happy.

Patrick said afterwards I was 'lit up' that evening, and told him I had met a remarkable man who really understood what he talked about. I have no recollection of this, but the strange night that followed I remember well. Inder's voice and presence permeated my sleep; it seemed he spoke to me for hours, and each time I awoke, which was often, I felt inexplicably that he was there.

The following morning I telephoned Alison just as she was about to phone me. We mutually agreed that the young man was quite out of the ordinary and had produced a profound effect on both of us. We also agreed we did not feel the contact mere chance.

The next Thursday he was again at the Lodge. This time more people were present, two of whom he had already met at the earlier meeting that neither Alison nor myself had been to. The atmosphere was congenial and he was invited to say more on the subject of spiritual development, so he talked of what he called God-realisation and the Path of Attainment. I remember him saying that in order to perceive God, one must 'unwind' oneself, becoming less and less rather than more and more; that instead of accumulating further knowledge, we had to relinquish the assumed knowledge we had acquired . . . our concepts of good and evil — opinions, prejudices, fragments of occult truths. Evil could be likened to a chain of iron, but 'good' was also a chain, albeit of gold; the seeker must ultimately transcend both good and evil, to find the Reality beyond.

He spoke of sanskaras, or impressions, which we accumulate from early life, or from life to life if we could accept the possibility of reincarnation — and which prompt our actions and motivate our thoughts. These sanskaras constitute the veil of self between the aspirant and God, and only one already Perfect (who has completed his or her own evolution) could finally wipe away their residue so that the soul might gain Realisation, or union.

Again he had the same extraordinary effect upon me. I listened enrapt to his words, and watched the light pulsating behind his features and about his head.* I did not then know who he was, but I did know he was a very special person. His radiation and innate authority stamped him indelibly with an indefinable quality. I had no doubt he was the Indian of whom

*Much of this account is written from an entirely subjective viewpoint, and many of the observations made are of a clairvoyant nature. A detailed description of the development of this faculty is given in 'Signals from Eternity'.

I had dreamed. Time and again on his face was imaged the reflection of another, and in this, and in the intonation of his voice, repeatedly I sensed the guiding influence I had termed 'Master'.

Once more Alison and I compared our reactions. We were greatly intrigued, and the inclination to believe he had been 'sent' to us was much consolidated. We speculated on the Teacher with whom he had apparently lived for some time in India. Alison said she had the queer feeling that the Teacher was following her everywhere she went.

At the third meeting Inder spoke of Christ; pure spirit incarnate in matter, made manifest on earth in the form of a man at certain periods of time for the benefit of all mankind. Did we really understand what this meant? Did we know what 'Christ', 'Master', 'Teacher' really signified? Something quivered within me and I felt myself become intensely alert. The subject, indeed, was nearest of all to my heart. Within the crowded room the very air we breathed seemed suddenly charged with the ancient Mysteries — the sacred gnosis of Egypt and India and Greece — the hidden teachings of Jesus ... Jesus, whom Inder said was one of the greatest manifestations of divinity the world has known, whose task was to impregnate the ethers with a blueprint; who exemplified and clearly demonstrated the entire Path of Discipleship from beginning to end ...

He then referred to his own Teacher, and the work he was engaged upon, and told us at last his name, Meher Baba, which until now he had not divulged.

When everyone dispersed he remained behind to talk with me at the gate. He said he did not normally speak openly as he had done this evening as most people in the West rejected utterly his definition of Christhood, and also the idea of the latent perfectability of human beings. As they could not detect either condition in the human form, they generally asserted it did not exist in a natural state, and he therefore rarely broached such matters.

I did not reject these statements. My past experience had convinced me that a level of existence far higher than our own watched over us, and I could readily conceive that to further this, such evolved ones could incarnate in physical bodies, as did Buddha, Jesus and Muhammed.

5

I passed on to Alison all Inder had said, and asked her how she felt about inviting him to a private meeting in one of our homes to talk to us more freely. It was becoming obvious that some of the Lodge members had lost interest and were increasingly aggrieved by the turn of events, and two had critically vouchsafed they thought Inder "talked too much" and dominated the meetings. This was hardly fair, however, as Alison and I had asked questions and urged him on, and he always stopped or withdrew at the least suggestion of another's desire to speak. He seemed to me the gentlest and most courteous of men.

Alison agreed a second meeting would be excellent idea and perhaps fairer to the Lodge as a whole; so we arranged to ask him alternate weeks to our homes, beginning with Alison's, as she was less likely to have trouble with Nigel, who was a sociable soul — than I with Patrick, who was not.

It is difficult to describe the gradual sense of illumination that occurred during this period. We were both deeply aware of it, and of the differing effects upon us according to our temperaments. It was like an awakening from sleep. Alison's experience was of calmness and peace, an imbuing of the whole world with radiance; mine was an intensification of feeling and awareness, a revivification of memory and an insurge of other-dimensional insight. We both perceived Inder's light, and accepted him as other than ourselves (although he always firmly stated he was simply a fellow-student). Eventually, we each recognised Meher Baba as a Teacher, or Master, from a very high level of spiritual evolution; but registration of this, as an inner event, came to us in different ways and at different times.

At the time of which I write, we listened to all things and neither accepted nor denied. It was as if we waited for something tangible and conclusive . . . yet there was no sense of hurry or desire. It was a blissful interlude, particularly for me. Nevertheless, the consciousness of swiftly moving events remained vividly in the background.

I decided to invite all the persons from our former group to the alternate meeting in my home, hoping they, too, might share in this acceleration of experience and potent release of energies. Therefore I wrote to Joan, Margaret, Lois, Betty, Rose and Mrs C. — inviting them along on October 8th to meet the young Indian who had made such an impact on my life and Alison's.

Rose replied to the effect that she would like to come but was otherwise engaged at present (this was our first contact since the episode at the Church). I extended the invitation to my mother, who, of course, declined as usual. She was not impressed by my comments on the Lodge meetings, and rejected immediately the possibility that Meher Baba could be a genuine Master. She said she would see what Mrs C. thought of it all. The others, including Mrs C., promptly said they would come.

On Thursday Inder brought some photographs to the Lodge, and a book, 'The Wayfarers' by William Donkin, concerning the Master's work among the masts (or God-mad) in India. We were both agog to see the photos, for they were our first intimation of Baba's appearance in the flesh. Alison told me afterwards her first reaction was "Oh no!" — which she quickly smothered, as other snaps revealed so different an individual it was hard to believe they were all of the same man.

Some interior perception had already prepared me for the initial shock of seeing the Master, for *shock* it must be if one has struggled long and hard to assimilate the concept of cosmic consciousness and all it implies. I was aware of an inner control of my possible reaction, a deliberate self-effort of restraint which thankfully proved needless, for at first sight I registered a positive response to him. Among the many photos, mostly swift snaps taken by devotees, were here and there gems of compassionate beauty — an expression, a smile, a gesture — all reflecting an inner completeness and a moving humility. For me they held a living quality, an essence of love that I learned later, to my sorrow, was perceived by very few.

That evening for the first time, Inder spoke to me *directly*, using my name. His remark was a simple insertion into the general conversation, doubtless unnoticed by anyone else, and concerning the book in his hand; but I felt he spoke to my very soul. There was a reverberation inside me, like the tuning of a hidden lyre. On other evenings Alison and I had consistently received the impression he spoke to us alone, despite the roomful of people — yet this was quite different. Previously it had been personally impersonal, but now it was impersonally *personal*. I sat in a curious state of stillness, utterly absorbed in his words, the numinous atmosphere in the room, and the living radiation of the man before me. Looking back in memory, the whole evening glowed with a golden radiance.

At its end, as we all prepared to depart, he threaded his way through the chairs towards me, and said quietly, "Nothing can prevent you from meeting him, Kate. You are ready *now,* and when you are ready, *he has to come . . . nothing* can stop it . . ."

No-one save me appeared to hear, and my heart quickened its beat as I murmured a completely inadequate response. I left for home in a strange and acutely sensitive 'lit-up' state.

The 8th approached, and I anticipated it with mingled hope and anxiety. Though firmly convinced that Inder was someone 'special', I knew of old the barriers that prejudice and orthodoxy can erect, and the sheer futility of casting oneself against them. When he arrived, a few minutes before we began to assemble, he looked so young (he was then twentyeight) and somehow defenceless, I had misgivings. Older people so often refuse to listen to the young, however truthful their words — and I realised, almost with surprise, that I desperately wanted them all to listen to Inder, and with open minds.

After a few minutes formality and apparent nervousness he began to speak as at the Lodge. Before long we were interrupted by two additional guests, a lively, attractive nurse known as 'Robin', and a young man named Peter, both from the T.S. Immediately afterwards the atmosphere became suddenly concentrated, and everyone listened in pindrop silence and with complete attention.

I was intermittently aware of the cross-currents in the room, and the individual reactions that lay beneath attentive attitudes. Betty was absorbed; Joan interested but non-committal; Margaret kind and tolerant as always, and anxious to set this young man at his ease — Alison contemplative — Mrs C. critical; Lois doubtful . . . They asked questions and received answers, and eventually the meeting was brought to a close. Inder told us that films were available, some made in India and others in the United States when Baba had visited a Centre there. It was arranged to show them the following Monday at Alison's house, and everyone present was invited.

As Mrs C. left, she said politely she would not come again as she felt quite sure that Meher Baba could not be *her* Master. The others were pleasant and kind, and Betty seemed almost in a dream. Joan was the only one who said she would like to hear more.

After the meeting, the nurse and Inder stayed on for a while to talk. It was my first conversation with him of a personal nature, and for some unknown reason I told him of my long-ago dream of the Sword. He said, "You notice it was *because* you had the courage to grasp it that eventually you *saw*." And this, again, registered profoundly within me. I had the uncanny feeling he had known of it all the time.

Patrick was not pleased that two young men had been present, and made it very clear he did not like so many visitors to the house. I tried to persuade him to be introduced, particularly to Inder, but he refused, and a cloud passed over my happiness.

On Monday I braved the elements and Patrick's annoyance and set out for Alison's. As I neared her home, Inder drew up beside me on his autocycle and walked the rest of the way with me. We stood talking outside the house for several minutes, and I realised all of a sudden what a charming man he was. Until then, the fact that he was masculine had not made any impact upon me, for whenever I had seen him, the direct perception of his radiation had dazzled my consciousness. Looking now into his face, I thought no human being could ever be more beautiful. He seemed to be formed of pulsating and luminous gold.

Alison's house was warm and welcoming, and Inder bewilderingly attentive. He treated me that evening, for a little while, as if I was someone of significance and very dear to him. It must have been equally disconcerting for Alison, with whom he had so far had more contact; but very soon Joan arrived and normality was again restored. The evening was spent mainly in dealing with her questions and a more general discussion on Creation and God. The previous week he had spoken of karma and reincarnation, and had also told us something of his earlier life with the Master. We learned that Meher Baba had observed silence since 1925, though this prodigious feat had not prevented him from leading a very active and *communicative* life. I had hoped all day that he would continue on these lines, not yet apprehending that he invariably centred each meeting around any newcomer (it was Joan's first attendance) and whatever queries they might raise. For some unremembered reason the films were deferred till the following week.

Patrick was not at all cooperative about the new arrangement. Until now, Lodge meetings had closed at nine, and I had been home by nine-twenty, which still left him time to go out. Now I asked to stay until nine-thirty, and with two buses to catch would not be home before ten. Reluctantly he agreed to stay in with our children, aged nine and eleven; choosing to ignore on principle that this was my sole incursion into night-life. His attitude evoked a warning signal in my mind. It was already insidiously apparent that there was trouble ahead.

The following Thursday Inder said something to me which seemed rather odd. He had previously told us, as a group, that the coming weeks held great potential for us, and in the future we should look back upon them as the most important in our lives . . . for they marked a new beginning; an opportunity that was the privilege of a few. There was to be a meeting of spiritual and universal consequence, in India, early in November, and he hoped we would all remain in contact at least until then . . . Afterwards, it was possible that those who wished to know more . . . would meet the Master.

In view of these statements and his personal kindness and attention, it was puzzling when he turned to me under cover of the general conversation and, lowering his voice, said with great seriousness — "Soon . . . *it will grow cold, Kate — very cold.* You will *think* I have changed . . . but *it will all be . . . in your imagination. Everything* will get harder . . . *very much harder —*" It was not possible, then, for him to say more — for this was apparently for my ears alone. Perhaps he would not, even had it been convenient, for I could have no comprehension of his meaning, only the lasting memory of his words.

I was still dreaming vividly and in such profusion, it was more than usually difficult to sort out what was seen and retain it in my mind. Almost nightly I would waken with the sensation that I was with Inder, as if he had just that moment faded from my sight; and often I heard his voice quite plainly as he finished speaking to me. Everything was intensified — mental activity, hearing, heart action, observation, etc. Some stimulus was potently received and registered, and it activated my whole being, body, mind and soul.

The foregoing rather lengthy excerpt simply established the commencement of a relationship, though the comment Inder made held the key to my imminent difficulties. What is imagination? In this context, it was in one sense the product of inference — in another, the apparent *meaning of a deliberately contrived series of situations impenetrable to the intellect. In both, what I* believed, *through appearances, was being said and done, was in opposition to what I knew inwardly and intuitively. The two were diametrically opposed, and the friction created between them made conscious a mode of perception formerly operative only in other-dimensional states, or dreams . . . as if two aspects of myself dwelt side by side in my brain and began to interact one with another. It was this interaction which produced the spiritual drama about to commence — without which there would be no story.*

A first move had already been made in Inder's singling out of myself for special attention, a factor which did not pass unnoted by others, particularly Alison and Patrick. Most registrations, of course, were subconscious, and many remained so — but some did not, and their upthrust into the light of awareness caused havoc. The move mentioned was pinpointed for Alison in the brief situation recorded, in which Inder held my hand and behaved almost like a suitor. These things I noted, *but without giving them weight or query, for they were in each instance immediately offset by some other episode, producing a confusion of impressions which each had to sift for himself.*

Now begins a further phase, a deepening of experience.

I arrived at Alison's on Monday to find great disorder; the room was disarranged, and a screen and cinematic projector were in process of installation. Inder was smoking and conversing genially with Alison, and after a few minutes Joan arrived, followed swiftly by Robina. He then talked to us for a little while, and told us we should all react one way or another to the films to be shown. They were "very poor films", taken by amateurs — but we would see the Master, and have a very good idea of his appearance. We waited expectantly. Alison's son, John, aged thirteen, helped Inder to operate the projector, and her daughter, Avril, eleven, joined us also.

We sat in a semi-circle before the screen, and the room was darkened. My stomach tensed, and I wondered if the others felt

11

as I did. I longed in my heart to be able to accept Baba visually. I knew if I could not, there would be a state of conflict in my mind, for a part of myself was already committed to him in a way I found difficult to formulate.

The films were in colour and four in number, lasting about fifteen minutes each. The first scenes brought me a swift sense of shock — I could see the living power in Baba's hands, and was momentarily afraid. I continued to watch with varying degrees of registration. It was as if a veil covered my awareness — he could so well be my conception of a Master, and yet . . . I was not sure.

The second film was run through, then the third. Suddenly it happened — some movement of his face, a captured essence permeating form — the way he walked, his gentle smile — all converged and drove a wedge deep into my heart. I saw the love and compassion that flowed through his body like light — and at that moment I *remembered* . . . fleetingly, through a veil darkly . . . My soul stirred yearningly within me. In my depths I knew him . . . His familiarity pierced me with forgotten joy and anguish . . . I *knew* him . . . I *knew Him!* The recognition resounded throughout my innermost self. I cannot describe how I knew, but I *knew* to the very core of me. Tears streamed down my face, unperceived in the darkness. Silently I wiped them away, and again they came.

Inder sat well behind us all, but I felt his eyes were upon me. An unknown grief welled within me which I did not understand — not a sorrow, not a sadness . . . an old grief, a tearing of the heart.

At length the films were over and a move was made to put on the lights. It had not been primarily an emotional experience, although description belies this — but an uprising from an interior fount.

I got up at once and walked quickly over to the fireplace, trying to conceal my tell-tale face. Inder rose immediately and followed me, as if, indeed, he had been watching all the time. He sat down beside me and said softly, "What did you think of the films, Kate?". I turned shamefacedly and caught the expression in his eyes; one that I had not seen before. I knew so much in that moment — who *he* was, who I was, and the nature of the tie that bound us; just for one moment, then gone. I could only say, "I *knew him* — I *knew* him. Inder, oh, Inder . . ." I bent my head and cried, and his arm was about my head, holding it in a strange way close to his breast, not in an embrace, but as a benediction. I was dimly aware that the others had left the room and remember asking why they had gone, as there was no need for this. Then Inder talked to me quietly for a few moments and I regained composure — the group returned, and our informal meeting was resumed. I have no recollection of his words to me.

Alison said afterwards that she, too, would have cried had not the children been present. She recognised Baba, just as I had done. But Joan's reaction was quite different. She told me privately there had been "too many women admirers" among the crowd surrounding him, which made her suspicious, also the way he patted and touched them. I had not noticed either of these things. It was most odd.

I telephoned Inder the next morning and apologised for my behaviour. He was calmly consoling, and said many people cried when they first met Baba and realised who he was. He enquired into my interior reactions and said I should phone him whenever I felt the need. I understood keenly that such a need was possible. My experience of the previous evening had produced an effect that at times was alarming. An intense, almost blinding light pervaded my head and gave place intermittently to a reaction of darkness and fear. I had bouts of inexplicable weeping for no apparent reason — the tears seemed to stem from a deep-rooted longing which I could not comprehend. These states alternated with periods of intense happiness or bliss. During the latter, I was very conscious of the *nearness* of both Baba and Inder.

The following day I telephoned again. The blackness had overwhelmed me during the night, and I had felt myself on the edge of a great abyss of nothingness into which I was much afraid I should fall. Inder told me little in a personal sense, but I felt much better after speaking to him — matters became clearer seemingly of their own accord.

I talked to Patrick concerning the films and again urged him to meet Inder. I thought this might set his mind at rest, for he would then see the type of man he was; myself still being foolish enough to imagine he looked as Godlike to others as he did to me. Nor did I realise at the time how emotionally absorbed I had become. My tears were shed in solitude and

13

their traces removed — but the bliss I did not try to hide, for it was joyous and I was happy, and this reflected in our home and was shared by my children. Patrick reacted against it, however, for it was not akin to "ordinary" happiness, and neither centred on himself, nor was dependent on his behaviour. He regarded it as foreign and undesirable, having also discerned it did not bring me any nearer to becoming the 'real' woman he wanted.

Eventually after much persuasion he conceded that Inder might visit us on Wednesday evening — he would then permit himself to be introduced. Inder agreed to come, reiterating I must be sure my husband did not object. At that moment Patrick gave every evidence that he did not, and we remained on good terms until our guest entered the house, whereon his mood suddenly changed, and he refused to leave the sitting-room to greet him.

Full of misgivings, I led Inder into the smaller room where our group meetings had been held, apologising apprehensively for Patrick's surliness. He stood hesitantly by the door as if to leave at once, so I asked him earnestly to stay. Judging by Patrick's present attitude he was going to be angry with me anyway, so I might as well take the opportunity now presented to speak with Inder alone. I found myself telling him about the School, and how I had closed the groups while still continuing the course work with the remaining postal students, feeling strongly that in the present circumstance I ought to conclude the whole thing.

He listened gravely, then made some remarks about the ego and how he hoped for better things for me than the postal school. Despite his youth he seemed so old and wise . . . so kind, yet at the same time, stern. Through my mind passed recollections of my own inadequacies — how tentative my efforts had been, how limited my knowledge. I remembered Phillip, yet said nothing. I had the curious feeling that Inder could read my heart and saw all that lay there — my ignorance . . . my stupidity . . . my somehow preposterous assumption that I could teach.

At length he spoke of Baba. I must have made a well-intentioned comment with some element of facetiousness, for he looked at me gently and said, "He is the *Lord of all the world*, Kate," and it entered my heart as a mild rebuke, and moved it

14

deeply in the strange way his words so often did.

Time passed rapidly, and Patrick, who had gone out at eight-thirty, was home in seemingly no time at all. I went into the kitchen to make tea for him and endeavoured cheerfully to put him at his ease, but he was withdrawn and disgruntled and still refused to meet our visitor. After a few minutes I heard him stamp off sulkily to bed. My heart sank, and I murmered to Inder to the effect that he had better go now. He did not appear to notice my embarrassment. Beaming and relaxed, he took ages to drink his coffee, talking amiably all the time as if entirely unaware of the violent waves of hostility permeating the atmosphere. These were so strong my legs began to tremble uncontrollably, yet Inder recounted humourous anecdotes, chuckled heartily, and was more animated than I had previously known him.

The clock hand crawled round half an hour to eleven-thirty, and he was just rising to depart when Patrick shouted angrily over the bannisters, "Kate!", and my stomach turned over. Still Inder lingered, buttoning his coat as if nothing had happened. Another furious "Kate!" came from the region of the stairs, and I hustled him out, fearing my enraged husband would throw him out if he came down.

Apprehensively I went to bed, and with good cause. Patrick was livid. He swore viciously about Inder — in *his* house, drinking *his* coffee, using *his* electric fire, talking to *his* wife. It was all so ridiculous, so totally uncalled for. I tried to pacify him, reassure him, finally point out to him that at thirty-four I was surely entitled on rare occasions to receive a guest — also that *he* had been willing for him to come.

But such reasoning was absolutely useless. After more recriminations he thundered downstairs and slammed the sittingroom door so forcefully the whole house trembled, and I lay waiting anxiously for the children to waken, which mercifully they did not. In a little while I felt I ought to go down to comfort him as he was obviously not himself, but he would not let me in. He held his weight to the door, and all my tears and entreaties were to no avail. I was suddenly very cold and very frightened.

At long last he allowed me to enter; he was not going to come back to bed but would sleep downstairs, etc. Eventually I returned to bed myself as I was shivering, to get up again soon

15

afterwards and continue my pleading. By this time I was thoroughly alarmed by his behaviour, and perhaps he was, too, for he suddenly gave in and went back to bed.

I lay awake for a long time that ominous night, trying desperately to understand his extreme violence and mental agitation. I did not recognise then, that his submerged intuition was signalling just as powerfully as my own. Like fading sunbeams the last shreds of my happiness dissolved and melted away. A faint semblance returned, on and off, during the next few days, but such moments were soon to leave me utterly for many, many weary months.

The following morning I informed Inder by phone of what had happened. I was still feeling extremely upset. He was kind and understanding, and told me to think of Baba and have trust in him. That evening I arrived at the Lodge some minutes earlier than usual, to find him already waiting for me outside.

The scent of crushed leaves underfoot rose like a fragrance as I walked towards him, remaining an integral part of my recollection. He greeted me gravely, his eyes sad and concerned; his manner restrained yet sympathetic. In the light of the streetlamp his skin shone palely ethereal, curiously alive. He seemed lit from within by an effulgence . . . My awareness quickened and a memory uprose, brushing the surface of my mind with anguished urgency. Who was he? *What* was he? . . . I could not remember.

He was aware of my disturbance and began to talk to me reassuringly, asking if anything else had upset me that I would like to speak of — perhaps something I had not felt I could mention before? His expression was calm and kind, almost tender. He said there was no need to be frightened.

But I *was* frightened, for increasingly my inner faculties reflected a pending disorder and change. The tremendous interior upheaval was bringing something formerly wholly concealed to the forefront of my consciousness, something even more agonisingly fraught with pain than my experience with Phillip. And he knew . . . dimly, as from a far-off place, I knew he understood. I heard his voice quietly speaking to me — "Don't be afraid, Kate . . . you may find thoughts rising within you . . . and feelings too . . . perhaps connected with *me,* which can disturb or frighten you . . . But they are not of your own making . . . you have not *just now* created them . . . They are *old*

16

sanskaras, * from former lives. We all have so many links with the past, some closer than others, some much more *Real.* The old loves are still there, and Real love *is never lost.*"

I stared at him, my heart doubtless in my eyes. His own eyes seemed misted with tears. Haltingly, I tried to express the confusion inside me, the terrifying depth of pain and emotion repeatedly perceived. The words would not come correctly, they stumbled and faltered — the cleavage between my mundane self and such powerful insights too great to bridge verbally and coherently. He led me gently, sentence by sentence — turning my perceptivity unobtrusively inward to what lay beneath the tumult. His voice came softly, "Don't be afraid, Kate. You are *perfectly safe.* Baba will look after you. There's no need to be afraid." The love in his voice was tangible, but held nothing of the man.

I was so close then to *remembering.* It was just a wisp away; the merest veil held recollection from me. To *know,* yet not know, was both bliss and conflict combined. I wanted to cry, but I knew there was more to say — that I could not evade the penetrating light he had cast into the dimmest recesses of my mind — that I must formulate *now* what my consciousness had dredged from its innermost source.

I told him I loved him . . . because of his light . . . The light drew me and held me and I was powerless to resist it. It linked with Baba . . . *was* Baba . . . and yet it was *him* too — in some strange way they were conjoined. Within my very soul I had found him . . . and the love I glimpsed there burned like a flameless fire — full-blown and vitally existent before my lesser self was made. There was thus no way I could *prevent* myself from loving him, and this unevadable foreknowledge made me terribly disturbed and afraid.

The words were not childlike, yet I spoke them like a child, and I felt like a child. It was a child's confession, not a woman's. But this is only a partial truth. It was the profession of a soul, as I later recognised, drawn out from the hidden depths of an existence long relinquished and forgotten. His words to me, as in all such moments, are lost. Compassionate and tender, they conveyed a total sense of understanding, and

---

* gross, subtle and mental deposits of accumulated experience.

evoked most vividly the awareness of the Master's actual Presence.

He lightly kissed me, and my stirring consciousness stabilised; my personality-self spontaneously reasserting. In the rapid fluctuation between levels, I existed momentarily on two simultaneously — that of soul to soul, and of lover to Beloved. Both swiftly passed, and I was again in mundane life, the world of form.

I cannot recall the gist of the meeting that evening. It centred on Nell and Edwin (the Dunston's) who were coming on Monday to see the films. I spent another dark night, and the next day wrestled with alternating light and darkness. I wrote to the three school students and explained that I was discontinuing the work, sending them each a parcel of books which I felt would most assist them. I tried also to read the books that Inder had left for me on his visit, but they filled me with such longing for I knew not what, that I wept repeatedly. I attempted to phone him and was told he was in London — so I wrote the first of many letters. He did not once reply to any of them, and seldom referred to their content or answered their questions, (I remember the first was about St. John) — but the mere act of writing relieved the tension in me, and sometimes in dreams he would explain what I had asked, and I would remember this clearly when I awoke.

On Monday morning I contacted him by telephone and told him of my interior cataclysm. He asked if I remembered my dreams of Saturday night which, oddly, I did not, although I knew I had felt most unhappy and distressed. He said I had been with him. He had experienced a "waking vision" concerning me which he would tell me of tonight, unless I could meet him beforehand. Was it possible this afternoon? I replied that I was free — the problem would be where to go. There was no public place in which I could safely be seen in his company, as Patrick simply would not understand. We considered Alison's, but Nigel was now complaining strongly about her current interests, so this, too, was abandoned. At length he suggested his lodgings.

I pondered this, knowing full well it would not have Patrick's approval, but as there was no doubt in my mind as to Inder's intentions and integrity, I decided to go. I had no suspicion of the storm that would later break about my head.

Nevertheless, I felt very nervous and apprehensive as I journeyed to Sedgwick Street. All my arguments would mean nothing to Patrick if he discovered I was meeting Inder alone; also I hated not telling him, particularly as it involved such a valued and aspirational relationship.

As I walked along the street I saw Inder coming to meet me. I felt rather surprised, having given the vaguest indication of the time of my arrival. He gazed at me in a strange way, and took my hand. I noticed his own hand trembled slightly and my inner anguish returned. We entered the room where he lived — a quite pleasant bedsittingroom, though nondescript and colourless save for a rose silk lampshade, his many books, a plaster cast of Baba's hand and several framed photographs. He motioned me to sit down, and took my coat; then he sat beside me. I observed he seemed to be gasping in a most peculiar way, scarcely audibly, as if overcome by some deep and inarticulate emotion. He was looking at me intently, and gently placed his arm about my shoulders. He said, a little shakily, "Tell me, Kate. *Tell me everything.*"

I started to cry, and the words gushed from me. It was as though he had unlocked my heart. I poured out all the things I had kept sealed away, the long years of struggle, endurance and heartache — all came out and were somehow absorbed in his commiseration. He held me tightly, his breath still coming in choked, short gasps. The flow of words faltered. I paused to look at him, wonderingly, His face was inexpressibly tender, his eyes intensely sympathetic and kind, his concern for me acutely real. I heard myself say to him, "Who *am* I, Inder — who *am* I?" and he softly answered, *"Who do you think you are?"* But I could only murmur, "I think — in some strange way . . . I belong *to you.*" His eyes blurred. He turned his face away and said, in a very low voice, "Yes, you belong to me. *You belong to me . . .*"

For one fearful moment doubt entered my mind. He held me so closely and was so obviously and profoundly moved, that I was bewildered. The queer, husky sound in his throat was perplexing. He said it was nothing, to ignore it, not to be afraid — but the thought had surfaced that I was alone in a bedsittingroom with a man I trusted, of whom I knew exceedingly little — and what an incredibly unwise position I had placed myself in. Then, just as swiftly, it was gone. There was no desire as such with Inder — or, if there was, it was utterly controlled. What moved him stemmed from some far deeper source, some knowledge of the past and of our soul-states that was hidden from me. I learned from this time onward the truth of all my former assumptions concerning him, for he was not as other men.

He told me then, that just as one had earthly relations, like brothers and sisters, one also had *spiritual* relations, and that our relationship was a spiritual one. He did not explain this, and gave me no chance to ask questions, continuing with one obscure statement after another which my mind found difficult to register. My inadequate recollection consists of his assertion that I had come on a long journey, *bound and blinded* and deliberately 'lost' in the world . . . Now he had 'found' me again, and would help me to waken from the long dream of life.

I did not know how to contain or comprehend his implications, and felt I was living in a lucid dream. Every few moments my consciousness made other-dimensional registrations, creating tenuous rifts in the web of shadows I had accepted as myself. There was a continuous sense of homecoming and a warm familiarity. He was so well-remembered, so *known,* so loved . . . Yet still my remembrance was through a haze. I saw with *his* reflected light. I *knew,* yet did not *know.*

He said I had come to him on Saturday night when my body lay asleep. He had taken me to Baba . . . the contact was "prearranged". They conveyed me to the boundary line of the planes — the perilous edge that demarcates the Great Abyss, the gulf between man and God. My faculties of perception were heavily veiled and my memory obscured. Unaware of both Baba and himself, I had moved away from them, to "cross *alone* the deep valley between high and beautiful mountains". He said he had asked if he might help me across — but Baba decreed I must do it unaided. Inder simplistically transposed his words — "If you disturb her now, she may *look down* and be frightened." He spoke as if to a little, loved child, concluding gently, "And you *crossed over . . . all by yourself.* "

I followed this visually in my imagination, and he would not elaborate further. I grasped he had given me an image, a glyph to dwell on, of deeply personal significance. Beyond this my intellect could not go.

20

All through our conversation I had intermittently cried, unable to stop myself. The tears rose spontaneously from a mingling of bliss and anguish that were rooted completely outside my comprehension, though I tried irrationally to relate them to my mundane life.

Perhaps to deflect my questions, or to stabilise my state, he told me how he, too, had wept . . . every night for four long years when he first came to England, crying himself to sleep "not for loneliness, or women, or anything like that — *but for God.*".

This information produced a sharply reactionary effect. I could not absorb it, and was shocked without knowing why. Confused, I uttered the first words that entered my head. They sounded flippant and glib. I said, "I suppose you never cry *now!*" and he replied at once, smoothly, as if the answer had been there before the question; "Not very often . . . though I *did* the other night, for several hours . . . *after I had seen you.*" He stopped abruptly, and when in amazement I queried this, said lightly, "Sometimes we cry for the things we must do to another that causes them suffering . . ." and I was even more bewildered, for he had brought me joy.

At this juncture he moved away from me and his air of seriousness lifted. The sense of intimacy at once dissolved. Reverting now to his usual demeanor, he smilingly leaned forward and pulled down a strand of my upswept hair, forming it carefully into a circle on my cheek and holding it there with a finger whilst he regarded me enigmatically. I asked what he was doing. He grimaced engagingly, considering me thoughtfully for a moment before he replied, "Trying to make you look a Princess!" Then he casually lit a cigarette and laughingly dismissed it.

There were some papers lying beside the typewriter on the table, and as I put on my coat to leave, he remarked airily that he had prepared them for this evening's meeting. Did I think Alison would mind if they were read? I said I was sure she would not, and gazed at the uppermost sheet with curiosity. It was a poem by Kabir, whom Inder referred to as a Perfect Master. I commented, heaven knows why, that I had the odd feeling I should one day read something written by myself in a former life, and recognise it. This was so inappropriate in view of the poem, indeed, lamentably egotistical, and I immediately

21

wished I had not said it. Inder smiled genially and made no reply, and within minutes I was on my way home.

The following morning Patrick sat bolt upright in bed as he awoke, and uttered, "Princess Kate!" loudly and clearly. When I asked what on earth he was talking about, he looked rather dazed and asserted steadfastly that he had said nothing at all.

The previous evening we had once more gathered at Alison's house. It had been decided to show all the films there as the lounge was much larger and more suitable for the purpose than the room in my own home, and I felt also that Patrick's uncertainty of temper was best not ignored. Nell and Edwin were present and Edwin immediately took over the projector, which left Inder free for once. I think Joan was there too, but cannot be sure.

Before running the films, Inder produced his papers and gravely handed them to me to read aloud. Having expected Alison to receive this request, I was unprepared and immediately nervous. Glancing hastily at the sheet before me, I saw at once that its content was quite new to us, and recorded certain information given by Baba on God-realisation (or Union with God). I forgot my apprehension and read it through fluently and with appreciation; then I turned to the second sheet, which Inder explained was the translation of an aspirational poem by Mira, an Indian ecstatic. I reproduce it here.

'Dearest, come and reveal yourself to me.
Life is unbearable in your absence.
Without you, my love, I am like a lotus without water,
And a night without a moon.
I wander day and night in anxious suspense, and the fire
Of separation is corroding me away.
The day finds me without hunger, and the night without sleep.
My lips are silent, yes, indeed, I cannot utter a single word.
Come and meet me and cool this fire.
You who see into the heart of things,
Why pain me any more?
Oh my husband dear, come for pity's sake, oh come.
Mira, your servant for ages and ages,
is at your feet.'

While reading this I had the most curious sensation. I cannot describe it, but something captured in the wording, or perhaps in the essence underlying the original, was acutely familiar; so disturbingly so that I paused at the end, staring dumbly at the paper in my hand for several seconds before passing on to Kabir. Although I did not look up, I was aware that Inder's eyes were continually upon me. He interjected, quite needlessly I thought, that the poem was not addressed by a woman to her lover, but by the soul to Christ,* and referred, in fact, to a profoundly mystical experience. I would like to have asked about this, but was requested to proceed with the third paper, the poem by Kabir, and it was not mentioned again.

Nell and Edwin enjoyed the films. They did not criticise, and Nell thought Baba "beautiful". She was much more matter-of-fact than Alison or myself, slower in her reactions; genuine and sincere. Her contact with Inder had in some way softened her, taken off the 'sharp edges' and curbed her somewhat unruly tongue.

Later in the evening, Inder discussed our varying experiences of the past week. Alison, too, had suffered a crisis and had felt depressed, but tonight we both were feeling better. I cannot remember Inder's explanation of these states sufficiently well to quote, though he did say, in reference to the films, that Baba, being "perfect and egoless" was like a mirror and would reflect the ego or soul-state of whoever approached him — thus we would see him "in our own image", and only we as individuals knew the type of registrations we had made.

This was difficult to grasp, more so than was readily apparent, and maybe we all deluded ourselves that we understood it at the time; but I am quite sure, looking back, that none of us did.

I spent that night in a daze. There was so much to think about, so much to remember and assimilate. The light in my head was overpowering, more so than I had ever known it to be before, and I had no idea how to cope with the way my life was moving. Baba was the only Reality, and centred in Baba was Inder — I could not dissociate them. I prayed perpetually, imploring guidance; for the fount of love that had sprung so

*In this instance, probably Krishna.

23

vitally to life in my heart overflowed at times and created fear in my personality. I sensed that its depth had not yet been plumbed by any means, and did not see how my daily existence could contain it without grief to both Patrick, and myself.

On Wednesday, October 31st, I experienced a sudden change in consciousness that was to affect my future course beyond all conjecture. While working in the kitchen at my usual tasks, I entered a condition of contemplative absorption, and felt myself inwardly raised up and wrapped in light. In the centre of the light was Baba, whom I registered as a Celestial Being — so close to me that He was tangible. As my spirit soared seemingly upwards, there was a rising sensation along my spine, and my awareness increased a thousandfold. I became identified with His substance . . . I was no longer 'Kate' but Baba . . . I in Him, and He in me. Exaltation poured through my soul — the joy was intense — I existed solely to praise and to adore Him . . . and the impulse of itself produced wave upon wave of ecstatic bliss. During this experience I knew, as a fact, that in Him we live and move, and have our being.

The rapture passed, and consciously and deliberately I dedicated my life to Him, knowing now beyond doubt who He was — and accepting Him fully and completely as an embodiment of Pure Spirit, a Christed One . . . and my Master.

A few nights later came a dream which set my mind in an unbreakable pattern. Baba hung me upon a cross that stretched between heaven and earth. He swung it slowly into motion, like a pendulum, and I knew I must remain there, suspended in space, until the motion was stilled and its balance was found. Inder stood at my feet as if protecting me, then both he and Baba raised me upwards . . . and upwards — until we no longer had form, and Baba was God Unmanifest. Just as form merged into formlessness and the dream dissolved, Baba spoke to me — not with words, but a profound and concentrated silence within my innermost essence. The soundless sound crystallised and became speech, which, still soundless, penetrated my brain. He said, "Inder is Joseph* *and* Baba. If you hold on, you will know *Everything*."

---

* the Teacher who made himself known to me in 1957. (See 'Signals from Eternity'.)

There are several incidents amongst the foregoing that leave me open to the worst kind of misunderstanding, yet they ought not to be omitted. My state at this time was primarily metaphysical, far more so than I then realised, and my inner vision was open and daily intensified. This enabled me to integrate a level of spiritual existence not registered before; one not merely perceived, but experienced.

These powerful insights were more real to me than mundane life, and I managed surprisingly well to hold them in balance and thus maintain my everyday normality. Inder accentuated the changes taking place by frequently drawing attention to these matters in the presence of others, initially Alison and Joan, and later, Rose and several more — evoking unspoken and possibly unconscious reactions which I eventually saw for myself, and which were obviously apparent to Inder. This treatment threw into sharp relief the unpolished gaucheness of my personality, and provided a fruitful source for reflex criticism in the future.

From this time onwards we were all thrust into a sequence of psychologically orientated events, and these gave considerable scope for all manner of deductions about ourselves and also each other.

It is clear to me now that Inder's work on myself was designed to bring into the field of consciousness the spiritual stratum registered. It is likewise beyond dispute that growth was initiated in each one of us, either via suggestion (which activated impressions latent in the ego) or by directed attention that brought the outer self into alignment with the inner. Some evidence of this emerged almost immediately.

Not least was the factor of radiation, impartially available to all who are in contact with a genuine Teacher, and absorbed according to one's capacity. It was this that affected Patrick so potently, quickening his inherent tendencies despite his unwillingness to participate, and it applied to others equally.

The strange 'throat-clearing', so easy to misconstrue, had a significance then entirely lost on me; for Baba Himself removed a blockage from my throat chakra many years later*, and Inder's preliminary activities (referred to again in the next few pages) were linked with this.

---

* described in Vol.III 'A Charted Destiny'.

The cross perceived in the dream symbolised a coming concrete reality, from which I was at last released in October 1976, fourteen years afterwards.

Have I the strength to wait?
What end have I to expect, that I should be patient?
Is my strength the strength of stone,
or is my flesh bronze?
Oh how shall I find help within myself?
The power to aid myself is put out of my reach.

Job 6. The New English Bible. (c) 1970
by permission of Oxford and Cambridge University Press
(author's italics. K. T.)*

It is exceedingly difficult from this point to chronicle time and events; things moved so swiftly in material, subtle and spiritual ways, and much that occurred is virtually impossible to describe save from a purely personal viewpoint. My own experience was quite different to Alison's, and again, completely different from Nell's or Joan's. Our links in common were the circumstances that encompassed us, but our interior, perceptive understanding and evaluation of these was vastly diverse.

During November, Alison and myself both oscillated quite rapidly between states of happiness and depression. The strangest thing about this was that our experiences were never co-existent in type — and it was as if we had been placed on opposite ends of a see-saw. Nigel now joined Patrick in strong protest against the meetings and our 'fanaticism' as they called it. Nigel had tantrums, was irritable and behaved childishly, but Patrick was violently aggressive and emotionally disturbed.

One Thursday, Nell and Edwin arrived at the Lodge in a ferment of suppressed excitement. They had both 'seen' Baba simultaneously — not clairvoyantly, but standing before them apparently in the flesh. From that time onwards both acknowledged him as their Master without further ado. Neither professed to understand the complexities that might confuse the more intellectual; they simply loved him wholeheartedly, and were happy and content. For Nell in particular, it marked the beginning of a gradual alteration in her normal characteristics. The rather hard and worldly facade she had worn for seventy years gently crumbled away, revealing the youthful, impulsive and affectionate nature that lay beneath it.

A little later Alison had a dream, or vision, which removed the last wispy veils of doubt from her mind. She saw Baba

29

reclining on a couch and radiating light like the sun. Kneeling at his feet, she felt an electrifying stimulus vibrate along her spine in what she described as "a very consummation of love". During this experience she said she knew ineradicably that he was a manifestation of Christ.

The day following my visit to Inder's lodgings, I mentioned the matter to Alison and suggested she might like to do the same, for until now she had not had the opportunity to speak privately with him. She at once set about arranging this, and in fact went the following Saturday. The result appeared to be a rather formal interview, though perhaps she did not recount it fully (I believe she did); either way, I did not pass on the things he had said to me nor mention the more personal factors, feeling deeply that these should not be spoken of.

Such weekday visits as my own had been, were rare, for he had to take time off from his employment for these purposes (he was a designer in electronics) and most of the private conversations recorded took place before meetings commenced, as frequently I managed to arrive first. There was nothing secretive in this, nor was it a special privilege, for Inder always stipulated the time he would be available at the Lodge, and it was up to us to make our way there as soon as we wished, or were able to.

Nevertheless I did go a second time to see him quite soon after the first occasion, and he was affable and friendly, with no trace of his former emotion. We talked of many things in a general sense, and his humour was so infectious and our conversation so natural that I began gradually to relax and slip back into my mundane, everyday personality — something I had not done before when in his company.

Suddenly, without any forewarning, he asked if I knew the level of my own development, and I was thrown at once into confusion. I gazed at him in silence, not really comprehending the essence of his question; nor did I have any idea of its answer.

His features had lapsed into seriousness, and his eyes were very earnest. "Don't you know, Kate, where you stand on the Path?"

Humbly I said no, I hadn't the faintest notion.

He placed both hands on my shoulders, compelling me to look directly at him. Then he said, very softly, "You are right at

30

the end, Kate . . . *right at the end.* You stand on the *furthermost* edge of the planes . . . facing the Abyss. And on the other side . . . lies *God-realisation!*"

I felt stunned, and stupidly empty of thought. If my surface self registered anything at all, it was disbelief; and when the capacity to think refunctioned, I wondered vaguely if he had presented me with some kind of test for the ego. Questions then began to formulate, but as always, although he seemed absolutely serious he would neither elucidate nor discuss what had been stated, and deftly changed the subject. Yet I noticed eventually that each time he touched this level of communication, his words activated and reinforced all else he had uttered in a similar vein, and afterwards their substance gradually infiltrated my consciousness. It was some while, however, before I realised he had made the same statement, in differing terminology, on three separate and dissimilar occasions.

One of the most remarkable things about Inder was that he could raise you metaphorically to heaven, and in a few minutes bring you solidly down to earth again with a subtle reminder of personal shortcomings; this presumably giving the ego no grounds for fresh growth. He now applied this technique — my first taste of it, and my quivering feelings temporarily crowded out even the recollection of what he had said before.

Having brought my senses to order again over tea and biscuits, I was about to leave when he proffered quietly, "If you are very careful — you can be *free,* Kate."

Once more the volcanic upheaval inside, and the sharp tensing of shock at his words. There was no hint of their significance, whether spiritual or otherwise; nor would he enlarge on them in response to my tentative enquiry, and instead sped me on my way in a most benign fashion. I became aware on this day that it was quite futile to ask him uninvited questions.

Some nights later, I awoke suddenly to find him bending over me, both hands placed palms downwards on my chest. At the instant I perceived him, some sort of voltage, like electricity, passed through his hands into my body, causing for several moments so much pain I cried out urgently, "Don't hurt me, Inder!" After a few seconds he disappeared.

This experience was absolutely clear and positive. I was awake and fully conscious, and saw him in a materialised body apparently as real and solid as his physical form. I *felt* the

31

pressure of his hands upon my chest, saw the pulsing light within them, and experienced its release into my flesh. It was very dark in the bedroom, but Inder's form was faintly luminous, and his colouring was as always — the only difference being that whereas normally in darkness one would hardly see another person — he appeared as clearly to my vision as if it were daylight. He wore his customary clothing — I even noticed the white shirt cuffs and the dark hairs on his wrists. Not having observed the latter before, I noted them when next I saw him, and they were just as I had seen. An equally strange factor was that although I had cried out, my voice produced no sound externally. It sounded *within* me, with crystal clarity, in the region of my heart.

I spoke of this incident to Inder, and asked if he had heard me. He replied, "Of course I did!" . . . but having acknowledged the experience, he was uninformative. I believed I understood the nature of it, and asked why he had increased my voltage. All he would say was, "I felt you needed it."

There was a quite specific effect. Almost immediately my awareness increased — not in a psychic sense, but in far more intangible ways. The non-visual 'seeing' became consciously clearer, and I was able also to register the thoughts and feelings of others without the use of any faculty save this strange attributeless one. I can only liken its action upon me to the burning away of a veil, and this in itself, ultimately led to a wider comprehension.

Another time, I saw clearly held before my eyes a series of charts and diagrams. These detailed the *impress* into matter of the prepared course of the New Age, and although understood, were not in a recognised language form. They were familiar, however, to that innermost essence that was the observer, and comprised a known communications system perceived intermittently in similar experiences. My recollection was of a compression of archetypes yet further reduced to symbols and signs . . . with the 'X' factor of instantaneous comprehension. Unfortunately the whole thing faded before I could grasp and retain it in my brain.

I knew that Inder had enabled me to see this data through the media of *his own* sight, perhaps by a process of permeation or identification. I cannot express this in any other way. He then deliberately removed the direct inference from my memory — like wiping chalk marks from a slate, and later questioned me closely as if checking that the erasure was complete.

During these brief weeks of intensive stimulation, he was very kind to me; kinder indeed than at any time since. Even so, I was always conscious that he held me at arm's length, and there was an inexplicable gulf between us not bridgable by ordinary means. I adored him utterly and was painfully aware of it; but my perception of his spiritual status and authority was ever-present and affected me accordingly. Yet I was completely unaware how nakedly I revealed my love, and did not know for some while that others observed it and critically misconstrued its source and motivation.

On some days, though friendly as always, Inder was quite unapproachable in a personal sense; but on others he became 'human' and accessible, drawing one into the warm intimacy and trust of the deepest friendship. On one such occasion I found the courage to ask what he had called me in the life in which I was closest to him. The question was unpremeditated, and rather a foolish one. I half-expected a rebuke.

He replied enigmatically, "What do you *think* you were called?"

I hesitated, not knowing at all what to say; a whirlpool of impressions suddenly swirled beneath my thoughts and rendered me speechless. He asked me again, and a ripple spiralled into my mind, demanding expression. On impulse I said, "Was I called Mira?" . . . He nodded.

"After the saint?"

He smiled and said nothing. I told him then that I had the odd feeling I had once called him Krishna, asking if that had been his name, and again he made no reply — so I requested that he tell me about Mira, my long-ago namesake.

His response was brief and non-committal. He seemed reluctant to speak of it, but said she had been a Princess who left the court and all her wealth to become a beggar, seeking God. A memory stirred . . . an image culled from sleep . . . a scene in a forest through which I had travelled barefoot. I dared not voice it, and asked instead how she had died. This, too, was ignored, and swiftly and charmingly he moved on to other things.

That night I dreamt he was with me in a vast room hung with rich silks; its furnishings ornately carved and opulent.

High above on the ceiling was sculpted my natal chart in delicate plasterwork, each planet represented by a glowing jewel. I noted that Neptune, a huge emerald, rose in the first house — not in the second as it rises now.* Inder made some comment on this, also on the Mars and Uranus conjunction on the Midheaven — neither of which I could recall on waking. He was sitting very close to me and held before my eyes two beautiful gold earrings, each set with a star and a pendant sickle moon. Smiling broadly he said, "Do you remember them? You used to wear them when you were a Princess! *When you were Mira . . .*"

The next time I saw him I mentioned the dream at the first opportunity; for it sometimes happened that when one had something to say, or conversely, when he did — animated conversations would arise all around him and thus make possible a brief space of absolute privacy. In this curious interval, which shortly came,† I asked if the information given me in the dream was true. He said firmly, "You are not supposed to know these things!" To which I replied, "Then why did you tell me in the dream?" and again I asked him, "Was I Mira?", feeling urgently the need to know, though I could not have explained why.

At length he murmured, scarcely audibly, "Yes"; and immediately Alison turned to him and our conversation was abruptly concluded. This confirmation, to my surprise, made no impact whatever; I registered it simply as information. But this was not, of course, his purpose in giving it. At that time, as I now realise, I understood nothing at all of his work with us.

Another night, when in a very light sleep, I was aware of Inder manipulating some chords (?) or making an adjustment to a point in the back of my throat. He was positioned behind me and I appeared to be in a sitting posture, at the same time conscious that my physical body lay supine and asleep. Apart from being within this finer body, I was also observing it, and saw a small, filmy web of greyish membrane which he was carefully clearing away. I heard him say insistently — "Tell me

* by Placidus.

† I once observed this happen while he spoke to Alison. I tried to overhear above the general din, without success, and this brought to my attention his conscious use of a specific technique.

about this trouble in your throat, Kate", and remember feeling suddenly uneasy.

I reported this experience at the earliest possible moment, for it vaguely worried me — asking earnestly what it meant. He smiled his most aggravating smile and said, "It means . . . you *have not been* quite frank with me!"

My heart lurched inside me and a deep psychological layer struggled and squirmed, but I managed to utter, "What do you mean?"

He looked intently into my eyes and said quietly, with disarming geniality — each word distinctly articulated, "I know *all about you,* Kate!" As he spoke, I apprehended with certitude the absolute truth of this — that every fault, every falsity, every grossness, every impurity I had thought, considered, imagined, uttered or performed in my entire life, *he knew.* The effect on me was shattering. I felt sick and unclean, and longed to flee from his sight.

I said uncomfortably, "I realised all things were known to you, though perhaps not in the drastic way I do now. Do I have to bring out all I didn't say before?"

He replied, "It is up to *you.* But I must warn you, everything that is not willingly yielded up to Baba, brought out and acknowledged, rises later to confront us when we least expect or wish it! I therefore advise you strongly to turn out everything you don't want before going further. This doesn't just apply to you, Kate, but to *everyone* in his contact."

I went home feeling incredibly wretched. Had I been less personally attached to him it would have been so much easier. To confess all my pitiful failings and weaknesses to one so dearly loved — whom I longed above all to think well of me, caused pain beyond measure; yet I knew it had to be done. The fact that he *knew already* was quite lost on my mundane self.

So I wrote to him — page upon page, recounting my life and where I thought I had erred. To the more worldly, the whole account would be laughable; only the prayerful seeker and struggling aspirant can have any understanding of my heartache. Most painful of all to describe was my pathetic 'love-affair' with Phillip* and its potent aftermath of unwanted desire

---

* non-adulterous. Described in detail in 'Signals from Eternity'.

35

— of which I was still inordinately ashamed. All the rigidities of my Puritanical upbringing assailed me remorselessly, and I gazed into myself with accusing and inquisitorial eyes. When it was finished I felt I could no more bear him to look at me. Alison and I were to meet him the following afternoon (a Saturday) and have tea in his room; but I knew I could not face him, and put a note at the end of my letter to this effect.

Early next morning Alison phoned. She said Inder had contacted her and asked her to give me a message; there was nothing, absolutely *nothing* in my letter to prevent my coming that afternoon — if I so wished, and my family circumstances permitted it. Strained and downcast I went, to be greeted at the door with a beaming face and an all-enveloping hug. I cried, as always, and he laughed at me, asserting cheerfully that there was no bad in me whatever I might think of myself.

I asked him when he had read my letter, and he replied, "Just now! I finished it as you came in!" So he hadn't read it when he telephoned Alison? No, but he was aware already of its content . . . His manner became serious and extremely kind. My tension eased, and I asked, rather nervously, if he had known about Phillip at the time I was in contact with him. He answered, "Yes. He is a *very good* man."

He also made other comments which I forgot virtually immediately, save in a most general sense. These related to "taking *sanskaras*",* a subject he mentioned repeatedly to me at different times, and which always glided through my mind in a dreamlike fashion, totally ungrasped. I tried to make rational links between these assertions and his obvious knowledge of my brief connection with Phillip, to no avail. All my questions yielded nothing. He smiled inscrutably and would say no more, and within minutes Alison arrived.

I did not comprehend to any depth that in the light sleep state referred to, he had cleared away from my throat centre the still-active impressions absorbed from Phillip, and that the entire incident was designed (at least as far as I was concerned) to draw my consciousness towards this point. It might be asked why he did not simply tell me if he wished me to know, but in this could

---

* the accumulated imprints of past experience.

lie the difference between information and knowledge; for one is remembered and the other experienced, thus making it one's own — and he was preparing me for imminent experience. This matter of the interchange or direct disposal of obstructive sanskaras was later reinforced by other incidents, and gave me an initial insight to the 'trial run' he afterwards set up in embryo. Without my realising it, he was awakening me to my future destiny and function, and many years passed before I knew the full measure of his work.

I told Alison of my act of confession and Inder's remarks concerning our need of it. For many days she refused to consider it for herself, but after a wretched period with Nigel she telephoned one morning and laughingly said, "I've at last capitulated, Kate! I sent it this morning!" She told me, days later, that her letter contained things she "wouldn't have told the Pope himself!" This very much surprised me. Looking at Alison's calm and happy face, I could not believe there had been anything adverse in her life to confess.

It was around this time that Joan withdrew from the Lodge meetings, perhaps because Ian, too, expressed derogatory views about Baba. Lois joined us twice and appeared to like Inder personally, but of Baba's status she was sceptical and unsure. Both she and Joan had noted the degree of deference given Inder by Alison and myself, and they considered that I, in particular, had "grown far too fond of him". So this left just two of us from the former group, and my past perception of Alison and I 'running parallel' thus externalised.

In semi-sleep I again had a strange experience. It seemed a square shutter was removed from the top of my head, leaving an aperture over which a fine film, like an ultra-delicate photo-negative, was placed. This was suddenly illuminated, and revealed geometrically — and simultaneously in symbol, a recurring archetypal 'event'. My brain translated this visually as a scene reminiscent of the Last Supper of Jesus, with an oblong wooden trestle set with many places. This was again shown in diagram or map form — each place being inscribed with a name, not in letters, but in root-sound and electrical* sign. The

* for want of a better descriptive word.

central place was for the Head of a governing body or Hierarchy — who could be designated a *Christ,* and the other places were, I knew, for recurring *types,* not necessarily recurring individuals. Suddenly I grasped my own 'sound' was among them, and perceived its sign, which I recognised — and immediately registered a whole host of facts that faded at once. I tried to retain them but, as happened so frequently, they were literally *withdrawn* from my brain consciousness.

This experience I eventually mentioned to Inder, who questioned me carefully about my recollection, asking where exactly I thought diagramatically my place had been, and what it all meant. I recounted the place, though the meaning had largely gone. He commented that what I had seen was existent throughout time, and the places were *functions* which were constantly fulfilled by relays of souls who afterwards "moved on". Strangely, after this conversation my memory of my 'place' disappeared, and I could not recall it at all.

On another occasion I saw a recurring pattern in my life which repeated itself in both large and small cycles, so that in unravelling the design of one minor cycle one would have, theoretically, the key to all future events on all possible levels. This too, was mentioned to Inder, who said my assumption could be correct. He suggested I try making it into a graph and to show it to him when completed. I eventually managed to do this, and to prove to my own satisfaction that the tiny inner 'cogs' or cycles were recurring correctly — when he confounded it by altering the sequence, or so I thought. For by the time I was ready to give him the graph, in June 1963 — he had changed in manner towards me so radically that it was no longer possible to discuss things pertaining to myself. It took me some years to discover that although I had drawn the graph accurately, the cycles had differing time spans — and some overlapped and intersected one another, without altering their rhythms, but modifying significantly their expression.

It can be seen by the foregoing that I swung about considerably between a higher form of consciousness and the ordinariness of my own personality, and when lost in the latter I had no real understanding of my own interior experience. These other-dimensional insights, so bewildering at the time, were given as forerunners — the precursors of a fully conscious, prolonged cosmic registration that occurred in 1977, and contained the quintessence of all the perceptions recorded throughout this account.

These glimpses were fed into my cerebral mechanism in small doses, in order to acclimatise it to much higher frequencies of vibration, and also to provide a framework of visual impressions which could later be used to anchor, stabilise, and project through the brain, fresh insights of even greater potency.

I think many persons touch cosmic levels, perhaps in meditation or other states, but are unable to imprint the experience sufficiently well on the memory processes to recall what has happened. They are left instead with the awareness of an inflow of bliss or a stupendous blaze of light. The purpose of the inner development which I have attempted to describe, is to make practical (and possible) the eventual retention of such experience in normal life, with a subsequent utilisation of the mechanism in activities that are generally non-apparent.

The prior necessity of a graded alignment and the gradual activation of the organism as a whole, can only be accomplished with the aid of a Teacher who has already perfected his own faculties. A series of text-book exercises cannot be made to produce the emotional 'steam' used as a crucible — to say nothing of further requirements; and Inder utilised the pending vortex of my disintegrating marriage, and the increasing stress of other relationships, to help create in me the required pitch of intensity. It is perhaps needless to say I did not see this at the time.

The next few pages detail the onset of the mystical 'dark night of the soul' elaborated so profoundly by St. John of the Cross.

Late in November I had a terrifying dream, so real I could hardly believe I had slept. I was struggling, struggling against an appalling weight of darkness; trying ceaselessly to lift myself towards the light which I dimly perceived beyond it, but I seemed shackled and weighted by another soul who pulled at me fiercely and possessively to draw me back. In my dream I did not recognise him, though I knew he was male and that his feet touched the earth. A little higher, in some subtle region, a woman clutched viciously at me and tried, too, to force me down into the choking dark.

I was petrified — more so of the woman than the man, despite the fact that his was by far the greater weight. After what seemed an age of agonised striving, everything blurred and became confused. Dimly I was aware that a Being, or Beings, came to me and released me from my bondage, cutting away the threads that linked me, first, to the woman, and then to the man. Swiftly a rescuer led me upwards, moving by levitation to a place that was safe. Beneath the ethereal form I recognised Inder, and he spoke to me reassuringly of the experience just passed through. When I awoke I felt shocked and desperately unhappy, wondering repeatedly what I had done to merit my chaining to such a fearful location and such violent people.

In the morning I telephoned Inder and told him of the dream, not being able to free myself from the lingering horror of its recollection. He said it was the reflection of a genuine experience, and not to be frightened, for Baba Himself had cut me away, he had but helped. Also . . . I was "not to blame" for my situation, and was "quite powerless" to extricate myself. The threads I had seen were objectified *sanskaras,* and when cut by Baba they vanished forever.

Puzzled, I asked if the man and woman were known to me in life. He replied, "Don't worry if you don't know who they are. It doesn't matter at all." His voice was gentle, and very kind. As I replaced the receiver something crystallised in my mind, and in a brief flash of illumination, I understood.

Patrick's antagonism steadily increased. He continued to upbraid me angrily after each meeting, and finally, at the end of November, forbade me to attend any more. This created havoc in me, and a state of tension difficult to endure. I tried to parry his ultimatum and by every means possible to heal the widening breach between us, but all I managed to do was to gain a little time in which to discern the major nature of the situation confronting me.

I had already found the greatest difficulty in getting out at all. Lois obligingly sat-in with the children for the first few evenings of the new groups, as the meetings had been extended timewise and it was now 10.15 before I arrived home. But I could not rely indefinitely on her cooperation in view of her increasing disapproval of my current trend of thought, and my mother's continued assertions on the subject for once found ready sympathy from Lois herself. I had paid for her services, and in order to do this had taken a temporary part-time job.

Later I tried having an *au pair* girl to live in and remain at home on group nights with the children — though there were still only two evenings each week on which I went out.

This easing of my predicament was of very brief duration. Within three weeks of the commencement of my new employment, David produced a severe attack of tonsillitis after months of robust health, and my absence during his illness confirmed my employer's doubt as to the reliability of married women. Patrick could not endure the Italian girl's inexperienced cooking, nor her 'foreign' presence in the house, and I was thus obliged to speedily dispense with her somewhat erratic services. My temporary position fulfilled its timespan and was not renewed, and the struggle against personal circumstance began all over again.

During the whole of this period (November to mid-December) I was acutely conscious of Baba. He seemed to be everywhere and in everything. His face was perpetually imaged in my mind, and his upsurging, all enveloping love pervaded my days. My understanding of this profound experience was small — much smaller than I then realised, but my intuitive feeling of his presence and compassion was very great. Yet always, inextricably, he was indissolubly linked with Inder, and I could not separate one positively from the other. I concluded that the only possible explanation was a quantitive one. Baba was my Master, my Teacher — of that I was certain. He was also Inder's — in the sense that Inder abided by his rulings; and Inder, indubitably, was my Teacher too. Baba was *Master of Masters* — the *Qutub or Christ* . . . yet . . . in some uncomprehended fashion — He and Inder were One.

December proved a dark, unhappy month. Although I saw Inder as before, two, or sometimes three times a week, my relations with Patrick were so strained and difficult that I lived with grief. Each day when alone, I dissolved into tears with the sheer misery of my situation, and the total impossibility of resolving it happily.

Patrick was still heavily dependent on me emotionally. He was accustomed to my fullest support in his business life, in the home, and in my wholehearted concern for his personal well-being — and now he quite obviously sensed a turning away. Yet I did not do this deliberately. I have repeatedly stressed that I loved him and wanted his happiness above all material things, but my inner life and its directive were not mine to control. In adhering to the spiritual path I stepped out of the niche carved for me by matrimonial subservience, a factor that Patrick found totally unacceptable. He was unwilling to change the rigid patterns of years and grant me, voluntarily, a modicum of freedom and self-initiative. Thus this precious assignation that could have brought great joy, instead brought sorrow and heartbreak through his fear, hostility and extreme possessiveness.

One morning as I awoke after dreaming vividly of Inder, I saw objectively a thickish cord, like an umbilical cord, linking my interior form to his own in much the manner of mother and child. I was aware simultaneously that my spiritual state, and every mundane condition likewise, was transmitted to him via this sensitive linkage — which registered at any given moment my level of being in its totality. Through the same channel some nutritive or organic substance was continually passed back to me. This perception clarified to some extent his function, and graphically bore out my increasingly conscious convictions.

Early in December I dreamt that he led me over mountainous terrain in thick fog to visit Baba. A mountaineer's rope was round his waist and I was firmly tied to the other end. Sometimes I saw him clearly just a little way ahead, but mostly he disappeared into the billowing mists, leaving me with only the rope to hold onto in a sea of whiteness. At last we came to a long, low building high on the mountainside, and here he deposited me outside a glass door through which Baba could be seen. About a dozen others waited, all men I think, yet I knew that Baba would see me next.

My mother's antipathy towards the groups was thinly veiled, waiting the inevitable spark to set it aflame. She cautioned me repeatedly regarding the "dark influence" around me and the fraudulent nature of "this man in India". I longed for her friendship and at least a glimmer of tolerant understanding, for our relationship was now a wafer thin veneer of conventional visits that barely concealed her damning rejection of all that I valued. She refused to listen to any proffered explanations, or to read as much as an excerpt from the books presented hopefully for her inspection — and shuddered when shown Baba's photograph. She felt, like Lois, that I had been led astray, and considered my persistent adherance to these controversial views a further proof of my delusion.

Because of my unsatisfactory situation and the pressures increasingly exerted by Patrick and my mother, Inder several times suggested I should write to Mani, Baba's sister, who dealt with some of his correspondence. This at first I declined to do, not liking to thrust myself forward with such personal problems, but Patrick now became so violently aggressive that I agreed in despair to write to Baba himself, for it was clearly apparent that either I must cease to attend the meetings — an unbearable thought to me — or my marriage would break down completely. Feeling grievously unhappy, I cried copiously over both my unwilling wounding of Patrick and the seemingly irreparable rift with my mother. I had little guessed the strength of my attachments, and my whole being suffered through the sheer intensity of emotional pain these links induced.

Conjoined with this was an overwhelming distress of another kind; an inner yearning that manifested as a burning, unquenchable and quite hopeless love for Inder, the nature of which was entirely non-physical . . . a factor that in no sense mitigated its reality. The pressures were thus interior and external.

In my letter I told Baba how I had cared for Patrick all these years, and had done my best to make him happy . . . and that now, in following what I believed to be His Will for me, I was undoing all that had been so painstakingly achieved. That Patrick was violently disturbed by my involvement, and my spiritual convictions about Himself infuriated him beyond reason. I mentioned, too, my unsought love for Inder, and my recognition that this might subconsciously have influenced my husband's behaviour. These matters covered eight pages, and I laid bare the whole situation, from all angles, with honesty.

Apprehensively I showed the letter to Inder before despatching it, anxiously watching his face as he scanned it — to gauge, if I could, his degree of approval or otherwise. He nodded encouragingly, and gently puffed a small and perfect smoke-ring that ascended like a miniature halo — a frequent habit of his. As he handed it back he said casually, "I suppose you realise, Kate, there is a distinct possibility Baba may stop you seeing me altogether."

My heart froze; but I knew His Will was the Law, and I could not over-ride it whatever it brought me. I was asking attention and help, and knew full well that I must prepare myself to accept whatever was given.

The morning after sending the letter, I dreamed I was running along a narrow pathway, so narrow in parts I had to use all my strength to thrust myself through. The sky overhead was dark and threatening, and two sickle moons hung low against the blackness. They both pulled with equal strength in opposite directions, but to break the magnetic ring that held them in place, each had to pass the other, and threatened a major eclipse. I watched the moons in terror; blood gushed from my heart and I felt its warmth against my dress. As I ran I cried bitterly. I wanted desperately to go home.

During the time I waited a reply, Inder was so buoyantly cheerful I could scarcely believe that Baba would deal with me severely — for I knew he was already aware of what was in store for me, and would surely not be cruel enough to so deceive me. At times he comforted me verbally and gave me hope that all would be happily resolved in the future — then, quite unexpectedly, he began to scourge me with his tongue, admonishing me for hidden faults, and advising me of the stern disciplinary obedience to come. I found this duality of inference and prognosis exceedingly disruptive, though it doubtless held in balance my psychological conditioning and the insurging prevision which threatened continuously to overthrow it — whilst he prepared me for events I could not otherwise have borne.

Just before waking one morning, I dreamt of Baba, and knew that my letter had been received and replied to. In the dream I sat in a very small room like a lift, and looking up, saw him standing in the doorway, his eyes intent upon me and holding an expression of infinite tenderness and love. As they met mine, I knew utterly to my depths that every minute detail about me was known to him; it was as though he looked through me, right into my soul. He entered the tiny room and sat beside me, taking my hands in his own. Tears came welling from my heart and flowed softly from my eyes as I absorbed the shining wonder of his beauty. Before me was Divinity made manifest, and I perceived within my spirit that he was *Christ*.

The words he spoke I cannot remember, they faded as I

awoke. But he explained what lay ahead, and also the reasons; and said I must *wait,* for prearranged purposes — and hold onto him in trust however hard the pathway — And in time . . . he would grant me the desires of my heart.

In Alison's lounge that evening, Inder told the assembled group, apparently with much pleasure, that Baba had definitely received my letter and plans were now set in motion for my future which *nothing* could alter or stand in the way of. He seemed exuberant, jubilant in fact, and my hopes rose despite my many misgivings. He then said that *everyone* whose name was placed before the Master *automatically* faced the last stretch 'home', and his or her earthly career was always *instantaneously and inevitably* marked out to the very end.

I was aware of some inconsistency here, a switch of emphasis that did not entirely ring true. I asked about traversing the planes, a subject he had touched upon several times with considerable emphasis on the trials and difficulties encountered by the genuine aspirant — and how this related to the liberation attained by so many who seemingly did not traverse them at all, having simply come into contact with Baba whilst still firmly anchored in the world. He replied that these souls were led "blindfold" through the planes so that they didn't get lost in the wonders they might see, as even these still lay in the domain of illusion. Their progress was thus very rapid.

I felt exceedingly puzzled. Why did Baba permit some to have consciousness of these states, and others not? His answer was that it depended on the nature of the work they were to do for him.

This left me with an enormous question mark. In his earlier statement I had registered a slight shift of levels halfway through; an ambiguity he had no intention of enlarging upon. I put forward other queries and he cleverly deflected them, pursuing more general lines of thought. Indeed, each time I broached this subject, which in those days was often, he adroitly side-stepped me and talked of something else.

As my personal life grew harder, Alison's eased in a striking manner. The onset was curiously deceptive, for Nigel joined us one Monday with the primary intent of wrecking the conversation, making Inder look a fool, and revealing to Alison how guillible she was. He commenced by confronting Inder with a barrage of critical comments obviously well thought out beforehand, which backfired in no uncertain fashion. With astonishing verbal dexterity and despite his limited command of the English language, Inder turned these statements back upon the projector, and in his good-humoured dissection of them, skilfully engaged his interest. The result being that instead of removing Alison from the group, Nigel joined us.

A pivotal point was doubtless his growing desire to know what moved her so profoundly, for since her 'vision' of Baba she had begun literally to glow with an inner happiness. She had always been a blamelessly obedient wife, and I think he recognised that her firm adherance to something in opposition to his own strongly expressed wishes, might well merit further investigation.

By February, to his own amazement, he had himself experienced an undeniable sense of Baba's Presence. This further convinced him of the realities behind Alison's convictions, and he secretly purchased for her a complete set of all the books available on Baba as a 'surprise'. She was not unnaturally quite overcome by this change of heart, and their marriage now blossomed as she had never dared hope for. As the weeks passed, others commented on her visible radiance and the aura of peace she carried, and it was this that eventually persuaded both Joan and Betty that Baba was truly "working for good".

Christmas came and went, and throughout the festive season Patrick subsided into a subdued state of displeasure and depression, but he ceased to be violent. For a short while the storm abated, and we had an uneasy peace. These five days of the holiday recess seemed to me an eternity, and were acted out like a charade. Each day I felt so ill with indrawn longing that I hardly knew how to bear it, and I thought if it continued I would die.

On December 28th, my letter from India arrived. It conveyed, quite simply, that I should have no thought of separation from my husband, and should live with him and try my best to love him; but to think of Baba *more and more*. Baba wanted me to know that *only love for God is Real*, and I should hold this thought at the back of all my activities.

In a few brief lines he confronted me with a paradox. All was to continue as before. My inner concentration was not to cease, rather to be intensified, and my daily life must at the same time

46

proceed as usual. Yet it was just *this* that produced conflict between Patrick and myself. He had not recognised its source and was still saying, it is this, or, it is that . . . Ultimately he, too, would realise it was my inner dedication alone that set us apart. That he was turned outwards, towards the world and the reality of life, and I was turned inwards, to the Reality of God.

The letter had a terrible and instantaneous effect. Inexplicably I felt that Baba had placed me in the palm of his hand and extinguished me. I was engulfed in darkness; sealed off at once from the throbbing flow of life. He had cast me out, abandoned me; and I did not know how to endure it. Helplessly I spun in the isolation of a Void, conscious of nothing save inner Silence and my own momentum. How I lived through that age-long day without displaying this to Patrick, who was still not at work, is quite incredible. Yet I behaved with complete normality; worked, cooked and shopped, and no-one guessed my nightmare state.

I telephoned Inder as soon as I got the opportunity. He was maddeningly cheerful and ignored my acute distress, remarking that oh! so Baba wished to liberate us both! meaning Patrick also. For some reason this statement crushed me utterly — perhaps because subconsciously I knew already what it involved. Throughout the three days following I lived in a black wilderness impossible to describe, and when I emerged it was to steady, unyielding darkness and grief.

Daily I cried myself empty, till my stomach felt raw and my mind numbed and exhausted. Nothing helped or comforted me. The darkness had eclipsed the light, and I was locked out — alone . . . in an empty no-mans-land between God and Creation. Words fail to convey this condition; it was ghastly. I realised later I had indeed been placed upon a cross, and now hung suspended in a timeless Vacuum.

My family were mercifully unaware of my distress. I wept in solitude and smiled when in company, wearing my face and body like an animated garment that insulated others from the harshness of my experience. My abstraction passed largely unnoticed even by Patrick, for early in January he slipped on the thick ice outside one evening and damaged a ligament in his arm. This caused much pain and kept him from his current job,* obliging him also to journey to and from hospital daily for

* he was a self-employed Builder.

treatment. He thus had miseries enough of his own without trying to analyse mine too deeply.

After Christmas Inder brought from London some photographs and films taken at the East/West gathering in India in November, and a recording of the arati played in Baba's presence. We first heard it in the Eachard Road sittingroom, with Nigel at his genial best. It was getting late and we were all rather sleepy from the built-up warmth of the blazing fire, for it was a bitterly cold night. Inder appeared to be dozing, his eyes were closed and his mouth gently relaxed. I looked at him as the last beautiful words were sung and saw his lips moving with them — the expression on his face unutterably poignant. There was an intense purity and devotion, and an ineffable *stainlessness* such as I had never before seen on a human countenance. I perceived his essential self for once without the cloak of his authority, and this gave him an air of vulnerability that pierced my heart — not the childlike vulnerability of man, but the pristine nakedness of the soul before God. It was the only time I ever saw him like this.

In January he became ill, at first with a chill which he neglected, soon followed by bronchitis that narrowly missed becoming pneumonia. At the worst stage of his illness I managed to get to him daily to prepare soup and a thermos and make sure he was alright, and Alison and Nigel called in the evenings to provide whatever he might need. At his insistence the meetings continued throughout his illness, and we met in his room.

During this period he was physically very weak and his chest gave much pain; but he made no complaint, and his passive acceptance of suffering was a lesson to us all. Once he was violently sick, and this did more to impress me with the normality of his humanity than anything else had done. Having been so conscious of his spiritual attributes, I frequently overlooked the fact that he suffered in the world in the same way we did.

Halfway through his illness, I dreamt he came to me. I knew my body was asleep, yet the dream was so real it was hard to grasp I was not awake. He drew me into his orbit, and a new world opened before me; a world filled with work, and joy, and a tender love.

In the strange dual-consciousness of such experiences, my

48

obtruding mundane self could not accept that this fulfilment was for me; there was a barrier in my mind . . . yet clearly I heard his voice against my ear — "*The time is fixed,* and *nothing can alter what is to be.*" Then followed sentences that registered profoundly in my being and faded immediately I awoke. He repeated all Baba had said to me of what would occur in the years ahead — making plain these things *must* happen *and must be courageously endured,* concluding with "*then,* and *only* then . . . you will come to me and share my work.*"

I lay between sleeping and waking trying futilely to retain his words, to bring back into focus the strangeness and impact of his impartation — aware that inwardly, on some rarified level, I *already knew.* It was impossible. No trace at all remained, and eventually I gave up and slipped into sleep again. In my dreams I sought him, wandering hither and thither like a wraith, crying his name in my heart with increasing desolation. But he had gone from me and I could not find him.

I awoke next morning with a weight inside me; a grey and clouded premonition of the future.

He took me into the wine-garden
and gave me loving glances.
He refreshed me with raisins, he revived me with apricots;
for I was faint with love.
His left arm was under my head, his right arm was round me.

Song of Songs 2. The New English Bible. (c) 1970
by permission of Oxford and Cambridge University Presses

All through January I struggled to make efforts, and obey Baba's instructions. Every day I wept, unable to stop myself, and my grief was searing and terrible. I wept for Patrick and his loneliness and despondency which was like an open wound in me, and I wept for Inder, because I loved him with a burning longing in my heart that grew steadily more intense, and caused a fiery reflex pain in the physical heart itself.

An obstacle to any possibility of renewed harmony with Patrick (or so I then believed) was my own lack of physical responsiveness, and by this I do not mean lack of affectionate expression. Never having had the same needs as he, this had already proved a sore point throughout our married life; yet I had never denied him in any way (nor did I now) and always treated him with much love and very real affection. Now, unhappily, my entire mechanism, both physiological and psychological, was in abeyance, and I could not make the required responses even if I wished. The love and affection remained, but to Patrick in his insecure emotional state, these were considered insufficient, and worthy of nothing save anger and resentment.

He would not accept that I wasn't being perverse, and as he could not understand my interior life, or even the fact that it existed — much less the effects of spiritual dereliction — I could not hope to make him happy. Thus Baba's instructions were a yoke of iron to me, and filled the future with vistas of emptiness.

Whichever way I turned I could not help myself. My life was focussed on Baba and its fulcrum was Inder; and much as I adored Inder and longed to be near him, the love of its own nature proved a purifying fire, and I did not once feel any physical passion in his presence. I can only describe my experience as an intense yearning to become *one* with him — *to be lost in his heart.* It was fundamentally, as he had said, a spiritual relationship; and coupled with the mystical path I was compelled to tread, it was impossible not to be drawn away from all physical things.

When Inder recovered his health again, our meetings were increased from two to three a week, with Nigel attending on Mondays and Saturdays. These now consisted of the four of us (though not for much longer) and took place at Eachard Road, the Thursday Lodge being left to Alison, Inder, myself, the Dunston's, two rather half-hearted Theosophists and various others who came from time to time.

The substance of the meetings differed greatly. Inder talked to us on anything and everything, but their essence lay in the *effect* they had on each one of us, and this had seemingly nothing to do with the actual talks. Our concentration on Baba, and proximity to Inder, produced a gradual interior transform-ation of which most of us were conscious, and which we could also witness taking place in each other. Alison radiated happiness and peace. Nell shone with cheerfulness and content. Edwin dropped his reserve and became friendly and talkative, generating a quiet tranquility. I can say very little of Edwin, for he was already eighty-two, and his health quietly and gently faded during the winter months, keeping him often from the groups.

Nigel alternated between enthusiasm and neurosis. His health was not good, though nothing really serious seemed amiss with him, and whatever his physical condition it was clearly underlaid by a deep and struggling aspiration. He dominated many of the meetings with his questions and the often boisterous assumption that it was all too simple; but he was inwardly overwhelmed and could not conceal it. There was a tenderness and sensitivity that sought release in him, and the veneer of the worldly and self-assured businessman crumpled and crumbled agonisingly at times.

Nevertheless they were all happy in their daily lives and felt close to Baba, assured of his love, and deeply blessed; and only myself experienced an almost continuous inner loneliness and heartache.

Since December my inner light had vanished completely, and I felt that the Master had rejected me for some basic lack I was too blind to see. After the powerful inflow of illuminative experience from September onwards, my condition of darkness was little short of unendurable. I could not equate it with the fluctuating states of the past, for this 'night' was the longest, darkest and most terrible of all, and gave no glimmering or foreshadowing of release in the forseeable future. Precognitively on occasion, brief intervals of light could be seen, to be swiftly surplanted by a yet more impenetrable dark.

Yet curiously, I could still 'see' Baba. His divinity flowered in those around me, and everywhere and in everyone I perceived the outworkings of his love and grace. While in myself I could find no trace of this . . . no light, no beauty; nothing at all. It seemed he loved the whole of Creation, but not me.

I spoke of this often to Inder, who treated it lightly. He said Baba had put me on "a fast train to God-realisation", and I should be grateful for the privilege of this kind of suffering.

In January I took my last service at the Spiritualist Church. The booking had been made many months ago — a tentative olive branch from the new committee; and though I had no wish to keep it, I felt that I ought to go. As this would be my 'swan song' I resolved to say a little of what was happening in my life, and hoped it would not be taken badly.

To my great surprise Rose was there. She said she had come on impulse, having heard I was speaker — and a strong impulse at that, as she should have been at work. This caused me to feel more nervous than ever, but I began to talk in the way I had planned, and the words to my relief came easily. Less than a dozen people were present and all listened attentively. Afterwards they talked of their own experiences, and there was an atmosphere of reverence and goodwill.

Before leaving, Rose called me aside and enquired how I was, and also expressed curiosity about Inder and our meetings, which she had heard of through friends of my mother. I could not with honesty say I was enjoying life, so I told her how much the new groups meant to us all, and how deeply we had each been affected by them. She listened intently, almost hungrily. I saw again the old Rose who had been such a friend, and in that moment I knew that she, too, would come to the feet of the Master.

She arrived the following Thursday, and each Thursday afterwards. Inder's approach to her was quite different to the mode he had used with Alison and myself. We discussed it together and noted with a certain awe his use of psychology. Rose also presented an entirely unsuspected facet of herself. She was feminine and worldly — subtly flirtatious — and Inder treated her with admiring respect and even with deference; then with much brotherly affection and laughter. Alison and I were temporarily quite disconcerted.

There was now a distinct change in his behaviour towards me. The insidious undercurrent producing self-analysis greatly intensified. He would permit me comfort for a brief hour, then plunge me again into the most agonising emotional turmoil with a few sharp words of criticism, or the most unjust accusations concerning my inner motivation.

This mental torture was not applied to anyone else, save in the mildest and most inoffensive manner, but to me his words were barbed and crucifying. He rent my psychology apart and placed it under the magnifying scrutiny of suggestion and inference, both publicly, or when a few minutes alone before meetings commenced.

Alongside this change in treatment, my marital situation worsened alarmingly, and despite my efforts Patrick spoke repeatedly of separation. He made insistent demands with which I was entirely unable to comply, and unless I 'changed' he would, he asserted, consider our marriage at an end. This being expressly against Baba's wishes — as he well knew, I grew daily more distressed.

In view of this, Inder suggested I write to Baba once more. But Baba was now in seclusion and all correspondence suspended, so I did not feel I could intrude my personal affairs on his privacy. With Patrick's increasing adamance, however, I grew frantic — and at length wrote in sheer desperation, showing the letter once more to Inder before posting it. He encouraged me to send it, pointing out at the same time that certain wording again left me open to the possibility of a further instruction — this time not to see him at all under the circumstances. In which case I would automatically be expelled from the group — *though,* he added consolingly as if it were an afterthought, through no fault of my own. So laboriously I rewrote it, panicked . . . and felt I could not send it after all for fear of the reply.

That night I had a vivid dream in which I went to see Baba.

He sat on a low couch and I knelt before him, looking up into his face, my arms pressed on his knees as if I were a child. I was very conscious that I was, indeed, looking at Baba, but my need overcame my awe. I said, "Father, I've tried so hard. Father, I've tried so hard . . ." and he smiled at me lovingly. Then he said, "Tell me about Patrick."

I remember thinking — Baba is silent, but *he is speaking to me* — for the words came clearly through his lips and not from the heart as in earlier dreams. I cried, "Baba, you spoke to me!" in great wonder. He smiled, as if greatly amused by my childishness, and repeated, "Tell me about Patrick!" Then I awoke, and as I did so I glimpsed Patrick packing his suitcase in a long hall, and looking for a door with a certain number on it.

I took the dream as an instruction to send my letter, and despatched it immediately. During the next few days Patrick's adamance wilted. He resumed our relationship as if he had forgotten the havoc so recently created, and for a short time we were again at peace.

February was an active month for the group. Rose came on Thursdays and brought with her several friends, none of whom were really interested, or came a second time; but they infused the prevailing atmosphere with change. And so did Rose, for she regarded Inder simply as a fellow student, and to my amazement considered him rather worldly. When she learned how I viewed him, she expressed concern and said she hoped I wouldn't be too disappointed. She regretted, too, that she couldn't endorse my perceptions in general, thinking them rather exaggerated. Inder approved her comments and encouraged her to make more. He even asked her advice and elucidation on matters which rose as the group enlarged, and so consolidated her impressions.

As a practising medium, Rose's viewpoint carried some weight, and was soon passed round to others outside the group, including my mother. Her attendance evoked further interest in our affairs, and highlighted existing attitudes; causing those concerned to carefully rethink or reaffirm their positions. And however Rose regarded Inder, she quite swiftly acknowledged Baba as her Master, and tried earnestly to become aware of her own inner linkage and to study all he had taught.

Joan was recontacted and found to be lonely and miserable. She did not need much persuasion to revisit us and came one

Saturday to Eachard Road, where Inder spent the evening dealing with her questions. She was worrying considerably about current world politics and the possibility of war, and her own impersonal concept of God brought her little comfort. The warm certitude she had felt in the days of our earlier groups had quite disappeared — she seemed depressed and fearful, and coming home in Nigel's car, began to cry.

Inder was immeasurably gentle with her — again, in a manner quite unlike his behaviour with the rest of us. With each one he expressed a different quality and a whole gamut of interwoven subtleties. Before saying goodbye, he told Joan to keep close contact with myself as she was in such need of sympathy and encouragement. I suppose this could be considered quite funny in view of my own situation, but she did as he said.

So Joan came most weeks also, and late in February Betty and Rupert joined us, and we watched together some newly received films taken at the East/West gathering. Betty was dismayed because she experienced no reaction to them at all, although there is little doubt she had 'registered' Baba on the day she met Inder in October, for she moved through the following weeks in a kind of dream, quieter and more at peace in her emotions than for many years, as Rupert confirmed. She said with commendable honesty that she "knew in her heart" who Baba was, but her mind blocked the knowledge and fought against recognition. Rupert withheld judgement, and both asked to come again, afterwards attending a meeting almost every week.

Among the profusion of dreams recorded at this time were several in which Baba gave me an indication of pending events. In one of these he pointed out certain things I had not yet properly grasped. They concerned two persons, a man and a woman, who jointly made a determined attack on me — one because I would not purchase what he was selling, the other aiding and abetting him for deeper and far more dangerous reasons. These latter were revealed symbolically, and produced feelings of acute distress which persisted on waking, despite the fact I could not recall what the symbols conveyed. Quite possibly this blurring of recollection was intentional, for in this instance direct foreknowledge of the inevitable would not have helped in any way.

Of a quite different nature was a very clear dream of entering an estate agents office, and asking for an unfurnished flat to rent with low outgoings. I seemed in despair about my living situation and with no expectation of remedying it. The agent remarked that, oddly enough, such a flat had been placed on their books that same morning, and wrote me an order to view . . .

On February 12th arrived the reply to my second letter to Baba. For days beforehand I had experienced much anticipatory anxiety, but when I picked up the blue airmail envelope I knew intuitively my fear of its content was unjustified. It was written by the secretary, Adi, and conveyed that my letter had been read to Baba despite the 'present phase of very little correspondence'. He was directed to inform me:

(a) I was free to take separation or divorce as I thought best in the interests of all concerned. Baba had no objection to this under the circumstances mentioned in my letter; and

(b) I could continue to love Inder Sain with a sisterly love for him in Baba Love. Baba sent me His Blessing.

I did not know how to take this, even bearing in mind the peculiarities of Adi's English,* for the extreme pressures under which I had originally written were now no longer operative. I thought this was very strange, to say the least.

Inder's apparent reaction to Baba's message overwhelmed me; I use the word 'apparent' because I knew perfectly well that he was aware of the approaching letter's content all along.

"It means something *unique!*" he said, beaming delightedly, his face aglow with warmth and good humour. "Something you cannot yet comprehend!"

Puzzled, I reread the letter.

"*Why* can't I comprehend it? *How* is it unique? It only says that I can have a divorce if it's in everyone's interest, and I doubt if Patrick will really think it's in *his*."

"It's in the *second* paragraph," he averred. "It *means*, Kate . . .

---

* It must be remembered that Baba observed strict silence and communicated by sign and gesture. All letters and cables were thus worded by senior disciples, who translated his wishes into their own mode of expression.

that one day, *you will come to me* and share my work. *Baba has given permission for this.* It lies *concealed* beneath the words."

My shocked consciousness re-registered the sentence from my dream. But I could not accept it. I longed to with all my heart, yet my mind lagged behind and could only argue its impossibility.

His tone softened, and his features became imbued with an indescribable tenderness.

"It is the *very first time* this has been done — the *first time* this *future* work will have been undertaken in this way.   It is something completely *new!* . . . And for *you,* this opportunity has never happened before! It will be the *first time* it is possible for you!"

He smiled radiantly at me. "I will welcome you, Kate," he said, and my inner self took wing. *"You will be my co-partner* and I will be so pleased to have you. *In all things* I will treat you as equal . . ."

He took my hand. His next words, spoken almost as an endearment, projected themselves hazily into my mind, came slowly into focus, and drifted away . . . *"You are a 'special one'* . . . But it will be . . . long time . . . *long* time . . . before you know what this means."

All thoughts ceased. Such statements were impossible to assimilate intellectually, and my essence, poised now in contemplative peace, had left the intellect behind.

But only briefly. By a slight shift of emphasis, the merest *nuance,* he anchored me firmly again to the flesh — and at once a curious dichotomy rose in my thinking process — a total *un*belief, yet at the same time an *equal belief* stemming from some inner core of knowledge. Again the two levels at war, though this I knew was an incorrect reduction . . . the operative factor was *time,* not levels, as I dimly perceived.

I yielded the effort to grasp these remarks, for having revealed so much with such precision, he was unlikely now to return to them and explain. Still looking at me, he lit a cigarette and blew giant smoke rings, his face alert and alive; and instead of 'closing down' as I expected, encouraged me with his expressive eyes to move away from these delicate points, but *not* away from this mode of communication. He was waiting . . .

I asked the first thing that came into my head. It had endlessly bemused me and I had not dared to query it before.

"If Mira was a sixth-plane soul as you said, why wasn't she given liberation when she died?"

He puffed gently with pursed lips to release the smoke and, still smiling, replied, "Mira *was* liberated. But don't think about it now." And I knew he meant I had as yet no hope of understanding this, or indeed anything else he had mentioned that belonged to this hidden dimension.

Before leaving the matter, I tentatively broached a further question.

"How is it that liberated souls can return to the world and make fresh connections? Surely liberation means the end of all *sanskaric* binding?"

"It does," he said, "but sometimes, if a soul is to return for special purposes, certain threads are held back."

The implication was startling . . . opening entirely new perspectives.

"This means, then, that these things are *already* known *before* liberation?"

His answer was yes, such things are always known, and every eventuality prepared for. Baba might even clothe an incoming soul with specially designed *sanskaras* that linked it specifically to former companions still trapped in illusion — who *by their implicit means* could more rapidly be led out. Certain situations were actually contrived . . . *created,* to facilitate this.

I asked if he would explain this to me. His reply was unusually informative, though I cannot remember it clearly enough to quote. The following is a part of it.

One way in which pupils were assisted, he said, was by releasing them from retrogressive *sanskaric* impressions which could block their progress or lead them astray. These impressions were the residues of former phases of experience — and certain souls were able to take these upon themselves and "burn them out" rapidly without personal entanglement or harm, or else were used as intermediaries, relaying them to the Master who himself dealt with them.

At the close of his unprecedented explanation (for there was substantially more than this) — quite casually he remarked, "You will have a *completely new life,* Kate! And to mark this new life I will give you a *new name* — one you will like . . . and you will carry *my name* as well . . ."

He paused, suddenly deeply serious; the pulsating light

61

behind his features so evident now, that my senses soared once more to little short of oblivion.

"When this time comes there will be *much* work to do . . . *many* people to connect with! It will be necessary to have a correct 'work' situation and environment . . ." (Here he said something I could not afterwards recall).

"There will be discourses every night . . . sometimes *all night!* Very strange things will happen, Kate . . . many will cross the planes and come close to God. People have *need* to grow and develop — to *open their hearts* . . . There will be many, *many* people. Much, *much* work. *You will be there with me.*"

I was held in stillness and light, my mind full to overflowing with whatever essence he imparted. I remember saying, "I suppose you will 'hammer' me all the time then, won't you?" not caring in the least if he did, as long as I could be there.

"Oh, no!" he replied. "Things will be quite different then. *Then* — you will *know me . . . as I really am!*"

He lightly touched my shoulder. The rapport he had created between us for one blissful moment reached a point of consummation and burst in ecstatic pulsations in my heart. The effect was apparently synchronous in the bodily heart itself — a simultaneous commingling of spirit and form which subsided within seconds, and my consciousness gently reverted to its mundane state. Inder stubbed out his cigarette.

"In the meantime, however," he continued briskly in his usual manner, "There are other things to be done! Books to write which can only be prepared by those with awakened insight . . . by people who can '*see*'. *Special* books needed for very special work . . ." His eyes held mine for a moment and then he swiftly and firmly passed on to matters concerning the group in general.

I had listened throughout without seemingly taking anything in. It was as if his words were covered with gauze to blur their impact, or were insulated in some way to form a screening process, and I simply could not absorb them despite the fact that I remembered them well. Months passed before they penetrated to any comprehendable depth, and even then I could not use them as a consolation, for their possibility of actualisation grew increasingly remote.

Whenever he spoke in this way his voice held a light yet subtle intonation I came to associate with spiritual truth. I had noticed before, and increasingly consciously after this particular evening, that the inflexion in his voice conveyed specific levels of understanding — like the scale heading a sheet of music. Sometimes he spoke spiritual truths, sometimes worldly truths, but most times a mixture of both. This produced the apparent confusion in understanding in many who heard him; they would all think he had said something different and assume that others had misunderstood. It always seemed to me that one thing was said on the surface and quite another lay beneath, depending on one's capacity to receive it. But in rare private conversations like the one above, he spoke openly in a different manner altogether.

That evening I hardly knew where I was. I did not feel in the least bit 'special' and any temporary reassurance was very shortlived; for during the meeting that followed this interchange, he plunged me once more into grief and despair.

March and April brought further changes. After a pipe-frozen winter, Alison and Nigel moved from Eachard Road to Weston, nearly sixteen miles from Cambridge, and the meetings were transferred to Inder's room. Everyone did their best to attend regularly, and Thursdays and Saturdays invariably found a crowd, leaving Mondays to Alison, Nigel and me. Occasionally Nigel missed Monday for some business function or other, and this unplanned event was considered by the female 'residents' as manna, a veritable gift from Baba, for then Inder talked to us on matters that never arose in the other groups.

We had already forcibly realised that attention was centred on any newcomer to the meetings or on those more obviously groping — and their needs and questions were probed and satisfied, regardless of how tedious this might at times prove for those who came regularly.

Once, when Alison mildly protested about a certain person's determined persistence regarding a particular subject, Inder actually spoke sharply to her, including me in the rebuke, and telling us both that if we ever interfered we should be publicly admonished. Furthermore, that we none of us had any idea for what purposes the groups were used. These were not "ordinary" meetings, but had been brought into being for specific objectives, and were utilised by Baba as part (a very *small* part, lest it went to our heads, but important nevertheless)

63

of his universal work. This was referred to many times in the coming months, and gave us much food for thought.

We concluded, rightly or wrongly, that the group was a miniature prototype, and the persons involved represented principles, qualities or energies that were manipulated within the group on a small scale, and would later externalise on one much larger.

A young man named Robert now joined us, and was followed soon afterwards by Rose's husband, Paul. So each Saturday Inder's room was literally filled to overflowing. The atmosphere at these times was electric, and Inder himself generated a dynamic vitality and magnetism which we all absorbed and reflected.

At one of these gatherings, when all of us were present, he brought up the matter of our possibilities of service. He said that each one of us, on entering the group, wore a 'mask' composed of all the facets of the personality. This mask, in its present form, had perhaps been with us for many years, and quite possibly many lives — but of itself it was 'false', and must be broken and dissolved away before we could hope to become sufficiently clear channels for spiritual use.

Some of us, he said, could yield up the mask willingly and without great difficulty — though the process might cause us pain; but others refused to admit their need of 'polishing' and thought themselves suitable vessels already. No force or coercion was ever used — we had our freewill and were not obliged to reshape our egos unless we wished. But he must warn us *all* that if we *did not properly prepare* before submitting ourselves for spiritual work — some day the mask would shatter and fall, to our greater humiliation and shame, and when we least expected it . . . leaving us naked and having to start all over again.

This unusually serious talk produced peculiar and unspoken reactions, and it was obvious that deep chords were struck in everyone present. The current of attention in the room subtly changed — as if energies were released of a psychic and psychological nature. These thrust themselves outwards towards manifestation: writhing and interweaving in an orgy of self-justification, and causing certain of us to squirm inwardly with revulsion. This particular impartation, to my knowledge at least, was never repeated — a factor of itself unusual; for whatever else Inder had to say to us was drummed in *ad nauseam*.

During March I became aware that Nigel's attitude towards me had changed. He began to make painful approaches that in my absorption with Inder I at first barely noticed — until he tried kissing me at each meeting's end with unbrotherly fervour. I protested without avail, and finally asked Inder to stop him, which he did. Alison appeared unaware of Nigel's potential defection and I prayed would remain so; but Inder made space to explain to me that Nigel was responding subconsciously to a former connection between us, and that he knew this himself. He had told Inder privately that he had "fallen in love" with me and remembered knowing me before. Inder indicated that his interpretation of the relationship wasn't quite correct, though he did not enlarge upon it, and I simply found it all an embarrassment.

It was around this time that I was shown, in sleep, an astrological chart for the group. Inder spread it in front of me and silently pointed out certain configurations of significance. I saw that Pluto was rising in the first house, and several planets were conjunct near the midheaven or somewhere of equal consequence. As I watched, the chart became activated and revealed a progression of events which culminated when a sudden, subterranean explosion burst through from the core of Pluto . . . rising up in a cloud of force that permeated, then disintegrated the entire group, and dispersed it. There was something strange here that I could not discern — a concealed element that gave *one* appearance at the point of eruption, but *quite another* from the height of the mushrooming cloud. And strangely, none of this could be retained. It faded rapidly on waking, leaving the strong impression that my recollection had been erased quite deliberately.

Inder raised his eyebrows when I told him, looking humorously askance. He had in the past disclaimed all knowledge of astrology, and quenched any stray enthusiasm held by odd members of the group. Now he said, in response to my rather indignant accusation, "Did you *really* believe I was so ignorant?" his eyes alight with laughter. But that was all I got from him, and he would neither admit nor deny the interference with my memory.

I was increasingly aware of this wiping away of remembrance, and often felt vexed and frustrated by my unaccustomed inability to recall the content of potent dreams. Matters I knew to be of importance which had been clearly and lucidly portrayed, ebbed from my mind in the oddest fashion as I awoke. I could actually observe them eluding me . . . Impressions and thoughts had a weight and substance, and could be perceived — along with images — gradually separating from my mindstream. As they disappeared from sight, all knowledge of their meaning left me, and only the memory of their unwonted erasion remained.

Until this happened with such unconcealed deliberation, I did not recognise my own psychic potency and perceptivity, or the way it coloured the whole of my life. Its partial withdrawal increased my consciousness of what had been mine, but of which I had been almost entirely *un*conscious. My past experiences had made impact on my inner development, yet little or no impression on my mundane awareness, and I registered this very thoroughly as time moved on. I had been deeply and soundly asleep . . . and saw that my previous perceptions of my own 'unconsciousness' were observed from finer gradations of that same slumber. Each stratum appeared to have decreasing substance and weight, but was still in a sense as illusory as the utmost unconsciousness itself. One could liken it to a fog . . . thick or thin it veils the sunshine, though one with greater density than the other.

Around this time, too, Inder made various statements, generally in reply to questions. Amongst these were the following:

Someone enquired what happened if prayers were offered to a long dead teacher who had perhaps moved on to other things, or even (mistakenly) to an individual who wasn't a genuine teacher at all.

"Masters have no ego," he replied. "They *don't mind* who you pray to in your blindness, *or in whose likeness* your limited brain projects them in dreams! *Whoever* is actually in charge of you, won't feel in the least bit upset if you attribute his care to someone else! All that concerns him is the quality of your aspiration, and your efforts to follow the highest principles of which you are capable. *Every genuine prayer is heard,* no matter to *whom* it is incorrectly addressed!"

He once told us the story of Milarepa who at first repudiated and strongly opposed his own Master. "This is not considered a bad thing by a Master," he asserted jovially, much to the amazement of his querist from whose persistent applications the story arose. "A man who powerfully opposes a Teacher *in his mind* will think of him all the time! His feelings of grievance will give him no rest, and his anger or hatred will bind him firmly, *by his own mental act,* to that Teacher, who holds him fast! And in a later life — not necessarily the one following, *of his own accord* he will become a close devotee or perhaps even a disciple. The Teacher on whom he threw so much hostility will *burn it out* for him — therefore both love and hatred can be utilised in certain cases. Here, it is the *intensity* of thought and the *continual concentration* on the Teacher that counts. But indifference — ah, that is another matter!"

Throughout April the meetings intensified and were well attended. I say intensified — though this is exceedingly difficult to define. On the surface they were perhaps less one-pointed than before, there being so many more of us in number and many fundamental differences in belief and approach that made unity of tuition more complex. Inder welded us together, concentrating external attention on the newest arrivals or those with consistently orthodox questions, but it appeared to me that considerable stimulus was at work interiorly, involving us all. This manifested in several ways — the most obvious being that everyone put forward their better sides and exhibited delightful characteristics that were often quite unsuspected of having existence. The men, for instance, became aspirational and most movingly tender, and the women exuded sweetness and devotion. And interwoven in their relationships was a thread of exquisite humour. Not all the time, of course — but in waves that rippled through the group and broke up tensions and cleared the board for fresh endeavours — Inder always at the helm and 'pulling strings', and at that juncture, most of us aware of it.

Despite the foregoing in which I participated to some extent, there still ran the parallel stream of my own personal woes. I continued to cry each day and for the same reasons, though by the month's end this was more controlled and in short bouts rather than the long, wrenching hours as before. Yet often when the meetings commenced my tear-puffed face would bear witness to my wretchedness beforehand, and this, as I came to perceive, beyond doubt was Inder's intention and by his design.

I was usually the first to arrive, and each and *every* time I would resolve not to mention, under any circumstance, the travail of the days preceding. But always I would start to cry when Inder had talked to me for a few minutes, not really knowing why, save that he made me so unbearably conscious of my separation from the light. The burning sensation in my heart and the agonised longing continued all my waking hours with only the briefest respites. Only his presence could assuage them completely — and this was tempered entirely by whether he gave me hope or despair.

In due time the whole group one by one grew exasperated by my misery, and with increasing resolution I determined *never* again to speak of it or display it, carefully making-up my face to conceal any tell-tale marks before approaching Inder's door or the portals of the Lodge — and it was then that I began to see aspects of his intent in operation, for within minutes, by adroit query or comment, he brought the subject to the fore — and also the tears, much to my detriment; and there was no way I could stop it however hard I tried.

No-one, naturally, understood me, and I could not blame them for this. Nor did I understand myself. To be aware of this appalling interior fire was not to comprehend it. I knew only that the Master drew me one-pointedly inwards towards Him — while at the same time debarring me absolutely from His presence.

For reasons of his own Inder continually pinpointed this state and its grievous workings in me, parading it before the disinterested view of my companions so that they knew full well the nature of my experience, but gave it no value; for no value was ever placed upon it, indeed quite the reverse. He always inferred the condition was transitory and could be transcended with correct orientation, thus implying my efforts were inadequate and that it was all very preparatory anyway (I can see now that this was true). Yet never did he state that my anguish was undesirable; the others merely concluded this by assumption, and later attributed the whole of this ordeal to the effects of marital disharmony.

One evening Rose told us of her own experience of Baba, already previously discussed with Inder. She had been reading 'The Theme of Creation' and pondering Baba's words, when suddenly she *knew*, in a profound moment of extended insight, that he was *God in form.* Simultaneously she had perceived her own psyche, and other, very personal things of which she had not been conscious before.

This experience affected her enormously. Her whole nature softened and deepened, and Paul was plainly quite overwhelmed by the fact. His own interest had already been caught and sustained, and his initial, rather hostile approach to Inder was now direct and friendly. That summer their marriage, like Alison's and Nigel's, found a basis of warmth and mutual understanding formerly unknown.

Betty, too, was touched by the flow of transformative influence so freely available. She was calm and gentle, quietly absorbed; stabilising her homelife and temperament to a notable degree. Even Joan, whose Anglican background created difficulties in the acceptance of a living Master, glowed with the inner brightness of a strengthened faith; and the rest unfolded in their differing ways like flowers to the sun.

I thus felt very much alone in the problems of my life; cut-off in an indefinable sense from these close comrades of the past, and very aware of the rifts that widened imperceptibly between us. Unaccountably I felt an outsider, excluded from the unity they shared — and as the vexation of the men became more openly evident, this feeling increased, and grew sharply worse when the women followed suit.

Since receiving Baba's letter my life with Patrick had been a little less chaotic. He swung backwards and forwards at weekly or fortnightly intervals between vulnerable sensitivity and a sullen aggression, but for a short while there was no more talk of separation. It was very curious to me that when our marriage could have been torn apart I was told to preserve it, and now I had been released from this under extenuating circumstances, those circumstances had subsided into some semblance of normality.

There were times when Patrick himself appeared to register things on an inner level. He did not, for instance, pit himself deliberately against Baba,* whom he was prepared provisionally to respect — but against my inability to "be reasonable" about the meetings and attend, at most, one per week, with no

* he had transferred this to Inder.

mention of my "interests" in the meantime. Sometimes he was tentatively 'pro', at other times violently 'anti', all things pertaining to the inner life of the Path. His feelings were fluid and ebbed and flowed. Occasionally amid the chaos we achieved a positive conversation, which he would afterwards go back on utterly, as if that facet of his understanding was again submerged beyond reach, and quite unknown to him.

One night I awoke to hear him muttering in his sleep. He was tossing about uneasily and I spoke to him gently, asking what was wrong. He replied that he was "crossing the planes" and trying to get from the first into the second, which was such an effort that it took all his strength. His words were quite clear and obviously spoken from a dream, but when he woke he had no memory of this and considered I had invented it.

About now came another sleep projection from the past of a former existence, and I found myself high up on the mountain-side in Tibet, in what I knew was a Lamasery. The room I sat in was large and low-ceilinged, rather dark, and sparsely furnished in carved and heavy wood. I was a young woman wearing traditional dress, with plaited hair hanging in braids and a close-fitting cap. Near me stood a wooden wheel in a frame, which I turned, and across the room, watching, was a seated Lama whom I recognised as Inder. He was giving me instruction.

The dream was exceedingly vivid, and when I related it to him he questioned me minutely on my recollection. I recalled some factor to do with the operation of certain principles, magnetic perhaps, or magical. He acknowledged the dream's significance without proffering further information, and I had the unlikely conviction that its content bore a direct relation-ship to the future.

Among the lesser prophetic dreams, in a very different context I saw 'X', another group member, 'cooking up' (quite literally, on a stove) some grievance against me which I saw would soon externalise. Rather warily I reported this, fearing rebuke for critical thinking. Inder listened amiably, and to my surprise agreed it was probably so. No more was said, and some days later the incident I had foreseen actually occurred. In the ensuing *contretemps* I came off worst and was very upset as a consequence, not having been guilty anyway of the accusation made against me. Inder, with sublime detachment, 'sat on the fence' and let 'X' have her say. In no way did he support me, and in fact gave credence to the other side. Eventually I had to apologise to 'X' to satisfy her aggrieved notions, this being the only way to achieve peaceable relations once more.

The following week Inder suggested I collaborate with her on some matter, and when I protested about her recent hostility and unfair attitude towards me, he said impassively, "That was *yesterday*, Kate." And I knew that whatever my personal feelings, I had to act as if nothing had happened, and 'X' had not behaved abortively. This simple sentence penetrated my psyche and lodged there as an instruction; one that I had to act on times without number in the years ahead.

Several changes now presented themselves. Rose and Paul invited us all to their home one evening, and for some months after this we met there regularly on Mondays, and before long on Saturdays as well. This, of course, created a change of emphasis in the body of the group, and what had once circulated around myself, and then Alison, moved on to Rose, though Alison remained prominent. Having once been the leader of the group, it soon became subtly apparent that I was now well and truly demoted, and this produced a subliminal range of reactions from all concerned.

Concurrently my personal affairs again began to suddenly deteriorate. Patrick, for no external reason, became exceedingly aggressive, and our life together was sheer purgatory. It seemed the vibration I carried had of itself an adverse effect on him and activated the jealousy and rage he repeatedly expressed. His belligerence was such that I believe he sometimes frightened even himself, and we once more rapidly reached a point when our separation appeared inevitable. Had he still been working all hours as in previous years the situation might not have been so bad; as it was, his work had slowed down considerably through his own lack of attention, and in May he became workless for weeks on end, and all his attention was thus centred on me.

Nigel tried to ease matters, perhaps at Inder's instigation, by arranging to meet Patrick for a private talk, explaining how he too had reacted with hostility to Alison's interests and the group, but in joining it had overcome his fears, and found something instead which brought them closer than ever before. After this Patrick made his first genuine effort to connect with us, and came one memorable evening to Rose's house and quite enjoyed it. Inder devoted much time to him, discussing politics and anything else he wished; and the presence of Nigel and Paul, both astute and worldly businessmen, compelled him to view the group in a more rational light.

Unfortunately, the second meeting he attended produced the reverse effect and provoked him greatly. He had watched (he said later) the "doting" expressions of Alison, Rose and myself whilst listening to Inder, and could scarcely conceal his anger. Obviously enraged, he left abruptly, and as I learned afterwards, went straight to my mother's home and cried when he reached there. This really unnerved me, for they had never been friends, and he knew how harshly she had berated me. Also to cry was virtually foreign to his nature.

At the peak of my heartache over Patrick, a dream brought comfort — not in my outer life, but the inner one from which my actions sprang. I saw Baba standing in the centre of a room with Patrick to one side of him and myself on the other, and I knew he had separated us. Silently he motioned me to look down at my feet, and smiled encouragingly. Stretching across the floor from Patrick to me was a golden cord that linked us indissolubly, and I understood that no matter what he did or where he went — however far away it may be, I could at a later time use the cord (in a manner not comprehended) to reach him for his benefit and consolation.

In contrast to my pressing difficulties, I found a growing comradeship with my children. They had always been very close to me, and now, mute witnesses to so much that was grievous, they drew yet closer, turning to me without criticism and with genuine love. This was a very real solace for which I deeply thank them both, for it sustained me increasingly during the coming onslaught of events.

The first Sunday in May brought a further change, and quickened the group-impetus considerably. It began with Alison and Nigel inviting Inder to spend the day with them at Weston, and proved the commencement of a regular Sunday gathering of all who could manage to attend, including the children. A few days before this first 'family' occasion, Patrick, having completed his current job and feeling bitterly resentful, took himself off to Middlesbrough for a week and left me to my own devices. So I was asked to come along too. I took Teresa with me, David having made a previous arrangement with friends.

It was a beautiful day with the soft warmth of an early summer, and I felt inexplicably happy. Teresa had met Inder twice before but not on a social basis, and to my great pleasure she behaved in an exemplary fashion — looking quite lovely in her white broderie-anglais dress and straw hat strewn with flowers. Inder made a fuss of her and talked and played with her to the extent of making Avril (who already knew him well) unreasoningly jealous. He also whirled her continually round and round by holding both hands, clockwise and anticlockwise — repeating this several times during the day. It was impressed on me that through this simple act he wound up, and unwound, differing patterns of *sanskaras* preparatory to their future expression.

Soon after our arrival and when our hosts were still busy with lunch preparations, Inder led Teresa and myself through the tangled profusion of bushes and weeds at the rear of the huge country garden, out to the field of young fir trees that bounded the property. His care of Teresa was almost strange, for he lifted her over brambles and nettles and carried her for some way in his arms, although she was a big child for ten and he not much larger. It was oddly like a symbolic journey, and conducted in silence. As we moved through the ragged long grass the sunshine grew brighter and warmer, and a softly luminous radiance permeated the atmosphere.

At length we sat down in the centre of the field, with Teresa cradled in his lap like a baby. He kissed her once, very gently, and held her close to him — as if he was overcome to find her again in the flesh . . . and the child herself was passive and still, in a way that she never was usually. Without speaking he took my hand in his own, and the three of us sat locked in what seemed a triangle of stillness. This released in me an ecstatic and upflowing bliss, lasting perhaps fifteen minutes, and passing as suddenly as it came. The rest of the day we all spent together as one close-knit family. It left a memory of happiness and light, a bright oasis set in a wasteland of heartache and bewilderment.

In May too, came change of a different order. The membership of the Theosophical Society whose Thursday meeting we shared, had gradually dwindled, and now only two or three people attended with any regularity, one of whom, the President, came only once a month. His view of things diverged increasingly from ours, and after several stormy and highly abusive Presidential outbursts (in which he indulged in some extremely personal remarks), the Lodge was dissolved, and we re-rented the room ourselves as a Centre for Baba's work.

The group had a visitor at Whitsun. Maud S., a member of the London group, came from Oxford at Inder's invitation and joined us at Weston over the weekend. She appeared very moved by the warmth and friendship with which she was received, which at that time prevailed at every meeting — making them utterly unlike (she said) the more formal ones she was familiar with in London.

That same Sunday Patrick also came to Weston and observed closely all that was said and done. He was in a rather better humour having been mollified by Nigel beforehand, and Teresa and David were with us. Rose and Paul brought their three children, and with Alison's two they made a lively party.

Patrick had already decided he disliked Rose, and made clear that he didn't care much for Maud either. Alison alone he regarded as "sensible", presumably because she behaved subserviently and Nigel was obviously well in charge of the situation. However, Inder soon annoyed him with what he felt was undue attention to myself; the conversation was considered "childish" and he quickly became restless and required us to leave. This was offset by our host, who offered to bring me home later when he came into Cambridge himself — so Patrick, anxious to get to his pub before lunchtime, speedily departed. He had tried his best to restrain his hostility, but the brief time spent with us brought sharply home to me once more the frightening extent of the gulf between his chosen way of life and my own.

Maud had stayed overnight with Alison and was to spend the following night with Joan. As the latter was not at the Sunday meeting, Nigel was depositing her at Joan's house *en route* home with Inder, it now being his habit to chauffeur him at every opportunity and remain afterwards for private discussion.

When we arrived at Joan's, I asked Inder if he would like to see baby Rachel, who was an unusually beautiful child, to which he smilingly agreed. So with Joan's permission we all trooped upstairs to the childrens room. The two older ones were wide awake, and Nigel promptly invented a bedtime story they both thought hilarious, and which probably kept them awake half the night with over-excitement.

Rachel, now sixteen months old, stood in front of her mother in her nightie, looking rather sleepy. She stared solemnly and silently at Inder, who quietly stared back. There came a sudden shout of laughter from the story group, and Maud and Joan at once looked towards them. In that instant I perceived a vivid interchange between Inder and Rachel. The child's solemnity registered a deep, still recognition, and glancing at Inder I saw that Baba was manifest in his body . . . I cannot describe this, only to say that Baba stood *inside* Inder, transforming his features into his own likeness, and smiling with overflowing love and tenderness at the little girl.

No-one else noticed. After a matter of seconds, it was over, and when later I told Inder I had seen Baba come to visit Rachel . . . he smiled at me serenely, and silently acknowledged it.

At the end of May Patrick again went to Middlesbrough, this time threatening never to return. I lived through those unhappy days feeling permanently ill and overburdened with guilt for being what I could not help. During his absence I experienced in sleep a vision more powerful than any preceding it, graphically pinpointing the growing fear and anguish in my mind.*

I was with a crowd of people around Baba, when suddenly he singled me out and drew me into his immediate vicinity. A man garbed as a Yogi fakir watched from the crowd and expressed great anger at what he saw, rushing out with a club in his hand as if to attack me. The Master took from him a silver watch, and the man, thinking I had removed it, advanced menacingly towards me with the vicious club raised ready to strike. I felt a rising flood of terror, and the scene at once changed.

I was alone now with Baba by the ocean. He leaned his back against a rock and held me closely to his heart, from which came soundless words that registered within me with crystal

---

* The outworking of this dream was not confined to the immediate future, as I later assumed retrospectively in 1968. Its core was locked in the events of 1976/77, and reflected both backwards and forwards in time from that point.

clarity. He said I belonged to him and was dearly loved, and that soon I would be attacked because of this. Yet no matter what happened, either now, *or in the future,* I must try not to be afraid — for he would look after me, and feed me with his own bread . . . He then placed a pellet of bread in my hand, embraced me lovingly, and disappeared.

I found myself in a narrow lane that bordered a cemetary, with the crowd surging restlessly behind me. Through the press of people I could see, clairvoyantly, that the man with the club still sought me, running hither and thither through the throng with murderous intent. Terrified, I cried "Baba, Baba . . ." fleeing wildly to find him . . . though I knew it was no use. For I must *stand still* where I was, and bear as bravely as I could whatever must come. So I stood quite still; and the Yogi saw me, and came hurtling towards me through time. Trembling with fear I awoke.

How long, O Lord, wilt thou quite forget me?
How long wilt thou hide thy face from me?
How long must I suffer anguish in my soul,
grief in my heart, day and night?

Psalm 13. New English Bible. (c) 1970
by permission of Oxford and Cambridge University Presses

As yet unknown to me, this last week in May marked the end of my special link with Inder; for despite the pressures he had subjected me to, they had been interspersed with informative kindness. Now the latter, too, would cease, and June brought the commencement of an applied state of inner dereliction, reflecting outwards into my daily life with a devastating equivalence.

The ensuing weeks increased also the internal stimulus at work in the group. We continued to meet regularly as before, and all those who accepted Baba as Master, excluding myself, seemed unbelievably happy. Yet I could not but perceive that certain things were happening to them, and that these observations were sometimes at variance with surface appearances.

I had known them all fairly well in the past, and some of them very well, and had noted (as with myself) the 'best' side they turned uppermost at meetings and services, and the more functional side that held sway in their everyday lives. It appeared now that an *interior* separation was being effected in everyone, and the spiritual attributes were gently and silently winnowed from the purely physical. The spiritual part, in freeing itself, emerged in ever growing and often bewildering beauty; but side by side with the loveliness of their light I watched the exudation of subtleties formerly unindicated and unseen. They were negative qualities, already present in the psyche, and previously held in check by time and circumstance.

These intensified, as if the sun that drew forth their spirituality also lured forth the weeds, so that they interlinked, one person's with another's, in a most subtle fashion. I believe these undercurrents were unobserved by any save myself — and certainly no-one alluded to them in the context described. Nevertheless, some consciousness of their presence beyond doubt existed, for to my amazement and distress the negative traits I witnessed were soon attributed to *me*. Circumstances moved in such a way that it would appear to others I was behaving in a certain manner, when to my own awareness I was not. My motivations were continually distorted and misconstrued. And incredibly, Inder deliberately fostered these conclusions — sometimes to my face before others, but frequently in my absence. When the latter occurred, news of this invariably crept back to me through Rose or Alison, or even via a person outside the group, to whom one of our members had obviously been talking. The fact that Inder insisted we were not to discuss internal affairs with the curious made not the slightest difference.

On Patrick's return from Yorkshire, he commenced to question me incessantly about my feelings for Inder in a way he had not done before, and I soon learned why. He had been through all my papers one evening when I was out, and had discovered the notebooks in which I recorded my dreams. The notes covered a three year period, with as many recollections from before that time as I could muster — and inevitably the most recent year was full of references to Inder.

I had made no attempt to veil the symbolism of my dreams. The records were kept purely for my own benefit, and were intended as an objective research project to assess the degree of reliability of my perceptive faculties. Unfortunately Patrick regarded the notebooks as a kind of diary, and had even shown the most recent one to Lois, asking her opinion of the contents. She told me later she had declined to comment, save to remark on the way I had looked in November, and that she thought there was a spiritual bond of love between Inder and myself.

Apart from my dismay at this unauthorised exposure of my most intimate experiences, I knew with sinking heart that this, unhappily, was the worst possible thing she could say to Patrick, who could not discriminate between spiritual love and its physical counterpart.

As his suspicions grew and festered, his hostility did likewise, and before long it created an effective ban on any directly personal contact with Inder, and thus all private conversations ceased. Alison was requested to come early on Thursdays and to arrive at the Lodge when Inder did, Patrick having threatened scenes and violence if ever he discovered us alone, however innocently. The Lodgeroom had been my last outpost of communication on a spiritual level, for Rose's house where our meetings were otherwise held, was a hive of intellectual activity, and group conversation no longer encompassed matters of this type.

I now became aware that Inder had cut me off completely. The onset was intermittent, and I found it ludicrously difficult to grasp that this was his serious intention. His attitude switched to a cold indifference and aloofness that the others attributed to Patrick's aggression, but which I knew was quite incidental to it. Hurtful in the extreme though this was, it was made yet harder to bear by the psychological dissection that he stepped-up and continued almost without respite. At every meeting he sent me reeling with his critical assessments of my condition, or with a subtle diatribe on faults which I found hard to accept were my own — yet to those listening they were, it seemed, quite glaringly apparent, and most definitely *mine*.

He practically lived at Rose's house, then for a time at Alison's, then Rose's again. Both husbands welcomed him and did not appear to mind how often he called. As social visits to my own home were quite impossible, I soon ceased to be included in the general exchange of hospitality, and this frequently left me quite stranded. Once in a state of desperation, I telephoned Inder at Weston and was smartly upbraided by Nigel. He told me with scorn that I should stop behaving like an immature schoolgirl, and be calm and peaceful like Alison. As our circumstances were so utterly different, I felt the injustice keenly and was even more upset.

Inder's comment on this and the other cruel judgements that spasmodically filtered through to me, was that the critic's should "hold up the mirror to themselves and leave others alone" — but he said not a word of personal rebuke to any of them. In answer to my frequent protests he would make mild remarks of general censure that quickly turned round on myself, for whatever he uttered in this vein was considered *ipso facto* to refer only to me, and I soon gave up my pursuit of adjudication.

My life at this time degenerated into a nightmare. Patrick's behaviour became increasingly disruptive and was fanned to fever pitch by my mother, with whom he had made a disastrous alliance. She filled his mind with fear, telling him I had been "hypnotised" and was under the influence of satanic forces — that Baba was a fraud, and Inder even worse. The effect of their combined hostilities on myself and, sadly, on my children, was harrowing in the extreme, and shattered whatever confidence and wellbeing I had left.

The pressures accelerated one terrible evening when Patrick brought Mother to Rose's home and publicly accused Inder of stealing his wife. My mother ignored me verbally, but looked at me with something so akin to hatred in her eyes that my blood ran cold.

The calmness I exhibited in the face of this surprised me; I heard my self speaking without tremor as I tried to induce them to see reason — appealing to my mother who ought, heaven knows, to have understood. To his credit Patrick wavered, but Mother was like granite. Teresa, who always came with me to Rose's to play with the other children there, said she and Avril had been "frightened of Nanny" because of the way she had looked. She seemed quite shocked, although she had not been present at the time of the outbrust.

That night Patrick slept at my parents home. Mother telephoned to briefly say he was there and not to wait up for him; also that he did not wish to speak to me. When I asked her to fetch him she curtly refused and slammed down the receiver. He arrived home at five in the morning, sullen and hard and utterly miserable. I implored him to try to understand my side of the situation, crying despairingly over the sheer irreconcilability of the unbridgeable differences between us; but words of themselves were futile. It seemed to him that his old, familiar world was in ruins, and the new one revolted him so much he could not endure it. Ironically, no-one ever noted that my world was in ruins too.

That evening was the sole occasion on which my mother met Inder, and I soon heard that she had told many people, including Patrick, that she had seen clairvoyantly two snakes slithering from his eyes — her vision thus proving him to be an occult and evil man. The following week she sent a friend, who like herself was a medium of repute, to our public meeting at the Lodge; the friend afterwards confirming in every detail her perception. This dual indictment not unnaturally aroused formidable opposition and condemnation in the minds of others, and created virulent gossip and much ill-feeling against the group. It caused, too, the crisis in Patrick's mind that led him to the verge of mental illness, and brought us both untold suffering which words fail to describe.

My mother's judgements were damning in their effects, and I could not even begin to counter them. She was recognised amongst all of our acquaintance as a devout Christian — a mystic whose vision was unimpeachable and whose integrity could not be denied. Her mediumistic abilities accorded her a local status of the highest order, and it was obvious from the start that we waged an unequal battle — one that she would inevitably win hands down.

She turned her attention now to my father, who until this point had been prepared to concede that my personal interests were as valid and legitimate as Patrick's, and had even told him so. Both Mother and Patrick at this crucial juncture led him to believe that I was involved with another man in a worldly relationship — a thing abhorrent to his Puritan mind. He did not confront me with these 'facts', feeling too embarrassed to do so, and I did not know of them until too late.

When at last I understood what was happening behind my back, and of what I was accused, I visited my parents and tried to undo Patrick's misrepresentations, so readily seized upon and given root; but they solidly refused to listen to my explanations. My mother decreed I was lying and deluded, and my father could not bring himself to oppose her. Eventually he came down fully in support of her judgements, and I was unable to convey the truth to him at all.

My mother's virtue made her quite invincible. She predicted my speedy downfall through the betrayal of my intuition, and every setback I encountered — and they came thick and fast — fuelled her righteous triumph. It was ghastly to be on the receiving end of it all, and I felt at times that I was living in a dreadful dream from which I would never waken.

Yet Patrick was sorry for what he had done regarding the scene in Rose's house, perhaps sensing the far-reaching effects, or merely through drawing adverse attention to himself before Nigel and Paul — and he wrote Rose and Paul a letter apologising for the unpleasantness in their home, an act I thought took real effort on his part.

During this period he met Inder several times by arrangement, inviting him to Metcalfe Road, not alas in friendship but rather in the spirit of an armed truce, in which he sought to discover exactly what held my attention so constantly, and by what means.

These talks were held in private and I was not allowed to participate, but I learned, little by little, what had been said of me and felt very perturbed as a consequence. Patrick had blamed me squarely for the disintegration of our marriage, and Inder had sympathised with him and proffered nothing in my favour. The meetings, however, soon yielded precise results, for whatever Patrick requested concerning myself was eventually granted him, and the only measure withheld was my actual dismissal from the group.

He told Inder he would not object so much to the meetings if I went out an hour or so later — so Inder insisted I do this. Nor could I be out later than ten, as this too was stipulated. If I could not get transport in someone's car, or collection by Patrick, travelling time must also be deducted. And he felt every Sunday at Weston was far too often, even if the children enjoyed it; so Inder required that I join them not more than once a fortnight, and the in-between Sunday I must give wholly to Patrick.

There were other restrictions as well . . . my books must be kept out of sight and I may not read at all when Patrick was present. Anything pertaining to my inner life and personal interests was now unmentionable, and in general I must behave like a submissive and obedient wife. Patrick remained completely free to do as he chose.

These rulings became operative concurrently, and I rebelled strongly (though silently) at the injustice of my limitations. I was expected to accept them cheerfully and with good spirit, and Inder made clear that if I refused to try, I would be acting against Baba's wishes. So I tried my utmost, and externally managed quite well. But in my mind and emotions I'm afraid I didn't do well at all — something within me slowly died, and Patrick's casual acceptance of the rightness of my bondage, and his total lack of concern for how I must feel, did nothing to help.

A number of strange and unhappy dreams arose in which I was doing things I abhorred, but could not prevent, and these distressed me acutely. There was no prospect now of reassurance, for I could not bring myself to speak of them to Inder in the presence of others and he refused point blank to speak with me alone. Even more disturbing was the awareness that he actually witnessed these dreams in manifestation — and sometimes I saw him openly observing me, curiously intent, as if I was in some way being monitored.

Repeatedly I sifted his past comments through my mind in an effort to clarify what was happening to me, also in a desperate search for consolation. I remembered he once said that many of the things that pained me were not my rightful heritage at all, but were "thrown over" me, like a veil, to be "burnt out" as an act of service. I did not know if this was really true and certainly dared not assume so, for what I experienced was absolutely my own experiencing and horrifyingly real. On another occasion he had remarked that when we "take burdens", we must carry them in every sense as if they were our own;* and without the comfort of his wisdom, I had no choice but to do this, and suffered accordingly. To my rational mind it all sounded insane . . . *yet I knew it was true.* And in the end, it was this knowledge alone that sustained me.

At the end of June we received a communication from India saying that from the first day of July, Baba would enter nine months close seclusion, at the end of which he intended to break silence. This long heralded event, linked to the hierarchical structure of world affairs and planetary evolution, had been prophesied time and again as having profound and far-reaching consequences for humanity as a whole, and for each individual in his own special time and manner. The release of power inherent in this stupendous happening — the uttering of the sacred Sound, or Word, drawn out and expanded from the root of the evolutionary processes by an Incarnation of Cosmic Divinity and Purpose — would ultimately reveal to each human unit its own Christhood — such was Baba's promise.

Inder spoke to us all with great seriousness on this imminent new phase. He called it "Baba's Feast", and said we were all invited to partake of it. He warned us that the proximity in time of this occurrence would create increasingly problematical circumstances — Baba had said that immediately prior to his

---

* such highly concentrated karmic residues are *not* incinerated in the subtle or desire body; and only in the earliest period of training does the pupil experience *in toto* these substances in their natural state.

Manifestation it would become so difficult to hold onto him, even his nearest and dearest would think him insane and have to let go — but to those who remained to the end he would reveal himself, and they would perceive the hidden divinity behind all Creation.

Sunday, June 30th, was a special day for the group. It was the last day of "preparation", and tomorrow would mark for each one of us the beginning of a new chapter — a time of test and trial, as Inder said, that would, if successfully accomplished, lead us into fresh fields of endeavour and the definite opportunity of service to God and the Master.

To celebrate the occasion we gathered at Weston, where it had been pre-decided to make Alison a small token of our affection and love for her efforts each Sunday. Inder provided a large bouquet of carnations, and the group, too, gave her flowers. Even Patrick, chastened and unsure, contributed a box of chocolates. Perhaps most significant of all, Nigel with deep solemnity gave her a new wedding ring to symbolise their spiritual harmony.

It was a sizable gathering. Rose, Paul, and their children; Joan, Ian and theirs; Patrick, myself and Teresa; Nell and Edwin; Robert, and surprisingly, Lois . . . Betty and Rupert were on holiday at the time, so did not attend.

After the frivolity and presentation, things quietened down, and Inder's following talk was serious in the extreme. Every now and then my eyes turned to Patrick, who listened intently but with evident disapproval. He was twisting his knuckles together in a manner that barely concealed his desire to use them on Inder's head, and my heart filled with foreboding.

It was already apparent that those present diverged strongly in their feelings towards Baba. Lois found the whole ethos unacceptable although she was very polite about it. Ian was sceptical, and Joan wavering. Rupert had recently tried to draw Betty away, and Betty herself was inclined to doubt whenever the peaceful mood left her. But the rest of us appeared solidly united, and our sense of commitment was beyond dispute.

Many of the events that swiftly followed our day of Celebration are best forgotten as far as my own life was concerned. Patrick produced scenes of emotional violence far surpassing anything before, terrifying myself and our children; and all the

*carefully adhered to injunctions, efforts and supplications bore
no obvious fruit. Parallel to this was Inder's growing coolness
and withdrawal, and the increasingly close-knit comradeship of
the rest of the group, which left me firmly in the middle of a
kind of no-man's-land.*

*The interior sensation of anguished longing became acute,
resolving into an intensity of feeling akin to burning. It was an
agony, located in my heart, that at times proved so all-pervading
and unbearable I truly thought I would die. In those formative
years I had not yet discovered the works of Sufi Mystics, and did
not know that what I suffered was a recognised state — a
symptom of one's nearness to the Godhead, or approach to one's
Source.*

*I walked alone in this strange country, forsaken by family and
friends alike. Ignored, or rebuked, by the Teacher; and
compelled by duty, instruction and love, to fulfil my worldly
obligations to the letter. This treatment was soon to crush me
utterly, although in retrospect I can see that it did not have to be
so severe. The pain of the inner journey was unalterable, and the
techniques Inder used were part of this; but the outer life
troubles were governed entirely by the behaviour of individuals,
and this to a large extent was under their own control.* *

Wednesday, July 10th was the thirty-eighth anniversary of
Baba's Silence, and the group kept it in the manner he
requested. We all fasted from eight in the morning till eight in
the evening, meeting at Rose's house to break the fast together,
with a meal prepared by Paul and herself. Inder also kept
silence for twenty-four hours, and scribbled comments to us if
the need arose.

I had found the day exhausting beyond reason. The absence
of food for such a short period did not seem sufficient to merit
such fatigue, and I wondered why it should be so. During the
following night I had an extraordinary dream — Patrick, myself
and the children were travelling in his van at tremendous speed
when suddenly an electricity pylon loomed in front of us, into
which we crashed. As I whirled through the air from the impact

---

* It should not be assumed that the activation of a Teacher decrees such
hardships are inevitable. We all have our freewill and can use it to be cruel or
kind, whatever the circumstance.

I saw below me a huge lake into which I was obviously destined to fall. I thought, quite consciously, "I'm going to die now, I must think of Baba," and repeated his name over and over again as I plummeted down into the water.

In the morning I telephoned Inder and tentatively mentioned the dream, fully expecting to be rebuffed. Its impact was still with me, and I wondered uncertainly if it portended an accident and the imminent demise of my whole family. Inder remained aloof and impersonal but allowed me to relate it, and then to my surprise expressed approbation — and no, he did not consider our time was yet! So, please, what *did* it mean? There was, of course, no answer; he skirted the subject affably, and only after saying goodbye did I realise he had made no comment at all.

That evening at the Lodge, as the meeting drew to its close, he suddenly broached the matter of my dream and asked me to recount it to the others. Then he told us it was a very *important* dream, and deeply symbolic. It indicated that the dreamer had reached a stage when the Master was more *real* than this world of illusion. When one could consciously face death and think only of Baba, forgetting all else — *then,* indeed, the bonds of matter *were broken.*

I could scarcely believe my ears. Having become so accustomed to public admonition for the slightest faults and shortcomings, to say nothing of more serious things — it was overwhelmingly joyful to find I had unwittingly pleased him. The effect was revitalising; I left for home feeling healthy and alive again — this unanticipated resurgence of my former wellbeing revealing clearly, by comparison, how far behind me I had left this priceless condition.

Immediately afterwards the discord in my personal life reached a climax, and this state was harshly overthrown. A measure of its seriousness was that Inder, of his own accord, sent a cable to Baba on my behalf regarding Patrick's violence and my distress. The swift reply brought me nothing save a sense of blankness. It said, "Kate and Patrick should sort things out for themselves, but Kate should know that looking after her children is being with Baba."

Alison was present when the cable was read out to me. She commented that it seemed to her that Baba was giving me "the world on a plate, so to speak". I could not see it this way. Inder

90

was spending a great deal of time with her at Weston, and her own life was very pleasant and comfortable. I thought it was she to whom Baba had given the world.

At the height of our misery, Patrick again asked to speak to Inder, with Nigel as witness. He had consulted a solicitor and fully intended to terminate our marriage and lay the blame at Inder's feet. Instead, at the veritable twelfth hour he decided afresh to unite with the group, largely, I think, through Inder's sympathetic attitude and total lack of hostility; factors that Patrick found a perpetual source of puzzlement.

Inder, observing my face when he told me, cradled my head in his arms and said gently, "He *must* have his chance, Kate. It is Baba's wish." And once more the efforts and heartaches began all over again.

Soon after this I dreamt that Inder took me to Baba and reminded him that it was "time now for Kate to have a change . . ." Baba smiled and nodded, then looked towards the dark corner where I had been placed — my hands and feet, indeed whole body, bound by thick rope. I hung my head, believing myself in disgrace, yet not knowing why. Then Baba said with great amusement, and as if he had just remembered, "Oh yes! and there's the other one, too, isn't there?"*

At that moment my mind opened and a shaft of light entered. I saw the nine months symbolic of gestation, and a child that would one day be born to me. Immediately I thought of Patrick, and cried inwardly, "Oh no!" but this thought was at once erased, and I understood clearly that the child, or whatever it represented, was Inder's. I then awoke.

It was at this time that the tempo of the meetings began to change. Previously there had been a firm feeling of unity, and the general interest was strong — but after Baba entered the new phase of seclusion, a noticable discord permeated the group. Nigel became restless, and Paul tended to get irritable with him. Rupert disapproved increasingly of Inder — doubtless through my mother's condemnations, and Joan appeared very disturbed in herself.

I became conscious that Alison and Rose were somehow 'cold' to me, and this, in view of Alison's past friendship, was

---

* this referred to his much later contact with my son.

perplexing. I thought it due to Inder's discussion of my affairs at the meetings which prevented the group from getting on with other things — but I could do nothing about this as he insisted it was all very important, and they would do well to listen.

Personally I would much have preferred to forego this attention, as it invariably placed me in the worst possible light against everyone else. And yet it was not that he said so much specifically concerning me that caused this humiliation — rather was it, as formerly, suggestion and inference — directed at no particular person, but which the others only too readily seized on and pinned onto myself. They thought me a drag on the group, and made little, then less, attempt to conceal it.

I was still too blind to perceive the reasons for this; too inwardly absorbed in spiritual travail: and too stunned by the harsh deterioration of my marital life and the concurrent loss of parental love. All round me lay the keys to my situation; to what Inder was doing, and why — yet I could not see them.

It emerged quite rapidly now that something was seriously amiss with Nigel, whose nervous health appeared suddenly to be breaking up. He and Alison developed some private difficulty of which I knew nothing; there was an atmosphere between them completely at variance with their so recent months of harmony, and the eruption of this into our grouplife was unexpected and catastrophic. Alison said he had asked her to give up the Saturday meeting as the strain of the pace we were keeping was proving too much for him. He had even cried, and his earlier convictions were giving place to darkness and doubt.

I sympathised feelingly, saying I knew too well how it tore at one's heart to see one's husband cry. She replied dispassionately that she had been "completely detached" from him and *was not* distressed — an achievement I was so far from realising I felt quite foolish to have mentioned it.

Nigel tried hard at first to retain his spiritual allegiance, and I watched with sadness the way he gradually slipped away from us. He and Alison had repeated discussions as Patrick and I had done, and then he, too, became emotionally distraught, though not in the same manner. Inder told Alison that if a genuine nervous illness was impeding him, it was her duty to help him through it even if it meant missing meetings, for *she* was his link with the Master, and it was vitally important for Nigel's wellbeing that he retain his aspiration.*

Alison's consistent reply was that Nigel simply wished to return to their former mode of living, and this would be wrong for them both. This may have been true later on, but at that time his struggle was real, of this I am certain. He asked Alison to word with him a joint letter to Baba asking how best to deal with their problems. Alison, however, felt it wrong and unnecessary to disturb Baba's seclusion with personal trials, and though Nigel pressed this several times with evident distress, she would not agree to write.

While this was going on, Inder reiterated repeatedly the need to obey the Master at all costs to ourselves. Using myself as an illustration, he inferred that my marriage was poised on the brink of destruction through lack of obedience, as Baba's instruction to me had been to live with my husband and try my best to *love* him — the second letter conveying merely a direction to be put into practise *only* if I could not do what was originally asked.

He added that sometimes people who had previously served were found wanting, and were then discarded, whilst others more promising were brought to the fore. I cannot recount the latter part of this talk, but it was obvious to all present that I was in deep disgrace through my inability to bring peace to my married life, and Alison, cool and collected, and in no way to blame for Nigel's inadequacies, was openly praised and promised all the opportunities that would have been mine had I proved worthy.

Something extraordinary was happening to Alison. I could neither credit my ears, nor my eyes, nor my senses. Inder's words did not ring true to me, and Alison's expression, comments, and auric emanations were incredible to my perceptions and I rejected them mentally at once. But her coldness towards me could not be denied. I knew in my heart that something had come into being between us that my friendship, however sincere, could not override.

* He once commented that neither Nigel, Patrick or Paul could gain access to a Teacher in this incarnation save through the link provided by their wives.

93

I did not understand until much later that these quite merciless onslaughts were actually aimed, not at myself, but another — who would probably have walked out and disconnected entirely from Inder's contact if this fact was apparent. It seemed he used me as a focal point or fulcrum, and several times he even indicated that this was so, but the general impetus of events was against my possibility of registering it.

Interwoven with these indirect admonitions were other workings; the building-up of specific aspects of certain egos — which had commenced (as I soon learned) and also continued, during the times I was not invited to be present. A point worthy of note is that it was made clear to the group throughout the twenty months of its existence that a normal, responsible pattern of external behaviour was desirable in an aspirant, the expression of which was an orderly life — with which latter, of course, I totally failed to comply. That this misfortune was through Patrick's reactions was never dwelt upon, the fault was always obscurely assumed to be mine, and Patrick was given consideration and encouragement in the light of this. My comrades readily accepted the hypothesis as literal truth, ignoring the quite obvious fact, as he did himself, that I did love Patrick, and endured numerous appalling situations not solely through instructions, in my efforts to mitigate the side-effects of his own inner development, which stirred up and threw out everything adverse within him.

There were many, and increasingly proffered, opportunities for me to take the line of least resistance and theoretically receive Inder's approbation, thus making things easier for myself all round. Perhaps the same criterion applied to everyone else. Such testing is traditional; yet strangely, those being tested are never aware of it, or else imagine that something quite different is being done. One could only act according to the situation presented, for in whatever one did, the Master could never be cheated or deceived — though surface appearances frequently indicated otherwise.

Patrick now decided that the crux of our difficulties was a sexual one. I was not "responsive", indeed, was void of sexual desire altogether, and he blamed my devotional attitudes. He also considered the word 'love' in Baba's instruction to me, meant sexual love, and I had therefore no business to be as I was.* His adamance on this point was immoveable, and as he had noted Inder's changed demeanor towards me and had also heard I was constantly under fire, felt on firm enough ground to approach Inder himself for clarification. This unheard-of subservience was of course 'loaded'; he knew very well that I regarded Inder as a spiritual authority, and tried always to align myself to his interpretation of Baba's messages. So when Inder agreed to see him as soon as he put forward his request, he insisted that I should go too. The thought of it made me feel sick, but as Inder, on being again approached as to the desirability of my presence, at once concurred to this, I knew it was unavoidable and had to be faced.

We travelled to Weston the same day, a Sunday, for a private interview, and were conducted by Alison to the secluded caravan in the grounds where Inder awaited us. He listened sympathetically to Patrick, who warmed to his theme and became quite eloquent. They both ignored me and discussed me as if I was not there. I felt myself grow cold and trembly, not anticipating the reaction he exhibited. At the conclusion of Patrick's forceful complaint and the query that accompanied it, Inder turned angrily to me and tersely repeated the whole of my instructions, demanding vehemently, "Why do you not *at least* make effort to obey?" then launched into a powerful tirade on my deficiencies as both an aspirant and a marriage partner.

Shattered by his anger, I tried nervously to protest and re-explain my position, but he rebuked me sharply for self-justification and was so severe in manner that I felt suddenly frightened. He stood beside Patrick and made clear that he firmly condoned his viewpoint. I could not credit it. It shocked me terribly to think that by 'love' Baba had meant desire, as Inder appeared to imply, and I was deeply upset to have this thrown up at me so harshly, in fact crudely, despite my previous explanations. But he was ironlike, averting his eyes from me with displeasure, and Patrick came away feeling exceedingly pleased with himself. For the first time he conceded that Inder was a good fellow after all and understood his own exasperation. No doubt this was why he had shown me such sternness in the past — because I was not obedient to either my God or my husband.

* It should be remembered I *did not ever* deny him a physical relationship.

By now I felt ill, and too scared to think coherently, for I recognised I was completely unable to move against the fathomless tide in me that ran counterwise to human passion. For hours that night I lay in turmoil, praying, and imploring Baba to reveal to me his will and show me the way. At length I seemed to cross a ring inside myself and enter a central, blinding light which transpired to be my soul — my 'I'; and I knew with solid certainty that whilst the light worked so strongly within me, and my body was engaged in trying to absorb it, I could not will against the current even for he who was my Teacher.

When at last I told Patrick, he was furious. He called me so self-willed I would even query the Will of God. But nothing he said could affect me. For a brief while I was secure in my citadel . . . but with morning came fear. Supposing I was wrong? My state no longer reassured me — I had lost my inner certitude and could only recall the severity of Inder's words. The thought of disobedience to the Master was shattering to me . . . as if I had betrayed everything to which I aspired.

I telephoned Inder, immediately blurting out my fear — "Inder, I have disobeyed Baba . . ." but swiftly and firmly he replied, "Don't be frightened, Kate — it's all right. There are some things he does not require of you, and it was already known you would not do as I asked."

That evening he told the assembled group (who knew nothing of the substance of this crisis) that on very, very rare occasions, so rare we must not even consider them in relation to ourselves — Baba gave instructions . . . *the disobeying of which* . . . constituted in essence the highest obedience.

Silently, the divine and loving Presence wrapped me round, and stilled the weeping in my heart. For that short hour, he granted me repose.

My days die away like an echo;
my heart-strings are snapped.
Day is turned into night,
and morning light is darkened before me.

Pity me, pity me, you that are my friends;
for the hand of God has touched me.

Job 17 and 19. The New English Bible. (c) 1970
by permission of Oxford and Cambridge University Presses.

In mid-August Edwin had a stroke, and Inder summoned the entire group to his bedside. It was a moving spectacle, for we had all been pulled in various directions, some almost to the point of no return; yet when the request came, everyone rallied. Patrick was reluctant but nevertheless took me to Sawston by van; Rupert transported Betty, Ian conveyed Joan, and Nigel and Alison collected Rose and Paul. Within an hour or so of contact, all concerned had congregated in Nell's small bungalow. She herself was dazed, and pathetically grateful for our support. Edwin was unconscious, and without him she was like a little, lost child.

Those that could do so were asked to stay the night. Inder said we could help Edwin, perhaps even to attain liberation, if we could turn his thoughts towards Baba as he prepared to leave his body; and Alison, Rose, Inder and myself stayed on when the others dispersed. Nigel returned during the early hours but did not remain with us, being too restless and disturbed. We heard him intermittently moving around uneasily in the sittingroom. Nell retreated to bed and tried to sleep, frail and wan with exhaustion and grief, and we promised to call her if any change occurred. The four remaining sat in vigil throughout the night, repeating the Master's name constantly in our minds, and for a short period aloud, like a mantra, at Inder's instigation. This completely unnerved Nigel, who came into the room and listened, then fled. But to Rose, Alison and me it was a profound experience which restored, however temporarily, our lost unity.

It was dim and cold in the old-fashioned, candlelit room, yet before long I noticed that Inder transmitted a soft effulgence that made it appear less bleak. A neighbour had placed a tangerine mohair cardigan about his shoulders against the chill night air, and this somehow enhanced the impression of delicate flames swirling lightly about his head. I had never seen him more beautiful, and my soul bowed before him in silent adoration. The night passed quickly, and remaining wakeful was extraordinarily effortless. And curiously, the harmony re-established between us was real and tangible; stripped of all discords, all barriers, all separation . . . leaving us nakedly heart to heart, and soul to soul. I shall never forget them as they were then, both Rose and Alison like lamps, lesser flames of the glorious blaze that was Inder.

We returned to Cambridge around 7.30 a.m., Inder staying with Nell to await a nurse and an ambulance. Patrick expressed great displeasure on my arrival, and the light and beauty still lingering in my mind ebbed quietly away. He said that Edwin would not die for a while, and there had been no real emergency. I ought to have gone home with my husband like Betty and Joan.

Edwin lived for a week without fully regaining consciousness. Nightly Inder took Rose along to see him, and did not appear to care whether I came or not, though he was pleased that Alison and Nigel visited regularly. On one occasion Patrick also went. Our former patterns then reasserted, and the bonds of unity loosened and frayed.

After Edwin's passing, a cable was sent by Inder to Baba on Nell's behalf, and she received a comforting reply. But he told us privately that Edwin had not been sufficiently conscious of God to attain liberation, for his last thoughts had been of his earthly life and he seemed to have forgotten altogether about Baba. Even so, we had helped him, now and in the future, by our concentration on the Master's name for his sake.

At the end of August he changed the format of the meetings, and in the following weeks gave us a series of talks on levels of awareness, stressing that everything registered by the mind and senses was affected by the state of development of our consciousness. He said that if we listened carefully we might be able to deduce to which level we belonged. The levels he divided into three conditions of being — that of beginners on the Path; those firmly established, and those so near to the end they were on the brink of Realisation.

The talks were short, concentrated and intensely interesting; but after nearly a month of meticulous application, to our disappointment he abruptly concluded them. Most of us, he declared, were receiving and applying the given information from the standpoint of the personality. This created incorrect perspectives and undesirable attitudes, and he must therefore discontinue this line of study. No amount of persuasion or vexation on the part of his listeners would induce him to grant us a further opportunity, and there was a definite sense of something lost. As to the level one had attained — I was none the wiser. It seemed I fitted the negative side of them all, without any correspondingly positive attributes.

Late in August I dreamt again of Baba. I felt unhappy whenever I recollected it, and certainly did not understand what it meant, but Inder said the dream was deeply symbolic. I had found myself in a cold and windy place, by a swiftly moving river. Baba was walking by himself over a broad common which I recognised as Jesus Green. I followed him with my eyes, my attention centred wholly on his movements, and at the same time I noticed that in his vicinity a young man was delivering a crate of eggs. Baba turned and came towards me, and I thought hopefully he would talk to me and assuage the loneliness of this bleak and empty situation. His face was serious, and all he said was, "*Who* is the man with the eggs?" Instead of answering, I tried to ask something connected with myself, which he ignored, and again repeated the question. Then he walked away. I hurried after him and cried, "Please Baba, may I come with you?" and he replied, "No, Baba wishes to be alone." I stood watching his retreating figure, feeling utterly lost and wondering where I could go — for there was no place else for me if I could not go with him.

Foolishly I associated this dream with the circumstances then prevailing; Inder's coldness, and the rather curt communications from Baba. It appeared to me that nothing could be much worse than my current predicament, and my state of mind well fitted that of the dream. Inder said this was not so. I therefore assumed something further would arise and I would again be commanded to negate myself for Patrick, whom I concluded was symbolised by the man with the eggs. Time proved me wrong, for the man was in fact Inder, and the dream foreshadowed the trial that awaited me the following spring.

Patrick was still swinging emotionally between a need to understand *who* and *what* Baba was, and a violent resentment

101

at this intrusion into his life, which later externalised once more as active hostility towards Inder and bouts of anger unleashed on myself. Night after night he got up, unable to sleep, and pored wrathfully over my books. He probably read the literature concerning Baba more thoroughly than many a devotee, and the effect on him was devastating. Passages which I had taken one way, he took in another, and a few brief remarks on the value of celibacy assumed gigantic proportions in his mind and incensed him to fury.

On my 'permitted' Sunday he would take me to Weston with the children, invariably leaving in a temper shortly after reaching there. Once he insisted on bringing us back home with him, and drove at such breakneck speed we were all terrified, missing death repeatedly by inches. It was like living in a perpetual nightmare.

On the last Sunday in August he hit rock bottom. We had suffered some appalling nights and I knew he was fast reaching a point of complete nervous and physical exhaustion. On that particular morning he had again asked to speak with Inder, and I was full of foreboding. Inder arrived with Alison around twelve, and for a while he and Patrick talked alone, then Alison and myself were asked to join them. Between them they analysed my behaviour, bringing up yet again the "faults" and failings that supposedly created such disruption in my marriage, and I listened incredulously, for even Alison said nothing in my defence, nor made the slightest protest at what she must have known could not be true. In the end I burst into tears and ran through to the kitchen.

Soon Patrick went out, apparently in a much better humour, and Inder and Alison came to say goodbye to me before leaving. I was rolling pastry and could hardly bring myself to speak to them. Inder's verbal cruelty and his blatant injustice had cut me to the core. In my view I had done nothing wrong save attend the meetings (if that was wrong?). Patrick had done nothing other than demand a return to his former way of life and my total compliance; an outworn state born of our past conditioning — and for this same conditioning we endlessly suffered, and I was beaten and weary with the senseless misery of it all. Added to this they had collectively made me appear the reverse of all I had striven for, and not one had put forward a mitigating word in my favour.

Inder remarked that he was taking Alison out to lunch, and would I like to afterwards go with them to Weston, as Patrick had agreed this? (it was 'my' day anyway). Morosely I said yes. But when Patrick returned he looked wan and ill again; he could not eat, and his untouched meal moved me inwardly to tears. He was so vulnerable — so in need of me — then, to my horror he began to cry, great choking sobs that rent my heart. Over and again he said, "I don't know what to do, Kate, I don't know what to *do* . . ." the great tears rolling over his fingers, dampening his shirt. And then he told me how he had come downstairs in the night and turned on the gas oven, determined to end his own wretchedness — how he had lain down but could not go through with it, and instead went into the street, wandering down the road in his pyjamas until accosted by a policeman who took his name and address.

I was shattered beyond words. Numbly I led him into the sittingroom (mercifully Teresa was away for the weekend) and talked to him as lovingly as I could. I felt unutterably bestial and cruel to have brought him to such a pass, and did not know how to deal with the implications. Nor did I question the truth of his statements. It did not occur to me to doubt him.

When Alison and Inder came for me, for the first time ever I had no desire to go with them, and I told Inder at once what had happened to Patrick although he had said I was not to mention it. Inder gazed at me very soberly and said, "You must make your own decision now, Kate — as to whether you trust Baba enough to leave Patrick *to him,* or whether you think it necessary to stay with him *yourself,* in case he tries again to take his life."

Putting it this way increased the agony. As a woman I felt I should stay at his side — disregarding the call of the heart, which could so easily be my own self-want; yet as a soul I was clearly aware this presented some test. It is easy to say one loves the Master and places one's trust in him; not so easy but nevertheless possible to demonstrate that trust when thrust into a situation from which one cannot escape . . . but I had a choice, and all my commonsense thinking, humanity, and love of Patrick as my husband had come to the fore. I wavered . . . then reluctantly said I would come.

Patrick had managed to pull himself together and made no demur. I implored him to phone me without fail a little later to

103

let me know how he was feeling, and said if he needed me I would return immediately.

Twice on the outward journey Inder asked if I wished to turn back. With all my heart I did, and fought it strenuously. The very roots of my life seemed intertwined now with Patrick's. I clung to him in my mind and I could not let go. All our years together crowded into my head . . . I was beseiged with bitter-sweet memories . . . with all he had meant to me. The youthful dreams I had woven around him, the unfulfilled hopes — all returned as clearly as if they were yesterday's, and the harsh-nesses fell away and might never have been. He was again my partner, my husband . . . the loved father of my children. I did not wish to be torn away from him: without him the part of me that was Kate would wither and die . . . and I knew this beyond doubt. My legs began to tremble and my stomach felt sick.

Yet something firm and calm at the core of me urged me on. Whatever lay ahead for us both was destined, of that I was certain. He belonged to Baba as surely as I did — had it not been so, we should not have been kept so firmly welded. Or so I told myself. I suppose it all boiled down in the cold light of rationality as to whether I dared place life literally in his hands. My own life, yes, for my natural inclination led me that way. *But Patrick's?* My spiritual need was *forcing* change upon him against his will, and my whole life's conditioning had been to defer to others, *to please.* It was *impossible* to act counterwise to this — *akin to destroying oneself.* I saw that the roots of personal attachment still remained *and had gathered force* . . .* he was my charge . . . *my child* . . . I could not *bear* to lose him. Did I, *in truth,* have strength enough to leave him to the Master, to let him face *alone* the desolate stretch I saw in store for him? Only those who have been similarly placed can have any idea of the pain of such relinquishment.

He telephoned at teatime and was in better spirits, and Inder suddenly thawed towards me and for a little while was kind. This proved to be our last Sunday at Weston, for Nigel stopped our visits after that.

Having thought about it, Patrick could not readily forgive me for leaving him on such a day, and afterwards felt he had been

---

* Perhaps because I had uncovered them.

betrayed in his hour of need. As a consequence he hardened towards me, and this made things even worse.

Inder now spent every Sunday with Rose and Paul instead of Nigel and Alison, which neatly returned my Sundays to Patrick exclusively; for whereas 'open house' had been kept at Weston, there were no invitations to Rose's — at least not for me.

Very early in September, a young woman arrived on my doorstep one evening in great distress. She was almost incoherent, but managed to ask for the "Spiritualist President". I explained that I no longer held that office, and this produced near hysteria, for she had been told to come to me and had walked miles in search of my former address, eventually tracing me here — please, *please* would I help her? I asked her in, and was given an agitated account of doctors and hospitals, and a medical report that decreed she was "mad" because she heard voices — and what the voices had told her to do. These things had arisen, she said desperately, when she began "seeking God", and the voices terrified her because they led her in the wrong direction.

It is difficult now to record all I sensed as time has blurred the memory, though I knew intuitively that she suffered some form of psychic interference with which I was not equipped to deal. Doubtfully I telephoned Rose and asked if Inder would see her (he now visited them daily), uncomfortably aware that this was not the type of request I should make. To my surprise he passed back a reply in the affirmative, and it was arranged that the woman should go to Rose's home the following evening before our meeting commenced.

By the time I arrived, Rose said Miss S. and Inder had been together for almost an hour, with instructions from Inder that they were not to be disturbed, so we sat in the adjoining room and waited.

Strange, discordant sounds were coming from the lounge via the closed interconnecting door. Inder was talking in an animated way completely unlike his normal manner, and the young woman giggled and laughed in a shrill, high-pitched voice that was rather unnerving to listen to. I began to feel sick, and suddenly perceived clouds of a thickish black substance seeping from under the doorbase. Although this was obviously a psychic observation, it was still unpleasantly real. I mentioned it to Rose, who said she had noticed it too, and felt sick herself.

105

A little later Alison arrived and after a while made confirmatory comments.

An insidious faintness crept over me and I asked Rose for a glass of water. She brought in three, and we each sat with one in front of us to earth the powerful exudations infiltrating from the next room. The woman became very excited, and both voices rose in a peculiar dialogue; but throughout the entire interview we had no idea what was said, for the discussion, loud though it was, remained indistinct.

Miss S. was there for two hours, and towards the end of her visit her voice quietened until we could scarcely hear it, and Inder's not at all. Gradually the blackness dispersed and it seemed the interview was over, for Inder called us in. Miss S. looked perfectly normal, shook hands with us all, and smilingly bid us goodbye. To my astonishment she was a well-spoken girl and not in the least as she had been the previous evening, nor could one associate her with the shrill, giggling voice. Inder told her to visit the group whenever she wished, and then she left. We did not see her again.

He declined to discuss what had happened, dismissing it lightly, and instead asked us individually what *we* had thought of it all. Rose and Alison told him of the nausea and blackness they had each felt and seen in varying degrees. He turned then to me and said casually, "What about you, Kate?" raising his eyebrows amiably to indicate we were friends again, at any rate for the time being.

I was afraid he would laugh but took the chance, and replied that I thought she had some dissociation of the subtler vehicles, initially induced by shock, perhaps in adolescence . . . and probably originating from unwise dabbling in occult matters during a former incarnation. This made possible the recent intrusive manipulation by several elementals . . . He did indeed laugh, though not unkindly, and I had the fleeting impression that in some obscure manner I had pleased him.

Around now came another* weird and most vivid dream of prehistoric creatures. I stood on a raised mound in a large rear garden in which my fellow group members were gathered, and numerous hard, squat objects came hurtling through the air and landed continuously on my heart as if accurately aimed

* The earlier one not included, nor its outworking, as it infringes a group member's privacy.

there. With dismay I saw that they were small, scaly 'monsters', *still alive,* and quite horrible to look upon. As each one thudded onto me it disappeared into my flesh and caused great pain — and with a stunned feeling of disbelief I perceived that it was Inder who threw them so unerringly, with this intent.

September brought its own troubles, which heaped on us purposefully one after another. Early in the month I dreamt that Nigel and I were looking at a recent photograph of Baba. He said it had lost its beauty for him, and he could now see only darkness and corruption. Then the photo caught fire — I did not see how — and its edges darkened rapidly with curling smoke. As the flames caught hold they flickered about Baba's features, which changed and contorted with agony, most terrible to see, as if he were actually being burned alive before me. Suddenly the fire disappeared, and the photo returned to its former wholeness, with Baba smiling directly into my eyes. I turned to share this with Nigel, who had stepped back when the fire began, to find he was no longer there.

I pondered uneasily over this dream, and felt its substance would soon work out into life. I did not know what it portended and tried to translate it symbolically, without any conviction. Then I allowed myself to forget it, for there were other things demanding attention.

I worried constantly over my children. Since the night in July when Patrick had smashed my pictures and forced me outside in my nightdress,† both were nervous of him; and at the end-of-term parent/teacher interviews, Teresa's teacher had said she was unusually quiet, and was she worried about anything at home? Her work was not up to its usual standard and she seemed unable to concentrate as well as before . . .

David, too, was affected. He avoided his father at all times and withdrew to his bedroom whenever Patrick was indoors. The atmosphere was fraught with fear, hostility and tension, and I felt trapped and desperate.

One morning, at Patrick's request I called on several estate agents to enquire after land. He was thinking of building again, and I hoped most fervently he would soon get himself back to work and occupy his time with other than my affairs. At the first office entered, on an impulse rising from a continual

† omitted.

impression of moving to that area, I asked if any unfurnished flats were available on, or close to, Milton Road. The young man in charge replied that, oddly enough, one had been given them that morning, on Milton Road itself — a very large flat over a suite of consulting rooms. It was leasable for six months at a low rental of £5 per week plus rates, and would later be placed for sale. If I was interested he would send me details within a few days, and arrange an appointment to view.

With racing heart I said yes, please do; afterwards wondering what madness had got into me, for I had no money at all of my own and no prospect of raising £5 per week or, for that matter, moving, without Patrick's consent.

Despite this I inspected the flat, as much from curiosity as anything else. It comprised the entire first floor of a Queen Anne mansion, having eight spacious rooms in excellent decorative order, a large garage and substantial garden. As I walked through the rooms, imprinting various details on my memory, it occurred to me that if I rented the flat and let four of them, I would make enough money to cover its outgoings, provide furnishings on H.P. and support myself and my children if need be, without taking outside employment. The doctor's wife in residence said there was no objection to lodgers providing I let the rooms furnished.

After careful thought I told Patrick about the flat and asked if he would help me to acquire it as a business venture. If I could successfully sub-let, the income would cover our household expenditure and, being still workless, it would be greatly to his advantage. He knew, of course, that I had other motivations as well. I was honest with him and said if he did not upset the children I would stay with him despite our difficulties, but if he frightened them again I would go to the flat to live if I obtained it. I also said that should he prefer not to assist me and make it a joint enterprise, I would try to raise a small bank loan or simply pledge credit before giving up.

Patrick told my father about the proposal to sub-let through the winter for profit. Father said whatever else Kate is, she has a shrewd head for business — so Patrick made me a loan and we embarked on the new venture with reasonable goodwill.

One morning in September Joan came to visit me. She had not attended the meetings very regularly of late, largely through Ian's scepticism and his condemnatory views on the state of my marriage, and perhaps her intention was to sort out for herself what the facts were as far as my inner convictions and outer life were concerned. As we talked, the embers of past friendship rekindled and we drew close again — and were thus completely off-guard when we were sharply intruded upon by Nigel, who banged on the door loudly, repeatedly and unexpectedly, and seemed in a strangely defiant, even inebriated mood.

He told us rudely and without any preamble that Alison had that morning severed herself from the group and would not be seeing any of us again. That myself in particular was not to try to contact her, as he had forbidden her to speak or write to me and she had agreed to abide by this. Her books were now *en route* to Rose's, and her photographs of Baba had been *torn down and burned* an hour ago along with all her snapshots and mementoes.

It was exceedingly hard to believe. Indeed, I could not at once believe it. *Alison,* who had been with me from the very beginning, whose faith was built on the unshakable base of perception. Nigel declared with satisfaction that he had forced a confrontation with her parents, and she had admitted before them that the group was spurious and Baba was a *fraud.* From now on she would speak *only* of Jesus Christ! He had spoken to Rose and Paul already, and had contacted Inder; now he was off to see Betty. Meeting Joan at my house had saved him a journey, but she was to tell Ian, and I was to tell Patrick! He left in a terrible kind of triumph.

Nobody else knew more than we did. Rose confirmed that Nigel had been to see them and had said he had taken Alison to visit her parents, after which she had yielded up "everything" completely, even to permitting him to burn her precious photographs before her eyes. The entire collection of books had been abandoned at Rose's home, mute witness to the fact that there must be some truth behind it all. I knew hollowly within myself that something dreadful had happened, although I could not accept that Alison's rejection was so damningly complete.

That evening Inder commented he was not greatly surprised by the turn of events. Alison had recently made certain remarks in his hearing that indicated a change of viewpoint, which I had to admit was so. He had withdrawn from Nigel and herself when the trouble between them began, and she appeared to resent this.

Patrick solidly supported Nigel's actions and said he should have been firmer with *me,* qualifying this by adding he thought that I was far more self-willed than the rest. The next morning as no hoped-for letter arrived, I disregarded Nigel's injunction and put through a telephone call to Alison, who sounded at first like a stranger. She said yes, she had definitely left the group and would not be coming again. Then she started to cry and told me how dreadful she felt — that she had betrayed Baba and everything she held dear. She said Nigel had bullied her incessantly and had finally taken her to confront her parents with the situation, telling them she preferred the break-up of her marriage to making any attempt to "give up" this hypnotic man she called Christ. As her father was just recovering from a heart attack, and held the most orthodox Christian views, she had wavered when facing him and simply could not go through with it. If he had died on the spot with shock she would never have forgiven herself, and could not have looked at her mother again. I knew too well the pressures she had been subjected to.

She said, too, she felt she had "let go" of Baba and could never get back. For some minutes we talked — myself asserting repeatedly that what was done could be undone, and not to despair — then at her urgent request said goodbye, for Nigel's car was entering the drive, and it seemed she was still prepared to abide by her promise. But she stressed swiftly that his report on her comments was untrue — she had not denied her convictions, agreeing only to forego her outward expression of them for the sake of family peace.

One week from the day she left us, Alison returned. Nigel had behaved in an impossible fashion. He had been overbearingly tyranical, and had assumed his authority over her in such a way that she knew she would be unable to bear it indefinitely, so she told him she had changed her mind and was coming back to the group. He stormed off to her parents and the scene she had dreaded passed without mishap. Her father survived it and was understanding and kind. Although her parents could not follow the essence of her beliefs, they commiserated with her for her "endurance" of Nigel without complaint for so many years, and on purely worldly grounds they comforted and supported her.

Nigel and Alison then separated. After the discord he

behaved very honourably, and agreed that although he could not any longer "put up with" the way she wished to live, there was no reason why they should not remain good friends. An agreement was legalised between them and she was given custody of both children, a house in her name, half of their possessions, a comfortable weekly income and a lump sum in cash. The house was newly modernised and freshly decorated from top to bottom. Nigel sent her sufficient coal for the coming winter, fenced her garden, and presented the children with another dog. A little later we heard that he had set up house with someone else. It seemed that Baba had freed her from all bondage.

All this upheaval naturally affected other people. Joan and Ian were seriously disturbed by it all, even more so when Patrick visited them one evening and told them all kinds of things which may have been correct from his viewpoint, but certainly were not so from mine. It passed through my mind that had Alison written to Baba as Nigel had wished, a quite different situation might have emerged, and by *not* writing she had perhaps evaded my problems.

I asked Inder cautiously why he had not encouraged her to do so, pending the obvious break-up of her marriage, and bearing in mind my own instruction to remain with Patrick whatever his behaviour. He replied coolly that it was probable Alison *would not have been able to do* what Baba may have requested, a remark that brought me no comfort at all.

The whole of this drama* was encompassed in a very short span of time, and by early October Alison was established in Cowper Road, and on excellent terms again with Inder. In the meantime, Rose's parents and her brother had journeyed to Cambridge especially to meet him, and had specifically requested that they might see Baba on film.

I watched his screened image and implored him in my heart to help me. The unyielding burden I carried weighed me down, and I hardly knew how to continue my life with equilibrium. I had seen others receive gifts of friendship and family approval; that where there were discords they were not bound

---

* Many details of this and other matters have been left out, either for lack of space, or through the natural feelings of those concerned.

to them, and fresh routes opened before them with ease and consideration. Why could it not be so for me, I wondered. Where had I failed him? And why was Inder, and everyone else, so disapproving? But there was no answer.

Alison's new-found freedom and the spiritual status that apparently went with it, upset me greatly. Patrick's hostilities continued and I did not know where to turn. The conflict in my mind was unbearable, and in a rare fit of rebellion the pent-up frustration and long-repressed rage boiled up in me and overcame my submission. I had been bludgeoned emotionally by Patrick just once too often, and confronted Inder on the subject straight away.

"*Why,*" I demanded wrathfully, "cannot *I* have a separation as Baba said in my letter?"

He regarded me blandly, and carefully puffed a perfect smoke-ring from the corner of his mouth.

"You *will* have separation," was his mild response. "There is no doubt about *that,* Kate." A significant pause . . . "The danger is . . . *that you might have it too soon.*" And he flicked the ash from his cigarette with great delicacy into the ancient Lodge ashtray, and turned to other matters in a nonchalant act of dismissal.

To revert to September. During this period Rose had a Church booking at H— and had decided that it would be her last as far as the Spiritualist Church was concerned. She said she did not feel she could talk anywhere without mentioning Baba, and this would hardly be generally acceptable. She explained the matter to the H— President, who still said, "Come along and talk to us, and bring your friends with you!" So one Sunday evening Alison drove Rose, Inder, Paul and myself to the church, where we were very kindly received, and were all placed behind Rose on the rostrum.

Rose has always been a splendid speaker, and this evening she spoke well, though was not at her best. Inder answered some questions, also Alison (the latter somewhat heatedly), as there was considerable dissention from a gentleman in the congregation. I sat listening, feeling the glowing strength of inner conviction and longing to speak to those earnest, upturned faces — so suddenly I got up during a lull in the questions, to say my piece.

To my horror my strength at once drained from me; my legs

112

trembled and my voice shook. I sounded like an emotional 'witness' giving a testimony, and eventually sat down again overcome with shame and confusion. I do not really know what happened, but as I was not a raw lecturer, it is my belief that Inder deliberately devitalised me and made me look foolish, for purposes that can possibly be surmised.

Rose and Alison talked to various people afterwards, and I was justly ignored. They departed for home covered in glory amid handshakes and warm goodwill. I was already in the car and suitably obscured when Inder drew attention to my discomfiture by loudly refusing to sit next to me, "in case Patrick sees me and makes a scene!" — the likelihood of this on that particular journey being too remote to even consider.

They dropped me at Metcalfe Road and went on to Rose's house, where I visualised all four of them merrily having supper together. Some time later, Rose and Alison jointly telephoned me in very high spirits to enquire if I was "all right", Inder having mentioned to them that I seemed rather upset. This, of course, confirmed my assumption, and rubbed the fact well in. I cannot describe the way the whole episode affected me, save that it was out of all reasonable proportion to the event.

In mid-September Betty became unwell with a threatened miscarriage, and was ordered to bed by her doctor and told to stay there. This was a late pregnancy as she was already forty-one, though once pregnant, she wanted the baby and looked forward to having it. At this time Rupert was trying actively to deflect her from the group, being again in close contact with my mother and much influenced by her, and the whole matter was obviously an embarrassment to him in his current office of President of the Christian Spiritiualist Church. Betty, as usual, kept a foot in both camps. Nevertheless, her personal psychic and spiritual experience had convinced her of Baba's benefici-ent working in her own psychology, and during her enforced stay in bed she asked if Inder would visit her and talk over the problems she had begun to encounter.

This he did with some show of reluctance, insisting that Rose should accompany him. I was there by chance when he arrived, as I daily gave Betty some small practical assistance, her child-ren being much the same ages as my own. Inder and Rose disappeared upstairs to Betty's bedroom and for a short while I heard the low murmur of indistinct voices — then Inder came

113

down, and to my surprise asked to speak privately with me.

Rupert ushered us into the sittingroom and closed the door disapprovingly, and Inder at once commenced to censure me severely regarding my *motives* in cleaving to Patrick when there was an increasing probability that he could alienate me from Baba. This was such absolute nonsense I was amazed he could suggest such a thing, and hotly countered it. So strangely unrealistic was the conversation that I soon found myself staunchly defending Patrick with wifely indignation, and aligning myself with him against Inder's seemingly off-the-mark criticisms.

He stopped abruptly, then in a softened tone spoke gently to me as if he was sorry he had harangued me, smiling in a way I had almost forgotten.

At this point Patrick violently interrupted the proceedings by hammering noisily on Betty's front door and demanding my return home. The unforseen interview had caused me to overstay the time allotted me and he required to know why. I left hastily, fearful he might cause a further scene, this time in the house itself.

I learned later that Rose and Inder left within minutes of my departure; and Rupert immediately told Betty there was "blackness" and "some very bad vibrations" in the room where Inder and I had talked. Betty wished to assess this for herself, and foolishly disobeyed her doctor's instructions by coming downstairs for this purpose. The result was a speedy journey to hospital by ambulance the following morning, and an operation to finally terminate her pregnancy.

Yet immediately before, during, and after the operation, as she told us afterwards, she entered a sublime state of certitude that Baba was with her and was, in truth, her Spiritual Master. So radiantly serene was she for several days, that Rupert temporarily stopped in his tracks, and conceded he could have been mistaken in his misgivings and hostility.

In the week following Betty's discharge from hospital, she found herself once more in difficulties. She had returned to the meetings whilst still weak and shaky, to find all else eclipsed by Alison's affairs; and Rupert, immediately outraged by the imminent legal separation, blamed first Inder, then Baba, and reverted irrevocably to his former attitudes. He was sure now that something was wrong somewhere — marriages did not break-up without reason, and the reason was indisputably connected with Baba, or so he affirmed. The group was therefore "black" and Inder was "evil". This sounded so like my mother's assertions I did not doubt she had been consulted.

Betty came in tears to see me, and said they had argued for most of the night, and she didn't know what to do. She could not bear to live like this, nor could she bring herself to hurt Rupert *as I had hurt Patrick*. Her words were like salt in a wound and a sword in my heart, but of this she seemed quite unaware.

At her request I arranged an appointment with Inder for her to discuss these matters, and went with her to Rose's house for this purpose one afternoon. Inder was very kind to her, but also very firm. At the close of the interview he said that we each had to make our own decisions in the light of our *knowledge* of Baba, derived from our direct experience. It would not be an easy path for any of us. Baba was a Christed Being and the world was the world. The world rejected Christ each time the Cosmic Principle made manifest as man, and Baba was no exception.

As we prepared to leave, he turned his attention to me and admonished me sharply for pride and lack of humility. I reeled inwardly beneath the fire of his words . . . what had I done now? What had I done? He said vehemently, "*Be* emotional if you want to! *Leave* if you want to! It is up to *you!*" and for some minutes he castigated me without mercy, more strenuously than ever before.

Betty just stood and looked at me with a strange expression in her eyes. I was dreadfully upset and had wilted visibly. Inder said a friendly goodbye to her and treated me with silent distain. Going home together she was bright and cheerful and we did not mention what had occurred. I felt, however, that if she *had* held me in any lingering respect from the past, she did not do so now.

On the last Thursday in September, Joan came with Ian to the Lodge to tell us she was severing her link with the group. She did not feel any movement could be based on spiritual principles if marriages were broken, and she also gravely doubted that "Kate's feeling for Inder was purely altruistic" in view of Patrick's unhappiness. Looking straight at me, with tears in her eyes, she declared I had all but broken her heart. She had loved me and trusted me, believing me to be a true aspirant, but she now saw that I had "twisted and betrayed" the truths I taught others. She publicly exonerated Inder from the slur she had cast on him last May,* saying she believed the situation had somehow come about in order to teach me a lesson — one that I had apparently not yet learned.

After she had gone I felt dazed and defeated, and deep inside me the tears broke afresh and flowed without cease. I had truly loved Joan, and knew she had once loved me, and I did not understand just where I had failed her. Those present, though criticising Joan for "letting go" of Baba, did not refute the charges made against me, nor offer any commiseration. Inder passed no comment on the matter.

Patrick and I had repatched our marriage as best we could, though it was still hard going. Every few days we suffered repercussions when he panicked, and fought strenuously to go back the way he had come. At these times he would tell me to "get out" and go to the flat to live, and at the beginning of October I decided to do just that. It was an odd situation, for having determined my course I asked if he would like to come with me, feeling he was not yet strong enough emotionally to do otherwise. And he, in his friendlier moments, said that he would.

I had already inserted a 'Rooms to let' advertisement in the local paper, and was busy providing furniture, sheets, crockery, etc. as Patrick insisted I must take nothing from 'his' house. He was still vacillating so much he was quite unable to sustain a decision and commit himself firmly to any one course of action, so there was no choice but to make any needful alterations myself. I knew my nervous system had had enough of constant scenes and recriminations, and felt my physical resources were fast running out. I longed for a place I could not be commanded to leave at the least provocation — where I could invite friends occasionally if I wished, and have a meaningful book by my bedside without being treated as a criminal. Baba had instructed me to look after my children and this I was trying to do. If it was his wish that Patrick should come too, then so be it — his welfare was still very much in my heart . . . yet I felt now it would only be possible to continue living

* this incident is not included as it is personal to Joan.

together on my own ground, believing blindly that this way things could be different.

October crept in, and Inder told us we were now entering a more subjective phase. Those that were willing would see more and more within themselves that needed to be put right, and the clearer their self-knowledge, the clearer would be their perception of Baba. He now gave each of us the opportunity for private analytical discussion, using Rose's dining room for the purpose.

Whereas formerly we had discussed external affairs and worldly matters that affected us, this was now discontinued and introspection encouraged. Several subjects were dealt with openly in the group — romance, for instance, and emotional attachment. I used to think this was aimed exclusively at myself, and discovered in due course to my great surprise that both Alison and Rose thought it referred to them. Also, unknown to me, Paul had previously expressed certain grievances about the display of affection between Nigel and Rose, and this and kindred matters were indirectly alluded to as well.

The private discussions, in general, were brief — though mine spun out painfully — much to the vexation of those waiting Inder's return. The fault was not mine, as I had no control over the duration of the interview. Inder questioned me closely on things I had mentioned in the past, and now he was more specific, delving deeply into psychological pressures, conditioning and motivation. Although I did not like this, it was a definite aid to understanding. Once I asked him why he always picked on me for this uncomfortable investigation. He replied, "Because you are willing! Instead of regarding it as a disgrace, why don't you also consider it might be a mark of favour on Baba's part? Not everyone is ready to see themselves. Mehera, who is known to be special to Baba, was often treated in this way when *she* was young."

It was a comforting thought, though fleeting. I did not feel in the least bit favoured. Inder was friendly during these private discussions, but scathing at the meetings that followed immediately afterwards; and when the sessions concluded three weeks later, he again resumed his stern exterior towards me at all times, save with rare exceptions. To the others he remained genial and pleasant always.

Yet there *was* a valuable compensation while the discussions

117

lasted, for being in his close company, and despite the impersonal work of analysis, the burning longing eased and became more bearable. It provided a needful respite, perhaps, in which to gather strength and bear even more.

Whilst the sessions were in progress, we went one Sunday on the long promised trip to London to meet Baba's younger brother, Adi. It was a lovely morning, a little chilly, even drizzly, but the sun shone through the rain mizzle and everything felt light and exhilarating. Patrick had been unexpectedly reasonable over my going — I had asked some days previously if he would like to come too, and though he declined, he had made no fuss. Teresa was to spend the day with her Auntie and the new baby, and David was still intensely occupied with young male activities. I therefore felt unusually free and relaxed.

Inder was in a delightful mood and disposed to be pleasant to me. For this isolated occasion he dropped all severity and let me sit next to him throughout the journey — a quite unexpected privilege. He looked extraordinarily handsome and exuded a vital magnetism, curiously enhanced by the immaculate dark suit and snow-white shirt that was his daily attire.

I told him of a dream of the previous night — rather an alarming one that I found most puzzling. Alison, Rose and myself were with him in a large room, each of us occupied with different tasks. He came to where I was working and drew two tiny gold snakes from my wrists, flinging them both away, wriggling like quicksilver. I cried out in horror for I had not known the snakes were there — one was vanity, and the other I think was pride. Then, with a swift movement he pulled a snake from behind my back. This one was passive and inert, a dull black in colour, and considerably larger than the other two. I felt sick with shock and implored him to tell me the meaning of it all, but he laughed and kissed me, and instead of giving an explanation, indicated the double doors at the side of the room and told me I must go through them. I walked away from him, without looking back, though in some part of my head I saw the others still busy as before.

The doors opened at my approach and I passed through to the hall beyond. A lamp glowed from the ceiling, very high up, giving just sufficient light to see by. Before me lay a flight of stairs which I mounted; these were thickly carpeted and my feet made no sound. At the top was a lift with an open metal grille, and I went inside. At once it soared upwards, at such speed my consciousness left my body and I could see only a whitish substance all around me. As I entered this, my awareness of God increased — I said, with feeling, "Baba, Baba, I love you . . ." then I lost consciousness altogether.

After what seemed a very long time I returned to my senses. The sun came streaming in through a window, and in front of me sat a mother feeding her children from a loaf on the table. I knew that something sacred and profound had happened to me.

Inder made no comment on the dream, though he heard me out with every evidence of interest. Then imperceptibly he drew me into the general warmth of the group relationship. Paul was with us, and there was an air of companionship that included me in it for the first time in months, and this expanded when we reached our destination, for Adi and Frenee received us as if we were part of the family. Their home was beautiful, yet cosy, and the whole situation delightfully informal. It had the healing effect of a soothing balm.

With Adi I experienced an immediate rapport; an intuitive recognition of having known him before. A young Indian was also visiting, named Jehangir, who had come with Baba's permission to study economics at London University. It proved a truly happy day, and I realised by contrast how acutely strained and tense my life had become.

On my return home in the early evening, Patrick was rather quiet. He told me eventually that he had felt so nervously disturbed in the empty house, he feared what he might do, and had telephoned the Samaritans. They sent someone to talk to him and were arranging for him to see a specialist for further help and treatment.

I listened, appalled. All the joy went out of the day, and the weight and grief descended again like a pall. I felt frightened and trapped. Whatever I did was hurtful to him. He required every moment of my time, every particle of my being, and if I did not give them he went all to pieces.

A week later he saw the specialist by private appointment, on his own, refusing my anxious offer to accompany him, and told me afterwards that he must have an X-ray as he was coughing a lot and had lost so much weight. An appointment had been made at once, he said.

When the day came and I ushered him off (he again declined my company) I waited in fear, and worried myself nearly sick with anxiety — chiding myself bitterly for not seeing the sharp deterioration in his physical condition. The worst was confirmed on his return. A small shadow had shown on one lung and he must go back in six weeks time. If there was no improvement he would have to go into a sanitorium.

This news devastated me utterly. I bowed beneath it and almost broke, believing every word he said, and crushing the signalling impulses that refused to accept he was ill. I was selfish, heartless, cruel . . . and observed with despair the continuing conflict in my mind. Weeks passed before I learned he had been to a dancing class, not a chest clinic; and there had been no specialist consultation, or X-ray, at all.

The London visit transpired to be of considerable importance to me, for Adi, Frenee and Jehangir all had later parts to play in my life, though the others present that day did not meet the first two again. My connection with Adi was of particular consequence, but outside the timespan of this record. Jehangir is mentioned again soon.

The dream too, had an imminent validity. The snakes, like the prehistoric monsters, relating to sanskaras of a certain type. These latter Inder made me deal with myself, but the former he eventually took from me. The last part of the dream referred to a mystical experience which came at the climax of my time with him, and was a much diluted reflection of the cosmic registration still many years ahead.

I did not know in those days how the Samaritans operated, and thus accepted Patrick's story as it stood. The unwinding of this was lengthy and has been omitted along with much else in the same vein. It should therefore be borne in mind that I was subjected to continual and intensive pressure in my marital life, greatly enhancing the effect of the treatment Inder meted out to me. The odd occasion, as on the London visit, when this was eased — served to alleviate a stress that could undoubtedly have damaged my health beyond the point of usefulness . . . as well as preparing the ground for other events. What I, and others, learned through the entire process was inaccessible at this stage, and could only become operative in the future.

We moved to the flat in mid-October, and for several weeks

Inder surprisingly stipulated the Saturday meetings should be held there. It was soon apparent that the others found this irksome, so it was by common consent discontinued. This caused me no great loss as there had been no chance of a more direct relationship with Inder — he always came and left with the rest, and generally went on elsewhere. Patrick was invariably out when they arrived, always returning long after they had gone, so there were no embarrassments or confrontations. He had again ceased contact with the group and had joined with those who had nothing good to say of it.

Rupert had broken his own connection in September, and at the end of October Betty gave up the struggle to appease him and left also. But worse than this; to explain her actions she openly stated the group was "black" and "evil" (how those words were repeated!) and even expressed this to my face. It produced a disturbing sense of unreality to hear her speak this way. No one ever, to my knowledge, laid blame on their own behaviour or conditioned attitudes.

My mother naturally heard of all that went on, and regarded it as confirmatory proof of the correctness of her judgements; Betty's assertions from a psychic standpoint, and Joan's from a purely Christian and moral one. Her comments reached me through various channels, for I had not seen her myself for several months. She refused to visit my home as Inder had been there, and the situation between us was quite impossible to resolve.

One of the charges she levelled against me was that I neglected my children. Nothing could be calculated to grieve me more, and no-one cared to refute her totally unfounded accusations. All Patrick's known past failings she chose to ignore, and his pronounced alcoholic tendencies she now laid firmly at my door, for I had "driven him to drink" it seemed. I floundered agonisingly in the web of lies constructed around me, and found it beyond my capacity to register the extent to which people would go, who had loved and been loved, to prove their point.

Slander and mental cruelty were but the beginning. In surviving them I invoked a more drastic punishment, duly administered in the future, and operative over a period of many years. Although I could not credit my perceptions, my inner faculties were nonetheless fully aware of these underlying traits and their ultimately expressed realities, and threw up repeatedly

121

in the form of graphic dreams the unabsorbed substance of their cognitions.

In November, perhaps alarmed by the tangible evidence of what he was instigating or supporting, Patrick appeared to come briefly to his senses and attempted to turn the tide.

Around mid-November, he appealed to me to give him a positive chance to make contact with Baba. He said my lack of physical response was still the root of his vexation with me, and because of the religious associations in his mind (he had been reared a Catholic), this stood between him and his own acknowledgement of the Master. He implored me earnestly to help him, and expressed with moving seriousness his underlying need, despite appearances to the contrary, to understand the principles which Baba personified.

This distressed me more than words can say. As mentioned before, the inflow of light to my mind had suffused my entire psychology. I was now better able to stabilise it, but his persistent unkindness, cruel accusations and hopelessly inconsiderate treatment had also played their own part in my withdrawal from him, and were now the predominating factor. I did not know if I could ever again be as he wanted me to be. In my heart I did not wish to make the effort, he had wounded me too deeply. Yet I knew with sad certitude that for as long as he deceived himself there was a barrier, created by me, obstructing him — the Master would oblige me to remove it if I could.

On the previous groupnight, and also on the one immediately following this conversation, Inder spoke to us searchingly and at some length on our individual surrender. As always, specific external instructions were not given, but beneath his words, in the strange 'inner' language he used, I heard him tell me plainly what was asked of me.

I prayed much, and I cried much, and in the end resigned myself to what I felt was God's Will. With a one-pointed effort that involved the Totality of my being, I moved *against* the current within myself, and turned myself to face the other way. I dimly sensed that it signified an ending — the point of culmination on a timeless, eternity-bound journey. I knew, though through a veil, that this marked the beginning of the Greater Mystery, the death in life — and paradoxically, the *end* of the beginning, the first stage on the gross-plane level, of total abnegation. Mercifully I did not grasp that it would repeat, and repeat again, and yet again . . . all along the line that comprised my existence.

Patrick had no idea how hard it was for me; how I had to move counter to every inclination within myself. Nor how often in the following months I would retch and vomit in the night as he lay asleep, beating my hands in despair and silent entreaty on the cold bathroom floor. Such states are beyond the possibility of description. They can only be experienced, and must by their very nature sound strange and unnatural to those not caught up in their laws.

For nearly a week Patrick reverted to a more youthful self and was pleased with me, cheerful and benign. He said he withdrew his remarks about Inder, and would come to the Thursday meeting to tell him he was now welcome to visit our home at any time he chose. He would invite him Friday evening and then for the whole day on Sunday (knowing quite well these times were usually spent with Rose and Paul) and he could see no reason why I should be left out ever again in the future.

On Thursday he came to the Lodge about eight in the evening and asked for a private interview. This was immediately granted and took place in an adjoining room. He commented afterwards that Inder "showed no ill-feeling or any prejudice at all" concerning their past relationship, a magnanimity of mind that never ceased to amaze him.

Our guest came on Friday as arranged. He and Patrick conversed together and everything was most amicable. After a while the latter became restive and went out, leaving Inder alone with myself without visible rancour. I had hoped so long for this to happen, and was oddly disappointed, for he was suddenly a polite, informative stranger, and not in the least like the Inder of former days.

Looking back, I understand now the impossibility of any other behaviour, for a relaxation of his role would have affected my state proportionately. I was only partially conscious then of how things really were — seeing everything through a golden cloud of spiritual light that blinded me to all save my own motivation.

He arrived early on Saturday, just as he had done elsewhere for so many months. Two films were to be reshown that evening for Patrick's benefit, and a full group was expected.

Patrick's geniality, however, was already slipping, and he refused to join Inder for tea while we waited the others. My stomach muscles tautened in the old familiar way, and I felt the same nervousness as I pleaded with him to at least behave courteously.

Later that evening he joined us and watched one of the films — both he and Paul moving restlessly throughout — and then he hastily escaped to his pub. I asked Inder if he would remain behind to talk when the group dispersed, as he always did this in their homes . . . but his cool compliance brought me no happiness, for as soon as we were alone he began to upbraid me. This time the fault was my inability to maintain an impersonal relationship with him — I had gone to too much trouble over tea and had treated him too deferentially, which "doubtless annoyed" my husband. *Why could I not* behave as Rose and Alison did? He entered *their* lives and was accepted by them as one of the family, without preference *or* personal feeling. *Why* could I not do the same?

I looked miserably down at my feet. I had not been aware that I acted so differently. Knowing indeed who he was, and loving him so intensely because of it, how other could I treat him than the way I did?

"What Baba requires is fire without smoke," he said enigmatically, and firmly eclipsed his cigarette in the ashtray. His manner then changed; his face hardened and became devoid of expression. He admonished me sharply for jealousy, possessiveness, resentment and other similar attributes, and was so harshly unjust I burst into tears and the anguished grief welled up again within me. He left soon afterwards, well before Patrick's return, and I stood outside by the gate and watched his dignified form retreating into the night, tears streaming despairingly down my cheeks.

I thought his rebukes were subtle blows aimed at the feelings that rose in me each time I was excluded; the sensations of abandonment and rejection, and the hopeless longing to be with him all the time in no matter what circumstance. In my ignorant blindness I no more connected his outburst with Patrick, than the much earlier one with Betty. Nor did I see that he had pinpointed for me the divergence between myself and the rest, and that it lay solely in my angle of perception.

Patrick was in a very black mood that night, and said he had changed his mind about "the bloody Indian" and would not have him here again. If Inder came, he would go . . . he had not cared for the film and the "whole thing" was rubbish. I reminded him he had invited Inder to tomorrow's lunch. His reply to this was, "Cancel it!", his attitude such it brooked no argument. When he slept I took my usual refuge in silent and hopeless tears, springing as much from Inder's criticisms as from Patrick's aggression and my own helplessness.

By morning he had quietened, though he reiterated he would not eat with our guest and would take his lunch in another room. I did not know what to do. Inder arrived to find him out; his demeanour was cold and severe and he required to know if "your husband" remained willing for him to come. I had to reply in the negative, so he asserted it would be wiser for him not to stay. Our meal was cooked and ready to go on the table — prepared, of course, with great care. I thought of Inder lunchless and leaving my home rejected and inhospitably received. It was too cruel; and made worse by Inder's attitude that clearly inferred my sole responsibility for this mismanaged state of affairs. He departed immediately. I heard later he went straight to Rose's house and spent the day there.

Patrick returned home somewhat mellowed and expressed surprise at the absence of our guest. It seemed he was disposed to play host and eat with him after all. I refrained from comment, though a thousand thronged for expression. I had learned to accept defeat and the vagaries of another's whims — especially those born of the conviviality (or otherwise) of immoderate drinking.

Despite what had happened, Inder made plain that Baba's first instruction still stood and, "If you have sufficient love for him you will obey it and let nothing stand in the way of this". So once more I removed my pictures and put away my books — which greatly pleased Patrick, who had so far shown no sign of repentance for his behaviour. There were no more meetings at the flat. I knew to press this would be pointless.

Patrick sold the house in Metcalfe Road and in December all the furniture from there was moved to our new abode. The home was arranged as formerly and I left my lovely room* for

* He had shared this pretty bed-sittingroom when we first came, but had made several violent scenes (not included) and gone back to 'his own' house. I gave him a separate room when he asked to return.

his, where the double bed was now reinstalled. It seemed to me I had achieved nothing by moving save a financial burden, for the lodgers remained, and I paid all the bills. My sole gain was a sitter-in, for one of my lady lodgers was a teacher who seldom went out, and she provided this service for me discreetly and sympathetically.

During our brief span of unity, Patrick confessed he had said many things about me, mainly to my mother (but some to Ian and Joan) which he had known at the time were not true, and he begged me for forgiveness. I answered to the effect that I understood his disturbance and we should now put these things behind us, adding that I would be grateful if he would first attempt to right this, which he promised to do. Sadly, he never did, and the opportunity to correct some basic and very serious misconceptions that could only be dealt with by himself, was thus lost.

I did not withdraw the response I had given, maintaining it, not exactly as Patrick wanted, but as it had formerly been all the years of our marriage. It made no lasting difference. However, the only thing he could complain about now was my attendance of the meetings, for which he no longer had the onerous, twice weekly duty of staying in. His social life expanded at this time and he began to frequent late night drinking parties. It became quite usual for him to arrive home at three or four in the morning, twice or three times each week. I protested strongly about it, without effect, for I felt he was not being fair and it also kept me awake for hours quite needlessly, as once wakened I could not readily fall asleep again. Sometimes he slandered me and called me things I would not wish to repeat, and his vituperative hatred of Inder was often frightening. At other times he expressed remorse and became vulnerable, childlike, loving . . . and kind. This side of him undid my puny defences and filled me with pity and compassion. *It also ensured* that my punished and bleeding heart did not harden.

Paul joined us for the last time at the very end of November, and Inder then stopped going to his home. There were no scenes or explosions, no backsliding or recriminations — it "just happened" (or so Rose said). No other explanation was ever given me, and meetings were thereafter held at Alison's house in Cowper Road, or at the Lodgeroom.

As an indicator for the future I produced a potent dream. Only four of us were left now (excluding Inder), namely Rose, Alison, Nell and myself, and I saw us sitting in a glass-walled room with many persons peering in from the outside. In the doorway stood my mother, wielding a sword which she tried repeatedly to make me swallow; and in the centre, in full view of all who wished to see, sat Inder — with four heaped piles of objects placed in front of him. These were shaped like astrological symbols, and he commenced to distribute them at once.

Rose and Alison received triangles and stars with accompanying flattery and praise, and Nell was given a smaller portion of the same, with warm encouragement. For myself was left the stack of little black squares that denoted further humiliation and pain, and I cried out at the injustice of it all; but he steadfastly ignored me.

PART II

THE TEST

Death in the midst of life

I know that thou canst do all things
and that no purpose is beyond thee.
But I have spoken of great things which I have not understood,
things too wonderful for me to know.
I knew of thee then only by report,
but now I see thee with my own eyes.
Therefore I melt away;
I repent in dust and ashes.

Job 42. The New English Bible. (c) 1970
by permission of Oxford and Cambridge University Presses

Inder gave us a series of talks on love, obedience and surrender that commenced in the latter part of November and continued until Christmas. In one of the earliest he placed great stress on differentiation, and said persons who were *devoted* to Baba (and were therefore devotees) displayed qualities of emotional love and personal attachment that indicated *they were still seekers* trying their best to learn how to obey. Conversely, those who had pure and unadulterated love for him were objective and *impersonal* in their approach; their feelings did not influence them *or* affect their obedience. These latter were ready for service. In time, the difference between the two conditions was likely to become apparent even in the small-scale setting of the group — in certain circumstances they would clash — and this could result in a separation of one from another, perhaps causing a cleavage in the group itself.

Rose and Alison blossomed under this descriptive exposition; it appeared obvious which category they fell in, neither of them suffering the tears and emotional turmoil which they all knew affected me. I struggled inwardly for a few minutes in an attempt to balance my past abilities with my present dereliction, then I let go entirely. Baba knew how much I loved him; whether it was devotional or altruistic, it was everything I had.

In practically every talk after this, a divergence was made between us. I was typed with Nell, though Inder stipulated we were widely different, and Rose and Alison were likewise classed together. The grading was never specified; it was simply assumed (or rather, inferred) that the latter two were ready for 'service' and for some obscure reason I was not. Nell openly said she knew she served Baba already, and this was never refuted.

Early in this period Inder began giving Alison his secretarial work. Formerly he had requested of her occasional letters connected with group affairs or the London people, but now he visited her quite frequently with his personal correspondence and other concerns. However discreetly this was done, it was always brought out eventually during one meeting or another, so we were all well aware of what went on. Alison also was very conscious of the privilege given, as soon became apparent.

We held a Christmas 'At Home' which accentuated the current procedure. Inder asked Alison and myself to type out some invitation cards to send to the London group and to any friends we might feel were interested, and I noticed he used all Alison's cards and my own were pointedly left. My observation of this was remarked on as "childish" but brought the small fact into highlight. Oddly enough, Mr. R. (invited by Alison) and Mr. and Mrs M. (invited by Rose) all accepted the invitation, and the five persons to whom I wrote did not even send me a reply. Mr. R. incidentally came several times before deciding that Baba was not for him, and this added to the overall effect.

The young Indian, Jehangir, whom we had met in London, also attended the 'At Home'. Afterwards Inder questioned me rather strangely on my "hypothetical intuition" and whether this "so easily deluded" faculty had made any registration about Jehangir — he being used simply as a random illustration, of course!

As my particular intuition had long ceased to be seriously rated, I knew that whatever I said would not prove to my advantage, least of all the assertion that he made me want to cry. For this foolish statement I was suitably reprimanded and my possible possession of any foreknowledge was publicly debunked.

Around this time I had two vivid dreams that I knew were precognitive, though I understood neither. In the first, Baba came to my house to visit me — not just to the upper rooms, but down into the basement as well.* His brightness lit the whole house with radiance and the dark basement became as light as day. I saw myself running through the streets to fetch Joan, and met her coming towards me — I cried, "Joan! Joan! come and see Baba! He is in my house!" and she replied, "Yes,

---

* This was symbolic. We have never had a basement.

Kate, I know — I was already coming!" And I awoke feeling happy and full of love for her.

The second dream was very different. Alison, Rose and myself were all interlinked, as if our limbs were woven together. We were placed on a hearthrug before a huge fire, and I saw that a cocoon had been thrown over us of fine and tenuous but incredibly strong cords. A feeling of deep love and friendship prevailed. Inder stood watching, then moved suddenly into our midst. I heard him say, "I'm sorry I have to do this to you, Kate," and he kissed me swiftly before sharply jerking the cords and throwing us all off balance. I saw something swirling towards us, like a cloud, and knew it had the power to dull the senses and stupify the mind unless one held firmly onto Baba. The cloud came upon us and, horrified, I watched first Rose, then Alison, fall asleep. Rose's sleep was light, but Alison slipped into a deep unconsciousness. Before she closed her eyes she said, "I love you, Kate", and I held her protectively in my arms. Rose was silent for a while and then her voice rose angrily in complaint against me. The cloud got thicker and thicker and the cords pulled us in all directions. The experience of pressure was alarming, and grew more terrible as unremembered factors conjoined. The end of the dream was lost to me, though as I awoke I saw Inder being violently sick and collapsing on the floor. I had the awareness he was radioactive and suffering bodily from an excess of radiation absorbed.

As a Christmas gift, I gave him a copy of Omar Khayyam's 'Rubiyat', which rather to my surprise he unwrapped at the Lodge. On impulse I had written inside the flyleaf: 'To my Beloved Master, in everlasting gratitude. K.' — Being so greatly discredited already, any 'hammering' as a consequence could not make things much worse. To my dismay, Alison picked up the book quite casually to inspect the plates, and opened the page where this message was inscribed. She closed it quickly, an inscrutable expression in her eyes — and I knew in that instant that Inder had intended her to see it for some reason, and manoeuvred things accordingly.

Soon after this, at the beginning of the New Year, he made an unexpected statement. We were sitting quietly together in the Lodgeroom, and for once there was a sense of harmony akin to that of the earliest groups. Inder had been joking and exhibiting the delightful humour that was one of his most endearing characteristics, and now he sat serenely smoking as we all basked in the heat of the big gas fire.

"I had a strange vision the other night," he announced suddenly. "I will tell you of it, and perhaps you can interpret it for me!"

We listened intently. Inder never mentioned his own inner life or experience, and none of us had ever asked about it with any success. For my part it had never been possible to do so; he controlled my queries far too firmly for unwonted intrusion into his affairs.

"I saw my own grave," he said. He looked carefully at each of us, and his voice was very cheerful. "It was in the centre of my room, quite a big one —"

Someone laughed, for he wasn't big at all — quite broad, but rather short in stature. He laughed as well, his face alight and vibrantly alive.

"Baba stood on the other side, and in order to reach him . . . *I had to cross my own grave.*"

I felt a sharp pang of tension in my solar plexus. He was trying to tell us something, oh, so obscurely — yet I knew it was important.

"*Did* you cross it?" I asked.

He laughed very boyishly and replied, "Of course I did! Baba embraced me on the other side!"

Alison asked him what it meant, and he turned the question back on us. What did *we* think it might mean?

"Does it mean you will die?" My heart seemed suspended in my throat. I could not reflect the general humour — my facial muscles refused to co-operate.

"Who can tell?" He puffed comfortably at his cigarette and blew a few cumulous smoke rings to give us time to savour this. "It is for *you* to interpret," he said, gazing directly at me for a moment. "Think about it!" And this is all he would say.

Some days afterwards he made another enigmatic utterance, again in a jocular vein. He said, "I once went to an auction and bought my own suitcase! Inside it *was one thousand pounds!* I left it in London, for Kate, when she needs it."

I noticed this did not go down too well with everyone, though we were all equally puzzled. The only indication he would give of its meaning, was that the suitcase had been his in a former life. The anecdote was obviously symbolic.

In January, Nigel approached Alison for a reconciliation. Iris had gone away for a while to give him time to "sort himself out", and he said if Alison would agree to attend only two meetings weekly he would like to reknit their marriage. He saw her daily, implored and pleaded — behaving generally (Alison said) like a young lover.

Inder told her she must make her own decision about this, and to remember it was important to her that she did not turn away from Baba. There was no question of this, however, for Alison's faith was glowingly abundant. The following week she agreed to Nigel's request, and it was decided between them that she should give up the Saturday group to leave the weekend free for family affairs.

So arrangements were made for Nigel's homecoming; yet a curious factor was Alison's uneasy admission that in his presence her framed photos of Baba lost their living quality and became 'dead' for her, and that "blackness" had for a time pervaded the house. Rose said this was because she was psychically absorbing Nigel's negativity. Inder made no allusion to the matter. He was as charming to Alison as ever, cautioning her kindly to be sure of what she most wanted . . . She replied it was done now — she had given Nigel her promise.

But the decision was taken out of her hands. The children were happy over the reconciliation and had made plans with their father for the Easter holidays when, having gained a victory, Nigel over-reached himself. He suddenly demanded of Alison a full and complete renunciation of the group, and also of Baba, as "this nonsense has gone far enough". All her tears and protestations left him unmoved. The lover had again become the tyrant, and with grief she once more said goodbye to him. Not long afterwards we heard that Iris was back and a new baby was on the way — news that Alison bore stoically. Inder simply remarked (at the time of the disruption), "If you had tried to go this way, Alison, the world would have claimed you again; but Baba does not lose his people so easily! Be more careful next time!" Then the subject was dismissed and life continued as before.

It was during the above-mentioned period that I experienced a pressing impulse to contact Alison and talk with her privately; so I wrote her a note and asked her to phone me if she agreed. She responded at once, and said she couldn't think why we'd never done this before! — our arrangement being to meet that same afternoon and have coffee in Lyons and a quiet talk.

Relations between us had been strained for many months, and I was very happy to renew the warmth of our old acquaintance. We selected a table in the teashop and found it secluded enough for intimate conversation. I had no real idea why I wanted to see her, yet the recurring impression had been insistent and felt of some consequence. Alison agreed that on receipt of my note she had felt the same. I started to talk, and suddenly the words flowed from me like a fountain — much to my concern, for I was leaving myself open to the worst of criticisms.

I told her a time was coming when she would neither be with me, nor with Rose, but would have to stand, metaphorically, at a point midway between us. Mentally she would be completely alone, and her only chance of surmounting successfully a trial to come, was to judge events solely from her heart — to do so from her mind would be to court disaster.

She looked at me wonderingly, obviously unsure whether to take this seriously. "What kind of trial?" she asked. "Can you describe it?"

I plunged on again, ignoring my recollection of Inder's recent scathing remarks on "feelings and intuitions". I said a situation would arise in which I should speak the truth, and Inder would deliberately distort it and make it appear that I was deluded. He would attack me mercilessly, and though I knew *now,* at this moment, that it would happen — when this time came I would be shocked and defenceless, and my foreknowledge would leave me. Worse for me would follow . . . Baba himself would appear to have turned away from me, and I would reap humiliation and disgrace. In this contrived event would lie a test for each one of us; not necessarily the same test; for *her* it would be of discrimination . . . and *something more.* The only way to perceive the truth was to hold onto the truth within and to detach oneself from the world . . .

I uttered this with a deep sense of conviction, and repeated the greater part of it. I don't think for a moment that Alison believed me, although she listened quietly. Inder had implied she had already acquired detachment, and I was so frequently berated for my intuitive appraisals they were no longer considered worthy of attention.

Inder was told of our meeting by Alison, and smiled wisely but made no remark. His smile could have meant anything, deprecating it or otherwise. The incident was soon forgotten, and Alison and I did not arrange a further afternoon out.

In January too, came a powerful experience in full waking consciousness. For quite some time, perhaps an hour, I was held in a state of interior absorption, my entire attention focussed one-pointedly upon Baba. It was as though I rose inwardly to some high place, and gradually became fused with a far greater life than my own; a life intensely rich and vital, whose essence was Love, and whose vastly expanded consciousness permeated me with Joy.

As I emerged from this overwhelming condition, some residue of it overflowed into my mundane self. Simultaneously I became aware of the inner essences of certain people — of Joan and Margaret, Betty, Lois and Ann. They were part of a large group of souls with whom Baba was working . . . I saw they were directly linked to him, and experienced in my heart wave upon wave of love moving from him to them. My personality began to register the inflow . . . I was *flooded* with love; *overpowered* by love . . . his love was so intense that tears were forced from my eyes and ran steadily down my cheeks. I could not move with the immensity of it . . . it seemed he used me as a focal point of transmission — as a kind of battery that stepped down and buffered the impact of such stupendous voltage. I did not retain the memory of why or how, but he brooded over them, enfolded them, mothered them . . . and his suffering for their separation from him was incredibly Real and acute.

When my consciousness descended and relocked into its normal state, I knew with absolute certainty I must contact them, for a reason which I had known, that was now withheld from me.

Later the same day I telephoned Joan — rather fearfully I must admit, in view of our last meeting. She was unyielding towards me at first, then melted suddenly and became the warm, loving friend I knew so well. The next morning I called on Margaret, then Betty, and finally Lois, and after this I telephoned Ann. I asked them all to visit me in early February for a kind of reunion, as I felt there was something unified and harmonious still existent on some level between us, and it would anyway be good to meet again.

139

Each of them save Lois responded. She was critical and disapproving and said she did not feel she could attend such a meeting. She knew I was on the wrong track, just as my mother said I was, and would before long suffer a serious setback through "dabbling with occult influences." I was sad and sorry over her attitude, and nothing I said could alter it.

Soon after speaking to Ann, the activating impetus waned as swiftly as it had come, and it was only as I approached the Lodgeroom shortly afterwards that evening that I realised what I had done, and the full extent of my temerity. I had acted in a haze of light, scarcely thinking at all, and now I came down to earth with a bump and grasped the external consequences of my behaviour.

Apprehensively I told those assembled of my experience and the instigations arising from it. There was a shocked and awesome silence, as if I had perpetrated the most appalling blunder. Inder's face was pained and solemn. Icily he said, in distinct and immaculate English, that he must warn me to be *very, very* careful when saying that things came from Baba. Instructions were normally given in black and white *on paper*, and it was most unlikely that I should be told to re-form a group that had already rejected him. Only the strongest and most trustworthy of his people would be charged with such a task — the risk of the ego rising and the soul again becoming distracted and lost in the world, was far too great — and *who was I* to imagine myself of such calibre?

I protested that I was not attempting to re-form a group.

"Then what *are* you doing, Madam!* — why should *you* bring them together?"

I had no answer to this, for I did not know. I knew only that it was Baba's wish.

He left me in no doubt of his extreme displeasure, and accused me witheringly of daydreams and delusions. It was apparent to *him* that I was rapidly becoming swamped by my egotistical desires to *teach* others what I didn't know myself, and in view of my grave danger he would like Alison to see me *daily* in an effort to dissuade me from this disastrous course of action. He would wish me to express to her, with honesty, whatever I

---

* He often called me 'Madam' when he was censuring me.

thought or felt about the matter, and my changes in viewpoint as the days progressed. This could perhaps prove helpful to us both! And Alison was to report to him the entire context of all conversations held. Had I sufficient discernment *left* to be willing to do this?

Inwardly I reeled, but I held my ground. Yes, I would see Alison, if he so wished, but I could assure him now it would make no difference. I *knew* I had been spiritually upraised — Baba *had* manifested himself to me, and I would go ahead with what he had indicated. Inder expressed exasperation at my "defiance" and then he ignored me for the rest of the session.

The next evening he arranged a private meeting with Alison and Rose at Alison's house, and impressed upon them the seriousness of what I had set in motion. I learned of this later and felt very perturbed and distressed as a consequence — and very shut out, for the meeting was not a brief one, and this was the only information I was given.

At each of the next two meetings Inder repeated much of the substance of the one before, but the following Thursday I found him alone on my arrival at the Lodge, and this, it transpired, was by arrangement. He embarked at once on the matter in hand and advised me sternly to undo my preparations and to have no contact with Betty or Joan who would without doubt draw me away from Baba. I was behaving foolishly, and was liable to end up in difficulties of the most *extreme* nature . . . *I listened with amazement and wondered why he should waste his words on me, for I knew he was perfectly well aware that I would pay no heed to them.

But Inder in full flow was a force to be reckoned with, and despite my conviction I wilted rapidly. Rose and Alison arrived at the conclusion of this tirade and took full note of his disparaging assertions and my deflated state. I was then obliged to listen to Alison's account of our daily meeting (which took place each afternoon) and was afterwards asked for my version. This was identical to hers, though I said in addition that she had been very patient and understanding the first day, but as I remained adamant in my intentions, I later felt a hardening

* This may well have been concurrent with the proposed reconciliation between Nigel and Alison. Regretfully I did not note the exact dates, not realising the possible significance.

towards me which increased with each visit. Alison agreed this was so. The subject was then dropped for other matters.

The daily visits continued, however, and on Monday, armed with Alison's verbal reports and my reiterated refusal to retreat, he again tackled me with severity. By now I was on my guard and presented a more composed facade that hopefully concealed my misgivings. The firm, unshakable core within me was becoming increasingly obscured by my fear of acting in opposition to Inder, for this it appeared was what I would have to do if I clung to the fruit of my spiritual experience. I found it as yet impossible to believe that he would maintain his attitude, for I knew that *he knew* I was telling the truth, and I prayed fervently he would acknowledge this before forcing me out on a limb.

He questioned me for some time on my "intuitions" in a strange way that alarmed me considerably. In the course of this his tone altered and the note of icy disapproval left his voice. He even blew the odd smoke ring — but his eyes never left me, and I felt uncomfortably aware that he had placed me metaphorically under a microscope.

"What would you do", he said, "in a situation like the one we have now . . . if Baba sent you a written instruction saying you are mistaken in your assumption and *should not* follow what your so-called intuition dictates?"

I replied that this was an unfair question as it had not arisen, and I did not know what I would do if it did — also, I could not accept that such a thing could happen.

This, he insisted, was not good enough.

"*If* you are prepared to answer honestly, you *must be more explicit!*" I did not miss the edge of sarcasm. My mouth felt dry and I longed for him to stop.

"Would you ever act *against* your intuition? — say, for instance, in the interests of *common sense.*"

My answer was no.

"Then you would *disobey* Baba's written instruction if it did not agree with your own views?"

I replied with some distress that I would not disobey Baba wittingly, and said again the question was unfair as I had no reason to believe that Baba in vision would say anything different to Baba in form. I hoped he would now leave the matter, but he persisted:

"Ah, but *if* Baba in your vision said one thing, and Baba in India refuted this, what would you *do?*"

Try as I would to evade a reply he would not be side-stepped. In the end, knowing I sealed my future in some way, I had to admit what I knew of my own mentation. I would follow the Master in my heart, nothing could alter that . . . though I could not concede there would ever be conflict between the two.

This seemed to satisfy him. He then proceeded to make clear to us all that Baba gave precise, written instructions simply to stop devotees falling into such traps — for how could they know if they were the victims of delusion? Literal, written instructions from Baba should always be obeyed as he could see much further than we could, and his advice was invariably for our greatest benefit. This he stressed over and over again, and Alison and Rose listened mutely, utterly convinced that I was deluded and incapable of direct obedience, and that Inder's words could have no possible connection with themselves.

At the next meeting he again dissected me, this time so thoroughly and cruelly I could no longer speak. I sat in silence, motionless and numb, wondering vaguely if I was going to faint. Nell was concerned and made coffee to "warm me up" as she declared I was "as white as a sheet". She did not really grasp what it was all about, but at least she was kind. The other two said not a word.

After two weeks of close observation, Alison was released from her task. It was quite clear, said Inder scathingly, that I would not go back on what I had instigated, nor retract my assertions; therefore he would wash his hands of me and waste no more time.

The foregoing presented an uncanny parallel to future events, a kind of 'trial run' . . . set up, perhaps, to ensure that things would later move as they should. It must also have been used to both test and strengthen me, for only by such increasingly applied pressure could I be sufficiently prepared to take what lay ahead without collapse. Words alone cannot convey the emotional impetus with which such contrived situations are permeated, and the whole episode constituted a very real ordeal.

The meaning of the above for the others concerned can possi-

143

bly be conjectured in the light of what came next, for nothing that Inder did was for one person alone. Each activity reverberated all along the line and produced an outworking of some kind with everyone in his contact.

Throughout the months of Baba's seclusion many subtle things had happened which are not easy to define and record. For the first three months everything quickened rapidly, and it was not difficult to understand how some had 'let go' without the necessary depth of conviction to endure the pace set. The next three months were akin to a cooling down process — the light receded, and we were left with only our own little lights to hold onto. Now another phase supervened, and it seemed to me a direct stimulus was at work of a much higher vibratory rate than before, so rarified it had no substance at all. It did not belong to the subtle realm, or the mental, reaching us from a stratum transcending them both.

Inder was ill for most of February. He complained of pains all over his body and collapsed twice at his lodgings much to his landlady's consternation. His doctor at first suspected heart trouble, and when this was disproved, could not satisfactorily discern what was medically wrong with him. He spent a good deal of time at Alison's home, and all the meetings were held there (to my vexation) as he said it was more comfortable than the Lodge whilst he was ill.

He complained, too, of loss of memory, which the others fully accepted as genuine. I found this hard to believe, for I could see the brilliance around his head that showed no congestion at all — as it surely would if his memory were affected. I became more than usually unpopular when I stated this, yet the following day he was his normal self again, and despite this remarkable recovery neither Alison nor Rose considered my comments valid.

I dreaded the forthcoming reunion. The subject was not referred to until immediately beforehand when I asked if anyone else would like to come. But Inder, it seemed, had already told Rose it would be inadvisable for her to do this as *she* was liable to criticise me unfairly in her thoughts. Alison, however, was clear of such things, and he specifically wished her to attend and to inform him afterwards of what transpired.

The meeting produced results, though unexpected ones. Out

144

of it came a renewal of friendship with Joan, and a close connection with Margaret, whom I visited afterwards for many weeks, and whose kindness was a staff to me in the midst of innumerable difficulties. It also drew forth a confession from Betty, who told me when the others had left that she was on the verge of a love-affair with my husband, a matter on which she sought my advice, though she begged me not to mention this to Patrick. But these were after-effects. The evening itself moved on its own momentum, for we quickly slipped into our former longstanding patterns of harmonious groupwork. In the course of this I briefly outlined the substance of Baba's teaching relating to spiritual evolution — of our ultimate ascent through the subtle and mental planes to our Source — becoming aware at the end of our journey of all that was unconsciously existent within us from the very beginning.

I embarked then on a personal account of the Master's entry into my life, describing the effects this had produced both in myself and on my environment. How I had seen his reflected divinity burning in Inder, and the way this had dazzled me and thrown me temporarily off-balance. I concluded by expressing regret for any actions and words of mine that may have caused them to turn aside from the Master — he who was our Teacher and Guide — a Manifest Christ. As I talked a deep stillness penetrated my inner being, and with it came the certitude of Grace. It was like a powerful healing essence, and I felt myself made whole again.

Alison, too, had something to say, and explained how Baba's impact on her life had been quite different to mine. She had become more practical, and also more conscious of her inner nature. Whereas the Light had blinded me to the world, it had unlocked the world to her and she had seen it in a new perspective. She brought out from her handbag a previously written paper and read it through to us. It dealt mainly with herself and Nigel and explained the reasons for the rift between them. I regret I cannot remember it clearly enough to record.

Inder arranged that the three of us should meet at Alison's house the following afternoon, and there we separately recounted our recollections and observations. His comment, expressed with unexpected kindness, was that if I had sought to undo any adverse consequence inadvertently caused by myself, I could rest assured I had done so.

Throughout February I was seared by his light. It had a surpassing 'whiteness' and transparency that was so ultra-fine and of such high frequency, my mind would feel burnt and blinded by its potency. One evening as I watched him I saw a dark cloud hanging over his head. At a certain point the brilliant halo about him appeared to absorb the darkness and in some way transmute it, throwing it back with tremendous ultrasonic force as light. He laughed heartily when I described this . . . and said perhaps I was right, as sometimes disciples were permitted to share the burden of Baba's work — after which he spoke a great deal of his health and the pills he was taking *in such a way* that it really seemed he was physically ill and aberrating mentally . . . though not to me, for I could still perceive with quite astonishing clarity what went on.

Alison strongly disapproved of what she called my psychism, and made this increasingly plain. All her years of sympathetic research into the subject might never have been, nor indeed her own past experience, for every time I mentioned some perception she would tighten her lips and usher Nell off to make coffee, or create some other diversion such as bringing in coal. Often there was a strained silence as if I had committed a major indiscretion — yet invariably I was *obliged* to bring out these things through subtly directed questioning by Inder. This was achieved in such a way that nobody else appeared aware of it, and I was therefore considered to be forever thrusting forward my own viewpoint and the everlasting dreams.

More and more preferential treatment was given to Alison. Inder praised her lavishly, confided in her, and gave her special jobs to do. Nell was directed to her each time she required clarification; and on any obscure point that arose, her elucidation was asked. Inder explained this was because she could be relied on to give a literal, objective summation without the discredited "romance and imagination", or indeed any personal colouring at all.

It seemed to me that Alison did this simply because she was blind to subtle implications — Baba's discourses frequently meant something entirely different, in my view, to the assertions made by Alison; but Inder reiterated firmly that Baba's words must be taken as they stood, without embellishment, for unless we were crystal clear channels, any presumed inner meaning could prove a distortion.

I noticed too, a sharp divergence in the group's understanding of Inder himself. As with the discourses and
instructions, his talks conveyed one thing to me, and another to
Alison and Rose. So the former was often asked to clarify for
my benefit — which she did literally and with admirable
directness, but it served only to illustrate to me that there was
more than one level of meaning in everything he said. Yet this
proffered truth was heavily frowned upon, rejected out of hand
and solidly opposed by Inder in person, and I did not understand the reason for this at all.

The situation projected itself in a dream which communicated my inner assessment of the facts and also confirmed my
emotional dilemma. But it gave no solution. It was simply a
statement of how things were . . . or so I believed. I dreamt that
Rose and Alison sat crosslegged on the floor whilst I sat on top
of a ladder. Inder was instructing us from a book (the written
word) and I could clearly hear them murmuring as he spoke —
"Why is she up there? Why *she,* and not *me?*"

Inder turned to me and said, "It is the ego within them that
speaks." So I replied, "If they have ego, why do you praise
them and persecute *me?*" thinking, 'Surely now he will vindicate
me', and looking to him in trusting anticipation. But he turned
away, and instead gave Alison a supervisory position in authority over me. I was *stunned* with bewilderment and disbelief. He
had acknowledged that what I had seen and sensed was
correct, and still he rejected me and promoted Alison. I could
bear it no more, and fell at his feet imploring him not to do
this.

During February the point was raised that I still regarded
Inder as a Master — a Teacher in his own right. How it came
about I cannot remember; certainly through no agency of my
own, for I had long learned it was a matter on which to keep
silent. Its resurrection annoyed Alison greatly, as by this time
she regarded it as yet another facet of my delusion. She openly
said to Inder's face that he was *like us,* though with more
surrender, a statement he approved. Rose agreed this entirely. I
asked Alison what had happened to her original assumption —
identical, verbally, to mine. She replied that *that* was a long
time ago, and she now realised she had been wrong.

The subject arose several times in quick succession, and on
each occasion Alison had much to say, with Rose in full agree-

ment. The one comment Inder himself surprisingly made and which should have evoked some remark, passed either unheard or unheeded by both of them. He said:

"If I was a Master and the time had not yet come to receive my Charge, Kate would still *see* me as one, although it would not, *in literal fact,* be true."

Nell's views on this had been tinged with reverence and were closer to my own, but when on Inder's advice she went to Alison for counsel, these concepts were firmly uprooted and she thereafter accepted the other's greater wisdom. She was also told it was unnecessary for her to pray, for Baba knew one's thoughts and needs all the time. As Nell's approach to God had always been by verbal prayer and the ritual of the Liberal Catholic Church, it seemed to me very wrong to deflect her into a path for which she appeared unsuited. This I expressed, to no good effect; for Alison, like my mother, had become invincible.

I cannot describe the atmosphere of the meetings at this time; putting it into words makes it appear petty and trivial, like childish resentments and quarrels, but it was not this way at all. We did not argue and there were no overt hostilities. We simply expressed diametrical points of view. This, however, was the least of it. The spoken word was polite. The subtle essence pervading it was cruel and destructive, and it was this hidden poison that wrought havoc in me. I knew I was secretly sneered at, derided and mentally punished for every observation made. And now these subtleties raised their waking heads and began to emerge — to manifest openly in the space they had been given by consideration and encouragement.

My intuition became labelled 'imagination'; my inner grief at the feeling of separation from God, 'unhappiness caused by my own lack of surrender' (from which they did not suffer, naturally) — my intense love for Inder, 'emotional devotion'; my worry and heartache over Patrick's behaviour, 'the results of too much attachment'. From this latter, too, my companions did not lose any sleep. Neither appeared in the least attached to her husband.

Perhaps these judgements of my state were true, though I do not believe so. If to be lacking in compassion is detachment, then I had no urge to acquire it. After a particularly painful session I said to Inder that I may as well give up now — for if the others were representative of the requirements for discipleship, I would never get there — I had no desire to become like them. He looked very displeased and made no answer.

There was a marked difference now in my reactions to them all. I felt myself hardening, though too late to help my vulnerability, and many times I cried hopelessly with loneliness and despair.

One evening, when questions were asked about the work of a Master, Alison enquired why direct answers were so seldom given, especially in response to personal requests for guidance and advice. Inder's extraordinary reply struck me as deeply significant. He said, "A Master will not usually tell his pupils where their faults lay, as words alone have little effect on a person who cannot see himself.* But he will *show* that person by direct experience how he is at fault, leaving no doubt at all in the mind. He will also indicate what is required to put things right. In certain cases — very rare indeed — he may even lead his pupils *in the wrong direction* to show them clearly the folly of mistaken attitudes and ways. He *will go with* them — *and they may afterwards believe him to be misguided* . . . but the lesson *will still have been learned.*"

No comments or questions arose from this. He went on to say that Baba did not mix levels of consciousness — he dealt with spiritual things in spiritual ways, and worldly things in worldly ways. People tended to get confused and would try to use one level in a matter appropriate to another, often with dire results. He used a favourite expression, "You don't need a hydrogen bomb to blow up a tree — a stick of dynamite will do!" Those beginning to 'see' were "a headache to the Teacher" for they only saw part of what was happening and were prone to misunderstand and interfere. However clear their vision, they *did not see far enough*. Yet in this in-between condition they were valuable, in that certain work could be accomplished with their unwitting aid. But when the veils dropped from their eyes, such work was no longer possible . . . and for them new ventures would arise . . ."

Love, obedience and surrender were frequently defined. A 'lover' of the Master was a devotee or seeker, moving towards the dedication of his life in the form of obedience. Unquestion-

* *(one without self-knowledge)*

ing and instant obedience to literal instructions was the aim and object of most of the Master's external dealings with his disciples. In this way they gradually eliminated the troublesome ego and became one with Him. Complete surrender was the ultimate level of unification, when pupil and Master were one in essence, and the pupil no longer acted in any way outside the Master's Will, and thus shared in his planetary work. This condition was rare and almost impossible to define; but obedience was open to all sincere 'lovers' who showed willingness to submit the personal ego to the shaping that alone made real obedience possible.

Late in February Alison's father died, and she missed several meetings and was very preoccupied with family affairs. Inder was still absent from his employment and complained again of frequent loss of memory. He had begun to look facially strained and unwell — even I could not argue this — but his strange state was subject to rapid fluctuation, and I remained unconvinced that it was due to actual illness.

The Sunday following this pronounced accent on his physical condition, he met Rose and Alison at Cowper Road without my knowledge, and the prevailing trend of events reached a climax. I learned, apparently by chance, from Rose the next morning, that Inder had told Alison she was to assume leadership of the group in the event of his sudden collapse, or if he was taken long-term into hospital or obliged to return to India. He appeared to expect some sort of development at the end of March, and Alison, he said, was the 'clearest' of us all and least likely to react emotionally to any circumstance. All his possessions, clothing, correspondence and books were to go to her in such an emergency, and she was to contact Baba on his behalf should any contingency arise. This last was most important, and he charged her in trust to do it. Rose said Alison was nearly in tears, and said she was "nothing without Baba".

This conversation, though brief, left me shattered. More so as Rose confessed she ought not to have mentioned the matter at all. It was the last straw. Try as I would, I could not accept that Alison was 'clear'. Her thoughts constantly impinged upon me, their criticism and contempt of myself like an actual force assailing my psyche. The sharp sword of her antagonism had torn deeply into my psychic awareness and frequently made me feel sick and unendurably burdened. Rose, who had borne the brunt of instigating any antipathy, did not exude anything like such deadly poison. Her anger was a whiplash, unspoken, yet unconcealed. Alison's was hidden and insidious, still waters running deep, but running strongly ever in my direction. Both Rose and Nell thought her an angel incarnate and made no bones about saying so. Rose also said she was convinced that Inder leaned heavily upon her, and looked to her for "advice and comfort" during his illness . . . It was, I knew, the very last straw.

At the Monday meeting I was surprised when nothing was said of this. Inder normally kept each of us informed of whatever concerned the group as a whole, and I had assumed he wished to make some statement himself, hence Rose's injunction. I noted that Alison glanced at him repeatedly, as if she, too, expected him to bring this to the fore . . . but blithely he talked of other things. Towards the evening's end I grew sicker and sicker inside as the cross-currents in the room became stronger. It was as though a giant hydra reared itself amongst us and directed its venom towards me, though outwardly all was calm.

It was time now for me to leave, and nothing had been vouchsafed. Feeling quite ill, on a desperate impulse I asked if I could speak with Inder for a few minutes privately — something I had never done before. It was a stupid thing to do and I regretted it immediately. He assented before I had chance to retract, and sent the others at once from the room. It was oddly like a confrontation, and I grasped sinkingly it was by design.

He waited silently, his face expressionless. He knew quite well what I wished to say. The atmosphere was fraught with tension, and the speculative thoughts from the adjoining room increased this. For a moment I could not think how to begin, then forced out a few words concerning the crux of my telephone conversation with Rose. I asked, dry mouthed, "Please, why is this being kept from me?"

He replied coldly, "Because you would probably have made a scene over it."

I knew then that all Rose had said was correct.

I told him I could not believe that Alison was clear of prejudice, nor that she had acquired the detachment she believed —

her attitudes and actions disproved it each day. He *must* know how she was to me . . . how hostile, disapproving and contemptuous. And to place her in authority over me . . . to make her my intermediary with Baba . . .

Suddenly I found myself on my knees before him, clutching his hand despairingly; struggling to withstand the inflow of intuitional impressions bombarding me, imploring his kindness and understanding. I remember saying, "Please don't do this to me, Inder, please *please* —" no longer sure of what I was afraid, aware only of a dark desolation in my soul and an agonised foreboding. His face was tense; he said sharply and explosively, "*Don't* get emotional with me, Kate!" — and I got up at once, utterly heartbroken, knowing I was defeated and could take no more. I murmured through choking tears, "I'm sorry, Inder, I'm sorry," as I stumbled to the door and into the street.

Blindly I walked to the bus stop. If I could have died there and then I would have done so. The searing agony of longing reached incandescent heights — my heart was burning, burning, burning . . . its central nucleus transfixed on Baba, Inder . . . Inder, Baba . . . Who would in no way acknowledge me, who had cast me out . . . My soul swung out into the timeless Void. I faced Eternity — alone, *alone.* I was on fire, a flaming nebula consumed with pain. Pierced to the core, I reached the borderline of my extremity.

Nothing made sense any more. All I had striven for was without purpose. If it were not for the persistent knowledge of my dependent children waiting for me at home, I would have wandered wherever my feet led, heedless and uncaring. Rose followed me to the bus stop a few minutes later and pressed a ten shilling note into my hand. She said Inder had told her to see I got home safely, by taxi if necessary. Silently she waited by my side, and I gravitated again to my daily life.

I declined the money and gave it back. It was soon apparent I had missed the bus, so I said at length I would not take a taxi, but would return and wait the next one. Cold, wretched and distraught as I was, the awareness had penetrated my mind that no other course was open to me. I could not leave the group until March ended, however grievous I felt . . . I must marshall what strength I had left, and face it out.

Wearily I went back, making no attempt to conceal the tearmarks or my abject misery, for once uncaring of my appearance, even before Inder. He sat in his usual place and looked calmly at me as I apologised for my behaviour. I told him the thoughts of others had been so concentrated, they had entered my solar plexus and caused intense distress. I had been unable to control my reactions — I could not shut them off. I simply did not know how to bear them. They were *hard* and *harsh* and incredibly powerful.

He contemplated me in silence and blew a gentle smoke-ring. Then he said quietly, and very directly, *"You will have to learn to bear them, Kate."* and I made some inner registration that by-passed my mind. He smiled suddenly and suggested I share the taxi Rose had ordered for him. I was grateful to accept it. Events (or emotions) had caught up with me, and I was now too tired to wish anything else. Although it was obvious whose thoughts I was principally referring to, Alison remained unperturbed and unmoved. I realised she did not believe one word I had said.

Going home in the taxi, Inder fed me verbally with kindness, and my energy began to return. He gently probed the roots of my experience and, ignoring the metaphysical overtones, asked mildly if my distress was through the many meetings held at Alison's home, and the fact that I arrived, and usually left, when the others were still engaged in discussion. I recognised some purpose in the way he turned my attention, yet I could not fathom what it was. I said one reason was that I felt unwanted and deliberately left out, and was seldom told what went on in my absence. He replied benevolently that things would change soon, and I revived at this, foolishly hoping the change would be for the better.

My sole comfort at this time lay in my relationship with my children. Whenever I arrived home they would both come to greet me, along with Tiggy, our cat. However depleted or unhappy I might feel, I was always able to conceal it from them, and we had much laughter and goodwill over supper. Teresa would come from her room once I was in bed and pretend she was a cat — this developed into quite a ritual; and David too, invariably crept in and recounted the events of the day at school. Patrick was out most of the time and the children did not seem to miss him, indeed they behaved more freely and cheerfully than I had ever known them to before.

It was around now that I was offered another house to rent.

The lease of the flat officially lapsed on March 25th, and I had been granted several weeks extension, if necessary, and had already made numerous enquiries of agents for further suitable properties. Unfurnished houses were difficult to acquire and this one sounded ideal. It had six bedrooms and two bathrooms for three pounds more per week than our present home — an amount that could quickly be made up with another lodger. There were also three floors, thus an easier privacy could be maintained . . . but to my great disappointment Patrick declined to inspect it. He said if I took another lease in my name he would refuse to come with me and would apply for a divorce — which placed me in an impossible position regarding Baba's instructions. He was adamant that the next house in which we lived must be his — he would buy one and "get things back to normal" — we would start looking now. So reluctantly I proceeded no further with the one on Barton Road.

We did in fact go to look at several houses, but they were either too highly priced; in poor repair, or needing extensive redecoration that Patrick did not wish to undertake. Eventually he decided that we should move into his current new house on Roseford Road when built. As this was still in the footings stage I felt very dubious about its completion on time, even with a second extension. But this was the way he said it must be, and I had to accept it.

He was still keeping very late hours, especially at weekends, and generally spent Sundays with his friends, so I saw much less of him than before. We continued to live normally together, though every few days he would flare up and say the most unpardonable things, behaving violently and aggressively as if the past few days of relative friendship had never been. There was no possibility of a mature relationship; we were poles and poles apart. He slandered Inder and Baba and everything I held precious — and any thus evoked protest brought fresh threats to break our marriage. We would reach once more the point of parting and he would then swing back again. It was distressing and exhausting, and sometimes I wondered how I managed to keep going at all.

One day he said he would give up the rather wild life he was leading as it was proving very expensive, and that he wished to give a 'thankyou' party for all the people who had given him hospitality. A party in our abode was an unheard of event, and I remembered all the years he had steadfastly refused to have a social life at all, at least at home. The date was arranged for a Saturday in March, and I offered to prepare sandwiches or do whatever catering was required. Surprisingly he did not wish this, and asked Teresa's help instead.

When the day came, and after arriving home from Alison's, I decided as a goodwill gesture to greet his friends on arrival and make them welcome, but it was nearing midnight before the first guest appeared — to me a very odd state of affairs. I stood at the end of the hall as Patrick and the man entered; he nodded curtly to me and the guest obviously had no idea who I was, nor were we introduced. I later saw two women in the hall who glanced at me vaguely as if I was a lodger. I soon realised that no-one knew I was Patrick's wife, and he had no intention of inviting me into the sittingroom.

The noise was bedlamic, with records blaring and doors constantly slamming — not our records either. Heaven knows how many people had been invited, they seemed to come and go all the time. Sleep was quite out of the question, and by 3.00 a.m. the children looked worn out. I noticed that the lights were periodically extinguished and shrieks of laughter came from the darkened room. It may have been the most innocent of parties, I really did not know, but the look on my son's face as he watched the women that teetered, giggling, back and forth to the bathroom, and analysed in his mind what it was all about, was suddenly too much for me. I stormed into the pitch dark sittingroom to be immediately forestalled by Patrick, who appeared to anticipate this, and demanded to know what was going on. He ushered me swiftly outside into the hall and asked me not to make a scene, so I told him simply to get those dreadful women out, I would not have them making such an exhibition of themselves in front of David. I learned later that they had been unaware I was his wife and assumed me to be an irate landlady. I learned other things too, but they are better left unsaid.

David remarked dryly, if that was a party he would never go to any. His father departed with the guests and presumably continued the festivities elsewhere, for he arrived home very much later — probably not realising what he had so carelessly thrown away. I spent the next morning removing drink stains

155

and ground-in ash from the sittingroom carpet, discarding endless bottles and in general feeling furious with Patrick for behaving so badly in the presence of his children.

I was glad March had at last arrived. Whatever happened I was determined to remain with the group until the nine months of Baba's seclusion transpired — though why this should be so important I could not conjecture. I did not expect him to manifest by leaving the body — this appeared to be irrelevant . . . for I was increasingly conscious that he was manifesting before us in other ways . . . though only myself appeared aware of it.

The light with Inder was dazzlingly beautiful. I adored him as always, and saw ever more clearly the perfection of his soul. To immerse myself in his radiation brought much solace, and I found I could begin to effortlessly screen out all else . . .

Early in March he gave several talks on the requirements of service. His words were quite obviously directed to Alison and Rose, and it was apparent to all that I had no place in them. But I did not really mind any more, for something that held bliss beyond words was happening to me. Outwardly my life remained as always — yet inwardly I became aware of Baba's presence, and this sustained and uplifted me in a way unknown before.

I knew beyond any shadow of doubt that he was there, within me and beside me, more Real than life, or suffering, or joy. He knew my every thought and every feeling; his love was an immensity that enfolded every life and embraced the whole of Creation. Nothing escaped his attention — nothing was lost; nothing was ever overlooked. He loved each soul with a love so intense, our fragile awareness could not contemplate the merest fragment of it. He was *Everywhere* and in *Everything* — All-compassionate, All-pervading. I understood at last the words from the discourse so frequently pondered . . . that suffering is born of compassion, and his Divine Compassion lies inherent in the pain of all separation and illusion.

I told Inder of this profound and infinitely wonderful condition. He said, "When you have such certainty of God's Love, things begin to happen." I did not comprehend then what he meant.

A further experience came to me some days later; the light retreated once more and I was plunged into darkness. This time I recognised many things of which I had been unaware in the past. I understood that this painful absence of light was the customary experience of humanity, and that they *did not realise* what their state was, or what it signified. I saw that all my life I had known some degree of light . . . and that I had *never* known how utterly dark the human condition really was . . . The terror and misery experienced formerly through the cutting off of light (or my descent into the denser levels of myself) arose solely because I had become *aware* of its absence . . . I was therefore conscious of aloneness — which, though an illusion, produces the deepest suffering possible in a soul that intermittently touches its Source . . . But to those to whom the light was unknown, the world and all its appearances, attributes, values and consolations . . . must, I saw, be a totally different place to the universe I lived in.

This perception revealed the world as a kind of film. Some lived *in* the film, and some observed it from the outside, though they experienced the 'living' in the same way as the rest. Many things were perceived concerning the fluctuating states of consciousness within, among them the unreality of human nature — the little bundle of impressions, conditioning and graded 'wants' that made up the life of the individual. Each 'want' when satisfied and outworn, paving the way for one finer — the imprisoned soul seeking step by step some balm for the pain of its unconscious longing for fulfilment — whether for wine or women, power or peace — or finally, the longing for God Himself. Even this 'want', I saw, must ultimately be transcended . . . and perfect surrender was the state when all longing and wanting *consciously* ceased.

For some hours I contemplated the nature of surrender, and found it to be the non-Being which preceded Being — the gulf between illusion and Reality; an egoless state wherein one experienced the 'film' in the fullest sense, but remained detached from it — knowing full well its illusory value, its purpose, its impossibility of perfection — wanting nothing because there was nothing to want — resting in God . . .

And beyond surrender — I could not reach; nor did I desire to. I knew the joy, the bliss, the *triumph* of Being — but through a veil . . . and there was no desire to lift it. For all things were safe, and had their time, their place, their ordinance . . . wrapped in the swaddling bands of Divine Love.

This state gradually passed, and I was in life again. Life that was colourless, raw and rough, but to which I speedily adjusted. Within a few days I awoke to recall a perplexing dream, both vivid and lucid, that left a deep imprint in my memory. I was again with Baba, standing beside him in a huge room where many persons were gathered in groups. In the centre sat my family, with whom he talked in a very friendly yet serious fashion. Although I stood close to him he seemed not to notice I was there, and I wondered what I had done to displease him.

We moved then amongst others in the room — some of whom he praised, and some he admonished. I felt increasingly disturbed, for those he praised, to my view, were behaving in a most unpraiseworthy manner, whereas those admonished were trying hard in their varying capacities to love others and work selflessly.

Suddenly he turned to me and upbraided me so severely for my unspoken observations that I was shattered, agonisingly, to the core. We moved again from place to place, with Baba remaining coldly aloof — and soon he commenced a quiet monologue, as if speaking to himself — in which he delineated minutely the psychological constitution of each person contacted — and I was astounded to hear my diagnoses had been correct. He had, of course, known all the time the hearts of those he praised so warmly, and sought to change them by means I was not yet equipped to comprehend.

At this point we stopped and Baba, looking very tired and ill, asked me to give him my shoes. Apologetically I held them out to him. They were like slippers, very old, and of soft, dark brown leather that flopped formlessly without a foot inside. Wordlessly he indicated I should place them on his feet, and I stooped down in the clean-washed gutter in which we stood, to ease them on. He was so frail and weary, and so very old. He held my arm and asked me to raise him up, which I tried to do, taking his weight upon me and gradually standing upright. Despite his slight frame, his weight was so great that the strain in the back of my knees was acute. I felt nervous of weakening and letting him fall, but eventually stood firmly, and walked along the gutter with Baba on my arm — dazed, and immensely grateful for the opportunity he had given me. People lined the roadside watching our slow but steady progress; and like a   rising nectar, soundless words from his heart overflowed into mine on a stream of light. He said, *"You belong to me."*

These words connected with the day of my birth, and I knew I had waited to hear them all my life.

I sent my mother a carefully chosen card on Mother's Day, with a painting of violets and much love — telephoning on Sunday morning to say how greatly I missed her and to ask if I might come to see her. She said I could come if I wished, though she must tell me now that my card was not with my brother's as she had torn it up on arrival. Lois had passed on something said by me of which she disapproved and she felt it was time this hypocrisy ceased, so the card was destroyed. Lois had either mis-heard or misunderstood what had actually been said, yet Mother would permit no explanation. She did not think Lois could be mistaken and began another lecture on my misdemeanours — at the conclusion of which she hung up on me. As usual I wept bitterly. In the face of such attitudes I was helpless, and I still did not understand why those I cared for attacked me so vindictively.

The Saturday before Easter week I mentioned to Inder my most recent dream of Baba (the dream of the shoes) and he asked me to retell it to the group. He then enquired if I knew what it meant. I was not at all certain, so he said, "When Baba 'bows down' to any individual, it is to *break their ego* — for this inevitably follows."

This was expressed in such a way that a personal inference was obvious, and I protested that Baba had not bowed down to me. He ignored this and made no answer, at least to myself; instead he threw the dream into the common pool for discussion, and it was at once apparent that to those present I had plenty of ego in need of shattering. I remained silent throughout the analysis that now took place, myself the unnamed and uncomfortable focal point.

When they were ready to turn to other matters, Rose said she was off to London on Saturday to see her relations, and Inder promptly arranged to travel with her as he was visiting Adi. He was as friendly towards Rose as he was distant to me, and I mourned unceasingly this blatantly unconcealed fact.

On Monday Alison reported a "very strange dream", and Inder invited her to recount it to us. She had been in a vast hall with many white-clad people who all held little white cups. She too, held a cup, given her by the man in charge of the proceedings. During some kind of ceremony they raised the cups to their lips, and it was observed that a stain remained where their lips had rested, while her own cup was stainless. The man in charge then said to the assembly, "My wife is *out* of all this, she has left no mark."

Inder commented genially that the dream *could* be a confirmation of Alison's 'clearness' and purity of motive. I listened, thoroughly ashamed of my own reactions, in utter disbelief. To Alison I think the dream was conclusive proof of all she had allowed herself to imagine.

We were at that time sitting in a coffee bar as another organisation was unexpectedly using the Lodgeroom; and suddenly, despite the noisy jukebox, I became aware of the slightest movement in my head, the merest brush of a gossamer wing — and instantaneously perceived, with graphic clarity, another interpretation of Alison's dream. I knew also that Inder had directed it there telepathically.

He had talked to us many times of the spiritual impact made by those who surrendered themselves wholly to God, and now affirmed that however ordinary these people might appear in speech and action, they still carried a potency assisting self-knowledge in all whom they contacted. Others might speak and act in exactly the same way, or even do things much better — but without the dynamic of the awakened soul behind it, there was no vivifying potency and no real magnetic attraction.

Rose and Alison wished to leave early that evening for some purpose of their own, their mutual friendship being particularly pronounced at that time. As we were in a public place, I asked if Inder would remain behind a little longer to talk, thinking it might prove an unforseen opportunity to put forward some personal questions. He abruptly declined, and I, in fact, left first; the three of them remaining in animated conversation. I felt rebuked and much at fault for asking, and more worthless and undesirable than the dust on the pavement.

Another time when something similar occurred, on a very strong impulse I walked back to the place where Inder normally caught his bus home, thinking myself quite mad as I could have sworn the bus had just gone. He was still there, and came towards me without any trace of his earlier severity. I stammered an embarrassed excuse for coming, and apologised for my resentment of what seemed to me the high-handed behaviour of others. For a moment he exuded a tender kindness that seeped into my starved heart and rekindled it to anguish. He said, his voice very gentle, *"Think less of the group, Kate, and more of Baba."*

I did not know he was preparing me for the severance to come.

My God, my God, why hast thou forsaken me
and art so far from saving me, from heeding my groans?
O my God, I cry in the daytime but thou dost not answer,
in the night I cry but get no respite.

Save me, O God;
for the waters have risen up to my neck.
I sink in muddy depths and have no foothold;
I am swept into deep water, and the flood carries me away.
I am wearied with crying out, my throat is sore,
my eyes grow dim as I wait for God to help me.
Those who hate me without reason
are more than the hairs of my head;
they outnumber my hairs, those who accuse me falsely.
How can I give back what I have not stolen?
Oh God, thou knowest how foolish I am,
and my guilty deeds are not hidden from thee.

*Psalms 22 and 69. The New English Bible. (c) 1970
by permission of Oxford and Cambridge University Presses*

On Thursday we had visitors to the Lodge meeting; two ladies from the Spiritualist Church who had contacted Rose. One of them I recognised as having once attended a group in Roseford Road — I had myself given her Rose's address as she was interested in healing, and Rose was a practising healer at the time. Now, to my dismay, the evening took a disturbing turn. This kindly, once rather shallow woman, had increased considerably in depth, stability and understanding from the days when we last met. She had suffered illness, and found help, and a deep faith within herself through spiritual healing, as had several of her friends. She was anxious to share this transformation in her life with people who understood, particularly with Rose whom she knew as a healer — and was plainly perturbed when Rose implied she no longer found healing acceptable. She asked Mrs P. if she had ever thought, "Perhaps God wants us to suffer —" and made further comments which heightened her air of bewilderment. I experienced again the same strange feeling as when Alison told Nell there was no need to pray.

Alison at that moment was expounding her views on Baba, and our visitors sat solidly unimpressed. Fresh from the compassionate warmth of Christ the Healer — Alison's remarks, with all due respect, were beautifully phrased, sincerely expressed, but barren of the igniting spark that sets the heart aflame. Inder blandly smoked and listened quietly in the background, allowing them both to have their head.

When the ladies had departed amid smiles and handshakes, it was generally agreed they had seemed impressed — though a thoughtful, retrospective assessment of Inder's comments revealed a careful ambiguity. I could not accede, when approached for my opinion, that either visitor was likely to join us as a result of the evening's work, and this did not increase my popularity. In my private view Mrs P. had been briefly distressed by the changed attitudes of one she regarded highly; then had swiftly returned to the safer entrenchment of spiritualism. Surely enough, neither she nor her friend came again.

To my own surprise I felt no disappointment at the way things were moving; it was obvious a grand anti-climax was at hand, and the intense pressure that had carried us along willy-nilly was not bearing towards any external and perceivable fulfilment. March had heaped humiliations upon me, and these did not lessen but progressively intensified. Inder would belabour me openly for attributes sometimes glaringly apparent in Alison or Rose, and to them he said nothing. They would listen to my repeated 'strippings' registering neither pity nor protest. Not once did either say one word in my defence, or repudiate the more flagrantly unjust accusations made against me.

Since the evening I had walked out of her house, Alison made no bones about her own biases and revealed them unhesitatingly. The briefest mention by me of any clairvoyant, telepathic or intuitive perception (always, of course, drawn forth by Inder) would send her at once from the room on some pretext, her face rigid with disapproval. It seemed she could not bear to listen to such rubbish any more, and would do anything, however rude, to avoid it.

Rose was patronising when I 'behaved' but sharp and cutting when I fell from grace, as I did frequently. Her own past mediumistic and clairvoyant abilities had conveniently subsided, indeed atrophied into non-existence; and her thoughts regarding my recalcitrant faculties assailed me like blows. When I referred to this and she denied it, Inder sternly rebuked me — yet I knew it was true. My solar plexus was tense and cringing beneath the wounds received.

But Alison's pious and self-righteous demeanour was the hardest to bear; it was like being with Mother all over again, and I trembled and was sick inside with fear and misery — and then at last with a burning indignation. No matter what I said, it was wrong — no matter what Alison said, it was right. And even if *both* were correct from our differing angles, only Alison's was given any validity. She was lauded, praised and approved. Nightly Inder visited her, and their discussions quite often included Rose. And conversely, in direct ratio, I was excluded and disdained.

Many times I felt I could not face them again, yet an inner impulse spurred me on. The meetings were ordained by Baba for our spiritual benefit and growth, and I knew I must attend them until he indicated otherwise. Sometimes I stumbled beneath the weight that was placed upon me, accepting inwardly that I was all that Inder said I was. I would pray in mental agony through these failings and my own perceived interior lack of grace. No words can describe the pain of it, and no-one could possibly understand who had not also passed that way. The soul uncovered in all its nakedness is intensely vulnerable, and only too ready to see each flaw reflected within it as its own.

At other times I knew it was all wrong — that I was none of these things. The weaknesses I knew to be mine were seldom mentioned — only those that I saw in the others, or *had* seen *in those not with us;* or in some that had *never* been with us — and I burned, literally burned, with a terrible sense of frustration and injustice.

It was impossible to confront Inder concerning these matters. He refused to speak with me privately, and on the now rare occasions we were a few minutes together before the others arrived, he either wilfully persisted in trivial smalltalk or, as said before, would draw out some thread of conversation that reached its culmination as Rose and Alison entered the door, invariably showing me in the worst possible light and ripe for the next onslaught on my quivering psychology — which was promptly made.

Sometimes I broke down and cried beneath it; or else sat silent, feeling so drained and ill I scarcely knew how to move or speak. On several occasions Nell grew concerned for me as she thought I would faint, but she was not present during the worst ordeals — I truly believe because Nell, bless her heart, would have interfered in my defence. She had no particular bias towards me, for Alison to her was a guiding light, an angel incarnate — yet she tried to be fair in her way, and would have intervened, I am sure, in the name of humanity.

These statements may seem highly coloured and exaggerated, and I cannot blame anyone for thinking so. In actual fact they do not touch the essence of the scourging to which Inder subjected me, nor can they adequately describe the anguish and suffering his treatment engendered.

The evening with Mrs P. left a deep impression on my mind and this, combined with other incidents, raised an insistent query that I could not ignore. When Rose announced she had invited someone else from the Church to attend Thursday's meeting, an activation arose in me akin to rebellion. I pondered gravely and wearily over the next few days, arguing with myself and trying to persuade my intuition that it was my ego and should leave well alone. It was no use. I accepted at length I could no longer conform to the groups requirements. The last thread broke when I visited my mother, on impulse, just before Easter. Relations were strained, but it was apparent that she had suffered through our estrangement, and her doubts and fears were not eased by what she had 'felt' with certain others in long past situations. I knew then with swift certainty that despite the harsh words and ostracism, these souls who opposed me were *inwardly* aware at least, that I had acted with integrity in the past, and my sincerity had been beyond dispute even to those who disliked me.

I therefore wrote a letter to Inder expressing my viewpoint, with a copy for Alison and another for Betty,* plus a note requesting the latter to circulate its contents to certain others. I include several excerpts:

'It is *because* of their past association with other members of the group and with myself, and the impressions they received, consciously or unconsciously, distorted or otherwise — and their unwilling but intense attention to more recent matters, that I feel compelled to act as I do now. I know that it is my duty to *them* not to compromise in any way with what I know to be true. You may call me egotistical or what you will, it no longer affects the issue. Because of my utter aloneness, and the attitude of Rose and Alison towards me (apparently supported by yourself), I can only rest upon myself, and act in accord with the deepest intuition of my heart.

'Therefore, with sadness, I must make it clear that I can no

---

* Betty did not do what was requested, so Joan was asked instead and accomplished part of it.

longer ally myself with the views of certain members of the group, particularly in their dealings with other souls striving in their own way towards the Master. I believe implicitly that "the wind should be tempered to the shorn lamb", and cannot accept that it is right to tell a person whose link with the Master is forged by prayer, that there is no need to pray — or to tell another whose conviction of His love came by spiritual healing that God prefers us to suffer. There are many instances, trivial in themselves perhaps, but assuming far greater proportions when they become the 'voice' of the group, which I cannot in any sense support.

'I do not wish to sever my relations with the group, only to make it clear to those outside who watch and listen . . . that my full and complete acceptance of Baba has not caused me to deflect from my former convictions, but rather has it confirmed and unfolded them, so that I know in truth, not just in faith, that *He is* everywhere, and in everyone — that *every prayer is heard,* every tear is seen, and every heartache taken to Himself.

'I believe with all my heart that the way to Baba is the same Way He revealed to us as Buddha and Jesus — the way of inner striving, aspiration, renunciation and obedience. These inevitably bring suffering, because of our inadequacies, and suffering causes us to reach out to Him in our hearts. Only in the conscious agony of our separation from Him can we grow to true perception. There is no other way to real service but the way of the Cross — the Crown can only be gained once this is surmounted, as those who have passed that way bear witness. They know the only indispensible is Love.

'But the cross is not for the 'little ones'. Their need is to awaken to the knowledge of God's mercy — only those whom He marks out to serve are passed through the refiner's fire. It is our ability to differentiate between 'little ones', and our yet younger Brethren caught in the law of karma — and those who are truly 'Babes in Christ' already treading the Pathway, which determines our dealings with all other souls. This is, unhappily, where the group disagrees within itself. The limitations may well be entirely my own, but I cannot go against the promptings of my heart. Consequently, I have sent the enclosed to Betty. The rest lies with Baba.'

In the letter to Betty I included the assertion that I knew Inder was himself a Master, though he would neither admit to this nor discuss it at the present time. Her letter was duplicated and a copy enclosed with Inder's. It was, inevitably, my swan song — though I had no idea then of what I had done. For Inder, it must have been the signal he was waiting for, that marked my readiness to stand at last alone.

On Thursday evening with palpitating heart I took the letters to the Lodge. Alison and Inder were already there; Rose apparently would not be coming, having gone to London as her father was ill. The letters were read in silence, then Inder said they would be discussed on Rose's return as the matter was serious, and the subject was thereupon dismissed.

The next day was Good Friday, and Inder visited Maud S. in Oxford. He arrived with Alison at the Saturday* meeting, and I had the odd feeling they had been talking about me, though I assumed they had simply met coming in. Rose was still away, and Inder was charm personified with Alison; I felt excluded and very much in disgrace.

On Monday I braced myself once more for the group's displeasure, and again Rose was not there. I had begun to feel like a washed out rag over the whole thing, and continued suspense did not help this.

Alison was unbearably complacent and had brought with her, to return, a book of Maud's that Inder had taken her on Saturday — I knew then he had been to see her for some reason in the afternoon; I dared not ask as I had been told before that what he did was not my business. After the usual verbal onslaught I must have looked as cold and ill as I felt, for Inder himself asked me if I would like hot coffee. I replied that I was all right and there was no need to bother, and at once Alison said would Inder like a cup, to which he replied in the affirmative — and she immediately got up and prepared two, one for them each. This must make petty recording, but the gesture in itself, with the manner that accompanied it, was like a sharp slap in the face and I did not know why.

---

* Most meetings were now held at the Lodgeroom at Alison's request.

Inder looked oddly at me. I felt, rather stupidly, that he seemed almost sorry for me; this being so unlikely that I pushed it from my mind. Later in the evening when he was reading to us, I had the strange feeling that Baba had placed a great weight on my heart — it was so heavy and intractable, my interior grief doubled and trebled until the tears welled in my eyes and ran down my cheeks unheeded. I no longer listened to the reading, being totally immersed in some inner anguish I could not identify. Suddenly Inder stopped, and spoke my name as a question . . . so gently I was bewildered and came back from my reverie.

I said I was sorry, I did not know why the tears came . . . it had just seemed suddenly there was too much to bear. Something indefinable in Alison's manner increased my bewilderment, and the following day* I learned the reason.

Rose's father died on Tuesday, March 31st, and on this day, too, Baba's seclusion came to an end. To those who had noted these affairs censuriously, he had given conclusive proof that he was not what he said he was, for he remained reasonably fit and very much alive, and he also retained his silence. But I was convinced I had seen him manifest both inwardly and outwardly — in my own interior consciousness, and in the person of Inder.

The latter was alone when next I arrived at the Lodge. He said he had something serious to tell me, and had called at Alison's and asked her not to come for another half-hour. Then he revealed that on Saturday afternoon, he and Alison had discussed my letter and had jointly sent a cable to Baba telling him that I was now openly stating that he, Inder, was a Master. Today he had received a reply and it was necessary to inform me of the content. He read it out to me. It was as follows:

'Be firm and admonish Kate Merton. Such false declarations cannot uplift you but on contrary will immensely harm your spiritual wellbeing. You should refute her claim declaring to all concerned you are simply seeker and lover of Meher Baba. My love to you. Meher Baba.'

I braced myself. The moment of shock passed, and I was

* During the last ten days of Baba's seclusion we tried to meet daily, if only for an hour.

filled with an extraordinary exaltation. I felt calm and sure, and ridiculously happy. I would not refute my assertion — I had no idea it would be used in such a way against me, but it was a sincere expression of a genuine perception. I told him I would not retract, indeed, would shout it from the rooftops if I got the opportunity, and would say it whenever applicable throughout the rest of my life.

For a few moments he beamed at me; then his manner changed. Baba had told him to admonish me, and this he did, with an efficiency that I shall never forget. My happiness fled, but the calm, deep assurance remained, though well overlaid with the reaction of shock, and the realisation of the significance of Alison's recent behaviour. When she came in, I could see by her face that she already knew the contents of the cable. It transpired that Rose, too, had been informed by telephone of my letter and all else that went on. I felt they had all conspired against me in the days when love and goodwill should have been at their height. I asked Alison how she could do such a thing — sitting with me for two entire evenings and watching my grief without saying a word. She said it was Inder's business and if he had wanted me to know he would have told me. She was hard and cold and quite pitiless. I enquired what had happened to her own belief that he was a Master — she replied that Baba had indicated he was not, and that was good enough for her.

Again the cross-questioning and ceaseless interrogation, formulated in such a way that I was obliged to admit I did not *feel* the truth of this assertion, for it was not a feeling; I did not *believe* it, for it was not a process of thinking — I *knew,* simply *knew* — and *Baba had told me himself,* not in words, but from the heart.

How absurd these things appear in the chill light of the intellect; yet I could not rephrase them, for I knew them with my intuition — that much maligned faculty, and nothing could dislodge such knowledge or take it away. I said I would contact Baba myself in the morning. Inder asked what I would say to him but I declined to discuss it. I knew that from now on I was completely on my own.

I had read somewhere that the five Masters who function at any one time are sometimes referred to as 'Jewels in the Crown of God' — and remembered that Inder had once, long ago, said laughingly that Baba had called him his jewel. The next morning I sent the following by cable: 'My life is yours Beloved, though my heart bleeds and my flesh falters. I know Inder is your jewel and you have but five. I can see Baba in Inder. Inder is Baba in Europe.'

When told of this, Inder said one shouldn't sent messages to Baba worded in this way and I ought to have asked him first; nevertheless Baba would be pleased I had communicated with him, and his reply would make me very happy. He then warned me that he must admonish me according to his instructions, and proceeded to do so with devastating thoroughness.

Rose returned on Monday and read my letter in the evening. She said she could only stay an hour as Paul was angry she had remained in London for so long. Inder immediately commenced to question me on my reasons for writing it, and despite the seriousness of his tone, she left shortly after. With meticulous detail he isolated motive, thoughts and feelings, and obliged me to bring out all I had registered with regard to Alison and Rose, in Alison's presence — an experience I found exceedingly discomforting. Alison passed no comment, serenely secure in my obvious state of disgrace.

There was no reply to my cable over the weekend and Inder said it was unlikely I should now hear further on the matter; he declared its wording was tantamount to telling God Himself that He was wrong and I was right. It was thus pointless for Baba to bother with me any more.

On Thursday he exhibited complete indifference towards me, treating me as a tiresome child of whom he had suffered enough; but on Saturday another cable was delivered to him personally, and this precipitated the worst trial of all. It read;

'Hold fast to my daaman and don't be deluded by praise of those who think they love you and who raise you to false status. Show this to all concerned. Meher Baba.'

In the evening I again found Inder alone and the cable was read out to me. My last shred of hope vanished; I could no longer harbour the lingering expectation of reprieve from what I glimpsed before me. Alison and Rose had already been called together in the afternoon to hear its content. Inder said he had told them they were not to judge me, nor to say anything against me to each other, to me, or to anyone else. *His alone* was the duty of admonition, and they were to remain impersonal and detached or he would be equally severe with them. This, at least, seemed promising.

When they entered soon afterwards, I tried to smile — but Rose averted her head with a gestue of such open disapproval and condemnation that I protested to Inder I had been judged already, although the cable said nothing directly involving me. Inder queried this with Rose, who swiftly denied she had even been thinking of me, her thoughts were elsewhere. In the haste of despair I cried out that this was not true — I could see her thoughts circling her head and every one of them judged and condemned me. There was a shocked silence, then Rose again coldly refuted that this was so. Inder accepted her word, and lectured me sharply on the unpermissability of voicing one's mental perceptions, assuming one *genuinely had them*. I retired defeated, as always.

That evening's onslaught was merciless and I have made no attempt to record it. Nell was present, and for the first time the scales tipped and she joined those on the other side. All four were arraigned against me, and I at last began to comprehend that the stance Inder had taken, on Baba's instruction, was that of an ego-orientated devotee.

The shock of this realisation affected me physically. I felt suddenly weak and ill, and the steadying power of my rational observations deserted me. All I could see was that however hard I tried, however earnestly I prayed, how lovingly I turned the other cheek — I was unacceptable to either God or man. I sensed strongly and frighteningly that everything had come to an end. It was all *finished* — the groupwork, the tuition, the meetings . . . *everything*.

Monday brought things to a climax. Inder literally flayed me with his tongue and finally formulated a comprehensive indictment. He heaped on my quaking self humiliation upon humiliation; each assay on my integrity like a thrown weight that bore me down into fearful depths . . . my selfishness, egotism, pride, delusion, emotionalism, self-centred wanting — all these and more were defined in explicit detail, and held before me with such gross and pitiless injustice I was dumb beneath it — my heart riven and torn with the pain of it all, my whole being wounded beyond measure by the senseless cruelty of the persecution to which I had been subjected for so many bitter weeks. I felt myself break psychologically, and observed with dispassion and muted shock the shattered pieces of my own disorientation. My one-time friends sat solidly through it, watching with censurious eyes my punishment, ignoring completely my distress.

I bore it till the evening's end when, trembling and exhausted, I walked uncertainly down the stairs and ran from them all to avoid the necessity of speech. I did not know how to bear the surging, desolating fire that raged in every cell of my body — I wished only to die and to be released.

During these latter weeks Patrick continued without break his own brand of persecution and I was crushed to desperation. Heartsick and verging on collapse I sent a second cable to Baba:- **'Inder severely admonished me. Says only perfection can perceive perfection. Deeply bewildered. Am accused of delusion and disobedience. Desite continued efforts Patrick demands complete severance from group and no further mention of Baba or marriage hopeless. No possibility of compromise. Your grieving child, Kate.'**

The day following, perhaps at the time this cable was received, the sorrow suddenly lifted . . . and for the span of several hours I was immersed in a profound serenity . . . a becalming sea of peace. It was an oasis in the most parched and windswept of spiritual deserts, and gave me a needful opportunity to revitalise my devastated system. It was also Thursday, and I braced myself to meet Inder again.

Mounting the stairs to the Lodgeroom with the waning glow of respite still enfolding me, a faint vestige of a far younger self stirred softly in remembrance — she who had gone so happily to meet one dearly beloved, not so very many months previously.

He was a little way ahead, and he stopped at the last flight of stairs (there were three) and turned to wait for me. The gesture was so unexpected I simply stood still when I reached him and gazed timidly at the revered features I knew so well. He was smiling, and he gently touched my cheek. He said, "I'm going to **get you out** of this rut you're in, Kate!" and placed his arm about my shoulders. Then he added, "But **this** can go on till the end of the year."

Not understanding, on impulse I caught at his hand and softly kissed it. He gripped my fingers and led me firmly and tenderly to the top of the stairs. Nothing further was said — yet

175

there was a feeling between us like a bird rising swiftly on the wing, and simultaneously an upward soaring in my spine . . . Another moment, and my universe would have burst into glory and sung like David to the Lord — but the moment was withheld, the flight was arrested, his arm was withdrawn . . . and we entered the Lodgeroom for the meeting that was to be my last.

There was no further admonition. Although he withdrew into his usual attitude towards me, it was sheathed in an inconspicuous consideration; and whatever harshness the others may have anticipated was not supplied. Instead, he quietly encouraged me to gather together the exploded fragments of my being, and to restore myself to life.

Half-laughingly I described to him a dream of a few nights previously. A man was distributing invitations to a wedding, about a dozen in all, and he gave one to me. I was quite amused because the giver had forgotten to put my name on it, almost as if he did not wish me to come. The invitation was in a plain brown box with no embellishment. I could not help noticing that all the others were carefully decorated in various ways, some extremely ornately, and very attractive to look upon, the guest's name on each box inscribed with many flourishes. One much larger than the rest displayed a red rose at its centre, and was trimmed with lace and ribbons like a valentine.

I took the box to my old home, the home of my childhood. Through the window I could see my father and brother busily arranging my mother's favourite furniture. I knew she was shortly returning home from a very long journey, and could see they were preparing a welcome. In the kitchen I showed them my box and, still laughing, picked up the single dark chocolate that lay inside, and ate it. Immediately a brightly lit square appeared in the top of my head, opening into an exquisitely colourful room. Baba and Inder stood inside the square looking down at me — then Baba lifted a golden rod and made a strange gesture — and to my horror all the light and colour drained out of everything, leaving only a dull black and white wherever I looked.

Inder made no comment on the dream, and spoke instead of the group's future. He said when Kate received a reply to her cable (and she **would** have a reply this time) everything would then be in order for serious work to commence. We had all passed through a time of preparation; some had benefitted more from this than others — and those that were spiritually ready would now be given certain duties to perform that constituted the beginnings of real service — while those still not fully prepared would have to be segregated and make good their deficiencies. This could be a lengthy process and might prove a matter of years, or even the entire lifetime.

There was a book he wished to write, and meetings in future would be utilised for this work. He would dictate it, and it would have to be phrased in correct English and placed into typescript. It would throw a clearer light on certain aspects of Baba's work and would one day be published . . . As he talked, I felt a strange coldness creeping over me. I remember saying, "I shan't be with you then, Inder, shall I?" and he did not reply. Nell said I was imagining things again, but her voice was friendly. She was relieved there was no disharmony tonight.

But I knew. The knowledge grew in my heart, and the light receded and was lost to me. I said to Inder, almost in tears that I strove to avert, "Baba won't let me see you any more, and Alison and Rose will have you all to themselves . . . *I can't bear it.*" — yet I managed to pull myself together, and the meeting closed on a cheerful note with no reference to what I had said. We all looked forward to the promised work which was to begin on Saturday.

It all came to a head on Saturday morning. I awoke feeling very unwell, the tension in my stomach quivering and acute. I had dreamt that Baba sent me a cable — he sat on the bottom of the bed as I read it. The words were not clear, though I knew they held severance and disgrace . . . yet he indicated that this was not as it seemed, but a ruse of some kind — a 'red herring' almost, to bring about some situation in his work. I heard him say, "Inder will be with you for many months yet," and instead of feeling comforted I experienced the reverse.

When the telephone rang I thought I would be sick. I was expecting it subconsciously, without knowing why. It was Alison, announcing coolly that Inder wished to speak to me. Then Inder's voice, crisp and cold. "Kate, there is a message for you from India —" He read it out slowly, twice . . .

'In reply to Kate's cable reproduced on this page, Baba wants you to inform Kate Merton that her severance from

177

Babagroup is preferable in the interests of all concerned, and that she should lead a normal loving life with her family whilst keeping her heart aglow with her love for Baba, because Baba resides in the heart of all who remember and love Him.' The letter was signed by Eruch, one of the Mandali.

Tears steamed down my face. I cried, "Oh no! Oh no! *I can't bear it!*" my body trembling, my fingers clutching agitatedly at the pencil they held. The message given, Inder said he would go now and tell the others. Brokenly, in a small voice I begged him to talk to me, to explain what was happening and where I had gone wrong. Griefstricken beyond shame, I entreated his forbearance and said I could not live without him . . . but he refused to listen to "weeping and romance", having other things to do. He rang off abruptly. It was all unimaginably cruel.

I cried as I had never cried before, the turmoil and internal rending quite outside my control. Mercifully the children stayed in bed late and were unaware of the havoc wrought in me, but Patrick knew midday by my silence that something was wrong. I could not speak unless spoken to — the numbing of mind made it impossible, and only gradually could I tell him about the message. It gave him enormous and undisguised satisfaction.

In the afternoon I wrote a brief note to Inder, the content of which I cannot remember; also one jointly to Alison and Rose requesting their forgiveness for any misjudgement of them I had made, and wishing them every success in their future work. I took both letters to the Lodge and left them for collection that evening.

Looking round the familiar room in which I had spent so vital a part of my life, I felt an unbearable nostalgia. I gazed at Inder's chair in its usual place and wondered if I would have the strength to endure my separation. I do not know how I got home that afternoon. I could neither feel nor think, and nothing was real any more.

I managed to hold back the weeping for most of the day, save for brief, solitary intervals, but at night I was deluged in earnest. Patrick tried at last to comfort me, soon giving up and falling asleep, for human comfort could not retrieve me from the abyss I faced. I wanted, desperately, God's love — and God had utterly forsaken me.

Alone in the Void my pierced soul cried out to Him, hovering between Creation and the Absolute, transfixed in solitude and silence amid fathomless wastes of space . . . and He would not hear me . . . had turned away and abandoned me. Nothing remained save a vacuum, and my own bitter grief.

The following day I retreated to bed in the afternoon, pleading fatigue as I felt so distraught. The weeping would not stop and I could do nothing to ease the rending inside. Patrick at first was kind — then, as I could not be comforted, became annoyed and once more fell asleep. When he awoke I was still crying and quite incoherent with inner pain. I no longer wanted to live. The light had gone out and even the darkness was no more — only stark, staring blankness remained.

Patrick grew disturbed by my mental agitation — he said if I continued in this way I would collapse completely. At the back of my mind I recognised this myself; in a split second of insight I saw myself crouched on the edge of a precipice, the merest hairsbreadth between me and destruction. The words Inder had used in a dream flashed into my mind — *"There is no short cut —"* and I understood with sharp clarity that if I persisted I would end in hospital, and this would be wrong.

I thought of my children and their dependence upon me, and this ultimately brought me back from the twilit place I had reached. Spent and exhausted, I slowly gathered strength and control before getting up, forcing my mind back to things of the earth in an act of submission. My children were my salvation. Without them I would have slipped my bonds, but they anchored me firmly again to life by their need of me. Teresa was spending the day with my sister-in-law and David was thankfully occupied with his own affairs. They were shielded from all that assailed me, and Patrick alone knew how I had cried.

The next few days are a nightmarish blur. In them I learned that even darkness and humiliation are staffs on which we may lean — for darkness can be seen and humiliation felt, and there was neither seeing nor feeling in the dull whiteness surrounding me now. The colour had gone out of everything and life was a barren waste — to be endured rather than lived through. Night after night I awoke with Baba's name on my lips, imploring his solace. I was totally bereft. There was nothing left to me of the life of the spirit, not even my dreams. Inder came no more to me in sleep, and only a confusion of shadows were retained on waking for days on end.

At the close of my second week of separation from the group, I sent a third cable to Baba in the pathetic hope that my punishment, if such it was, had been sufficient and could now be rescinded. Perpetually in the foreground of my mind loomed the memory of the letter seen clairvoyantly last year — 'There have been no doubts and no delays. I cancel all my previous instructions to you'. That night, Baba appeared in a dream and reprimanded Inder for allowing me to bother him once more. Moving towards me he placed two lettuce leaves and a tomato in my hands, sternly indicating I was to prepare a feast from them without continually troubling him in the meantime. I awoke feeling chastened, then into my awareness came the certitude that the 'feast' was a record in book form of my contact with Baba. This seemed quite incredible under the existing circumstances, though it brooded so powerfully in my brain that I was virtually driven at length to set down my thoughts, commencing to do so on April 29th (1964). My intention initially was to recount only the events of the past two years; I soon found, however, that to make any sense at all of my own actions to others, it would be necessary to go back further, then further still, until I arrived at my earliest recollection.

Patrick remained at home with me for two evenings only; the first time willingly enough, and the second with considerable annoyance, departing to bed early in a very black mood. Apart from these concessions, his evening life continued as before.

After a week in which I think he felt rather guilty, he wrote of his own accord to Inder and requested that I might be allowed to return to the group — I was so unhappy, and he now withdrew his objections. I told him it was useless to write to Inder, as it was from Baba that such permission must come. In prompt reply he received a curt, cold note from Alison to the effect that it was up to the individual as to whether they chose to obey Baba's instructions or not. Inder's signature was on the bottom.

The following Tuesday, Alison telephoned to say briefly that Inder had received a reply to my cable, and would I phone him. She was cool and superior, adroitly evading my eager questions concerning them all. My cable had informed Baba that I had complied with his wish though with much grief, and that Patrick was still dissatisfied and our situation was deteriorating; that we would be homeless at the end of May and Patrick's solution was to split us up and accommodate us separately wherever possible until August, when his new house would be finished. That my parents had again rejected me through my non-renunciation of past convictions. I concluded by saying that the children were disturbed by approaching homelessness, and gave my address in full for a prepaid reply. It was therefore puzzling that a reply should be sent to Inder.

Apprehensively I contacted him as requested. Dispassionate and aloof, he read out the cabled words as if to a stranger:

'Tell Kate Merton cable received and that she must not worry but try best to live loving and normal family life and keep Baba in heart. Meher Baba.'

He added in the same tone that if I found finances difficult he would reimburse me for my cable through Alison. I thanked him but declined. He, too, would not reveal anything about the meetings, their frequency and work. There was no doubt at all that I was banished with ignominy. Surely, my mind argued, if my severance was through Patrick I ought not to be in such disgrace, nor receive such callous treatment; and my misery broke afresh. I wondered also why the cable had not come to me direct — there seemed no point in sending it through Inder, unless to confirm in everyone's mind the fact of my exile.

We were due to finally vacate the flat on May 29th, and as the days passed it became increasingly evident we should soon find ourselves without a home. The new house was nowhere near finished. Patrick had been hugely over-optimistic concerning its date of completion, and the first week in May saw the roof tiled but the interior untouched. He made a half-hearted attempt to look at properties to rent, quickly abandoning this measure as nothing was available for less than a six month period, and he considered it impractical to sign a lease when the house would be ready "in about eight weeks". As an alternative to his original intention of separating us all, he suggested that myself and the children should go to his mother's home in Middlesbrough — the mere mention of this upsetting both children to the extent that I became frantic with worry. It was cruelly frustrating to see the days slip by with no effort made to change our situation. Patrick refused to trouble himself, know-

181

ing his mother would have us; and considered it my fault anyway that we were in such a plight. The children's distress he laid at my door.

I watched David with much anxiety. There were increasing signs of unease and nervous apprehension in him, and I grew angry with Patrick for letting it happen and rendering me powerless. He still felt viciously about Inder and repeatedly brought up our past connection in the most vitriolic and often sordid manner. If I had gone away with him for a week, it could not have been worse.

In mid-May I sent a further cable to Baba detailing my current situation, and the fact that three of us were soon to leave for Yorkshire whilst Patrick remained here in Cambridge. Baba had said we were to live together and had thus tied my hands as far as independent action was concerned. I now asked his advice.

I dreamt that night that I returned to the group. I saw myself unbrick a hole in the wall which I had bricked up some time earlier. The fresh aperture revealed a tableau set in a cupboard, with tiny figurines of Alison, Rose, Inder and Nell seated in a room exactly as I had left them. The figures suddenly came to life and I joined them.

This dream infused me with hope. I thought my cable would open up a way back for me, and got up expectantly for the first time in many days — but my anticipation was soon quenched by an inexplicable sensation, and I knew the end was not in sight by any means.

Rose telephoned me at work four days later to say that Inder had a cable for me, and would I contact him. I did, in sudden fearfulness, and he read out the following:

'Kate's cable to Baba received. Baba would want Kate to get adjusted according to the circumstances confronting her and bravely discharge her responsibilities *without referring again to Him* for advice and instructions. Eruch.'*

The world spun about me. The nucleus that was 'I' ricocheted wildly in the Void, then stopped — quite motionless, with shock. I heard my voice as if from a distance saying distractedly, "I can't bear it . . . *I can't bear it* —" and then the

* My italics.

182

confused and breathless jumble of words as I tried to explain that Patrick was hostile and sending us away — and how disturbed the children had become . . . that I would lose my job and Patrick refused to pay for the furniture† . . . and I felt too ill and wretched to cope with it all sensibly any longer.

All to no avail. Inder had long gone from me; he spoke like a stranger. When my employer summoned me a few moments later I started to cry, and he stared at me with exasperated disinterest. I struggled hard to pull myself together, though how I got through the afternoon I do not know. My mind was blank and I typed like an automaton.

That evening I went to Alison's house to collect my books.* There was no longer any valid excuse to leave them there, for the slight possibility that Baba would one day permit my return to the fold was no longer viable. If I may not contact him, it was exceedingly unlikely he would ever contact me, and my rejection appeared complete and conclusive. I asked myself a thousand times what I had done, for this was never made clear to me, and I could see nothing in my own behaviour to merit expulsion. Indeed, I now saw nothing at all. Baba was not there any more. *Nothing* was there — even life was a mirage, cast on the screen of a vast emptiness.

Alison greeted me with caution. She fetched my books and I was about to leave immediately when Inder arrived. My heart convulsed, and I felt myself shaking as I looked once more at the loved face and into those stern dark eyes. He motioned me to stay, and to sit down.

He had with him the cables that had been read to me over the telephone, and these were handed to me "to assure" me of their authenticity (which I had not doubted). He then showed me a letter received a few days previously from Baba to himself, which said if there was any possibility of attachment or personal involvement in connection with any member of the group, he was to conclude the meetings at once and leave Cambridge as soon as he had obtained satisfactory employment elsewhere. There would be spiritual work for him wherever he was placed.

† I had taken a part-time job to pay the Hire Purchase on the furniture, as our lodgers had to leave when the lease first expired.
*These had been left with Inder. He had upset me greatly by passing them on to Alison. I discovered this during our last but one telephone conversation.

'*Attachment* or personal involvement'? *Inder?* It was too ludicrous. Utterly beyond belief! I therefore did not take the statement seriously and let it slip through my mind and away. Inder commented briefly that the last sentence indicated he was shortly to leave anyway, and he would in fact conclude the meetings the following evening. Alison stood silently by his chair, a curious expression on her face. No other explanation was given, at least not to me, and Inder suddenly leaned back and relaxed and talked naturally to me as if nothing untoward had occurred since we last met.

By this time Rose had arrived, and he asserted with some emphasis that this evening's 'chance' contact had been arranged by Baba in order that certain things should be said to us all, one of them being that as the group from tomorrow would cease to exist as such, I was no longer 'severed' and could talk freely with Rose and Alison — and also with himself as long as the conversation remained impersonal. I asked if I might therefore be present when he visited, and he said yes, one of them would let me know when he was there and I could join them.

He then stated that from now on we were all *entirely on our own* and he could advise us no more, *save on matters of obedience* — as Baba's use of himself in the former manner had come to an end now in Cambridge, though it may well continue elsewhere. And whatever *had been done* for each one of us, *we must now learn to do for ourselves,* by *our own* efforts, and this would take *much* longer than the short while he had been with us. We had been *given* a quickened process of development *as a gift.* Now we must work to foster it and make it permanently our own. Help of this nature would not be proffered again till we had done so. It was up *to us* to consolidate our gain.

I felt very uncertain about the first part of this, concerning myself; the relief I should have experienced was not there, and I was full of misgiving and doubt. Also a very real sadness that Inder was going away. Yet there was a quite specific outcome from this meeting as far as my personal state was concerned. On the surface everything was much the same, but *inwardly* the terrible spiritual suffering and sense of isolation diminished to a borderline degree of bearability. I realised long afterwards that I had been monitored throughout the whole ordeal, and the 'chance' meeting served quite other purposes than those

184

mentioned. Through this means he alleviated the stress that could have overwhelmed me, and thus ensured that I survived the first impact of 'annihilation unto death' without mishap, and with all my faculties intact.

The next day I asked Betty if she would like to accompany me to the Lodgeroom that evening to say goodbye to Inder. He had said he would deal with the group's official closure as soon as he got there, after which I would automatically be freed from my instruction concerning it. So Betty and myself arrived soon after eight o'clock, expecting this to have occurred.

Inder, however, had not yet arrived, and Alison, Rose and Nell were still waiting. When he did eventually appear he seemed in excellent spirits and greeted Betty warmly. He brought with him a sealed envelope which, to my surprise, he immediately gave to me. He said it contained my letters. I discovered later that every one I had ever sent him had been safely returned to me. I wondered why they were given back, but he gave no reason and I did not like to ask.

When seated, he said he did not have to close the group at this juncture, it was really up to his discretion. He then referred to the sore issue of former meetings — that Kate had stated he was a Master . . .

Calmly he fixed his inscrutable eyes upon me.

"Are you now prepared to withdraw this?"

It was, perhaps, my last opportunity to avert disaster. Or, having tasted the consequence of stepping out of line, to step back in again. Or maybe some other kind of test? I did not pause then to think. I simply said "No!" very firmly.

"In that case," he remarked pleasantly, "I am already being involved in a way that is contrary to Baba's instructions, and the group must close."

For a moment his eyes glanced into mine, then moved coolly away, their depths unfathomable. In the short talk that followed he summed up the situation, saying the fault of the discord in the group had not lain with one alone. If each of us had held the impersonal detachment necessary for service to the Master, all would have been well. He stressed that none of us meant anything to him personally; his entire connection with us had been through instruction, not choice, and he would be no more concerned with us when he left Cambridge. We all listened in silence.

Betty departed as soon as Inder had finished, Rupert having come to collect her. Nell left shortly afterwards to catch the early bus, and Alison, Rose and myself sat on, but nothing more of significance was said, and within minutes the meeting broke up. I shook hands with Inder and reluctantly went home. It seemed a tame ending, and I could not accept that he had gone from my life. His insouciant friendliness had been like a veneer, beneath which was . . . what?

In the morning I telephoned Alison and asked if I might come to see her. My fear of her displeasure had crumbled away during the night, and I longed for her friendship and the renewal of affection between us. Surely she must feel this too? She seemed none too pleased by my request but agreed that I might come on Monday. Rose came too, and on the whole we spent an amicable evening together — though at one point it was apparent that the breach was not healed in any sense. Inadvertently I learned that Inder had been to see Alison privately over the weekend, and this impressed me forcibly that all was not as it seemed.

I had the uneasy conviction that my severance still remained operative, for Baba's actual instruction, clearly expressed, and conveyed to us via the much vaunted 'black and white' media of the G.P.O., had in no way been rescinded in the same manner. Immersed as I was in my own tribulations, plus my continuing certitude of Inder's powers of directive, it did not enter my head to question Alison as to how Inder (an "aspirant just like us" as she had so frequently defined) arrived legitimately, and to her satisfaction, at his recent decision. Namely, to allow my reintroduction into what was still, indisputably, a group situation.

During the ensuing week I grew more and more despondent. We were hurtling towards removal day and absolutely nothing was being done about it. Daily the children would ask where we were going to live and what would happen to us, and I could give them no definite answer. Margaret had agreed to take Valerie (our one remaining lodger) until the end of her course, and Betty offered to accommodate either David or Teresa, but more they could not do.

In desperation I phoned my mother, who had been particularly fond of David in the past, and appealed to her for help — asking if she would have him for a week or two to give us extra time. He would feel safe there in familiar surroundings.

She was unmoved by my pleas, and retorted frostily that having got myself into this mess I must get myself out. The children were *my* responsibility and I should have thought of these things before . . . she would consult my father, though as far as she was concerned the answer was no. A few minutes later she telephoned back to inform me that my father agreed with her and they would not take David. There was no sign at all of concern for his wellbeing; what happened to him would be part of my punishment. I would not have believed this of either of them until it happened.

Neither Alison nor Rose made any move to contact me, much to my disappointment. They naturally knew of my plight and were quite obviously unconcerned. I suppose it was childish of me to mind — but I knew that had they been so situated I should at least have enquired what was happening — particularly considering the close contact between us over so many months.

I was at my wits end. Only four days to go, and then our enforced and reluctant departure for Middlesbrough. My mother-in-law was still unaware of our imminent descent on her home; her son was so convinced of her compliance he had not as yet troubled to write.

I cannot describe how completely my mind rejected this solution. With every fibre in me I did not wish to go, and nor did poor David and Teresa. I had found my son the previous evening with a suspiciously tear-stained face — he who was brave and never cried — and my heart ached for him. Each wakeful moment of the night I had cried out silently to Baba, begging him to help us; and in the flat now by myself, I prayed long and earnestly in my effort to reach him. Yet I felt and sensed nothing, and sighing deeply I got up and went to the bureau drawer where Inder's photo was kept. I gazed at his reflected face and held it despairingly to my heart. Acknowledging my own foolishness I bent to put it back, and noticed a letter projecting from the bundle where it had lain, an old one sent the previous year by Maud S.

Idly I removed it, and just as indifferently commenced to reread its pages. It said, incredibly, that she would welcome me to stay with her whenever my circumstances permitted — I could come at any time, and if in difficulties could bring my children. The letter had long gone from my mind. I read it through a second time with a sense of bewilderment. Could this be the answer to my prayer? To stay with one of Baba's people would be like going home.

It occurred to me then that my instructions might well include all Baba's followers. Though I did not understand what was happening, nor could see why disgrace should fall upon me — I had to accept that it had. It must therefore be assumed I was cast out for some purpose . . . and I could not truly believe this had been undone. Before approaching Maud I ought first to find out my position, and I suddenly remembered Inder saying that he could still be consulted on matters of obedience . . .

As soon as the thought had entered my head, without hesitation I at once telephoned his laboratory, fully aware nevertheless of my rashness in doing so — to find he was absent "with influenza" and had not been there for several days.

Something quite irrational happened to me then. I cannot explain it, save to say he 'called' me, and I had to go. A note was struck in my brain, like the plucking of a delicate thread, soundlessly communicating what he required of me. I knew I was acting against all common sense, yet in no time found myself ensconced on the bus and travelling towards his lodgings: thinking all the while how mad I was, and that I ought to get off at once before I made an idiot of myself.

He was not at home. So much for my hyperactive intuition! His landlady said he must have just slipped out to the shops, would I like to wait? I declined, explaining that Inder had asked us not to come to his room, and I had only wished to ask something. At the top of the road once more, I saw him walking towards me. My legs felt weak and I was conscious of twisting my hands together with nervousness.

He expressed no surprise at seeing me, smiled unaffectedly and stopped to talk — did not seem in the least bit vexed. I apologised for coming to visit him and briefly explained my position, asking if he could tell me whether my severance included the London group also — as this was now the only group in England as far as I knew. His manner became grave. He said I must use my own discretion, the onus was completely on myself now and he was not permitted to help me at all. One thing he could say — if I decided to go to Maud's, she would certainly be kind and "look after" me without charging much for living expenses. However, if I would like to talk about things generally, not *personally*, he would see me at Alison's that evening . . .

I hesitated. With all my heart I longed to go, but the children had such need of me just now, and I did not feel I could leave them. I told him I was not much in the mood for general discussion and my children were both so disturbed by current events that I really must stay with them. He looked at me with a strange expression in his eyes, almost a tenderness combined with pity. I ejected the thought at once, but went home a little comforted. That evening I wrote to Maud, and Patrick wrote to his mother. Both letters requested accommodation.

The next morning I registered another strong impulse — this time to telephone Alison. I was troubled by this without knowing why, yet still felt I must. Alison was aloof and distant and I experienced a deep spasm of fear. Something had happened to revert her attitude to its former steel-like hardness.

After a few attempts at one-sided conversation, I asked if she had seen Inder. She said yes, he had called last night. Silence. Did he say he had seen me? Yes, but she could not discuss it . . .

Why on earth not?

What Inder said to herself and Rose was *their* business.

I was puzzled and increasingly annoyed. If Inder had spoken about me, why couldn't I know what he said? Our conversation of yesterday had not been a secret . . . But Alison was obdurate. She said cruelly that she had been told *not* to discuss anything with me, and that was sufficient for *her!* With a firm goodbye she rang off.

I cannot remember the whole conversation. The wall of hostility that left me seething on the wrong side, and the continual implication of secrets that I was forbidden to share, made me burningly angry. This uncalled-for duplicity by Inder and the calculated unkindness and eternal self-righteousness of Alison now reached a saturation point within me. She was insufferably 'holier than thou', and I longed to shake her exceedingly hard in a most unspiritual manner.

In that same moment a chord sounded in my heart, and I responded automatically. With lightening speed a resolution formed in my mind. Again I boarded a bus and within minutes was on my way to see Inder. I felt alarming inside. It was sheer madness to approach him again, especially after what Alison had said — yet something drove me on, and I accepted, after a swift mental battle, that some inner part of me had already determined the course I should take.

Once more I walked along Sedgwick street, inexplicably terrified now, my limbs forced along by my will. This time he emerged from the side street further down, as if indeed he was waiting for me. His face was like thunder and as he drew within earshot, he demanded angrily to know why I was *deliberately* causing him to break Baba's instructions. Then he abruptly turned back, and walked away in the opposite direction. I followed, imploring him to speak with me if only for a minute, and at last he paused, frowning heavily.

Shaking with apprehension, I asked what he had told Alison about me, and said I felt it grossly unfair of him to go to her behind my back when everything was against me and I had been so desperate. He replied he had told her *nothing* save that I should *not* have come to see him, and that I had not been interested enough in general discussion to meet him in a proper, *uncompromising* setting.

General discussion! When faced with the tragedy of my childrens situation, my needs were surely other than this! The sheer *injustice* of it incensed me. A surging fount of frustrated impulses created a rising vortex within me. I stood my ground and repeated vehemently what Alison had said, and asked him again why he did this to me — what had I done to *him?* His face was enraged but he did not answer, so I shouted it, hurling into the words the pent-up force of my impotent fury — *"WHAT HAVE I DONE TO YOU?"*

He matched it, fury for fury, rage for rage, hurt for hurt, and finally accused me violently of making a scene in the street.* After more bitter reproaches he moved rapidly away from me.

Deflated and spent, I accepted defeat and walked the other way to the nearest side-street — feeling as if my heart was breaking to pieces. When, by a roundabout route, I arrived at

---

* In this way, by the evocation of deep-seated emotion, a Teacher will loosen and remove accretions in a pupil. This incident was also utilised in other ways, and was reported to Alison immediately.

the bus stop — there he stood. He ignored me as if I were a total stranger, and I hovered there miserably, silent and ashamed. The bus came and he did not move, nor look in my direction, and I knew he intended to wait for the next one. As I boarded it, something within me died; perhaps the last spark of hope that had feebly glimmered on despite all things. For a moment I fully experienced my secondary self† in all its aspects — then it slipped from me like a sheath. In those seconds I told myself what an utter fool I was — a dull, very ordinary house-wife who had stupidly believed in a dream of love. While he, the adored of my heart . . . my most dearly beloved . . . trampled my very soul into the dust.

*   *   *   *   *   *

That evening a telegram arrived from Maud. It read, 'Yes, come here. Welcome. Maud.' and I blessed her gratefully.

A fourth impulse arose. Softer . . . in a much lower key. In a chastened mood I wrote a brief letter to Inder apologising for my visit of the morning. I told him of Maud's telegram and asked, as I was leaving Cambridge on Friday, if he would please come on Thursday to Alison's to say goodbye. (This arrangement was initiated by Nell, who had today confirmed it by post.)

On Thursday I went hopefully to Alison's and braved my icy reception. She had not cancelled my visit, presumably for Nell's sake. He did not come, though I knew he had certainly seen Alison. Some time later I discovered also that he visited her the following Saturday and tore my letter to shreds in her presence. He said I had *again* (for the third time) disobeyed my instructions by contacting him, and he wanted nothing more to do with me.

To revert to Wednesday. Hotfoot on the telegram a letter arrived from Maud, written in the sobering light of reflection next morning. On reading it I knew she had been having second thoughts, although the letter was very kind — the problem, I assumed, being my children.* A deep maternal instinct at once suffused me, and I telephoned several agents in

† the personality.

* This was incorrect. Her reason related to personal affairs of her own.

a last, belated hope of rented accommodation. One place was miraculously available to us — an expensive new flat that I had enquired after two weeks previously, in the forlorn hope that Patrick would take it as a temporary measure. I had made a tentative application and, hearing nothing, assumed it had gone to someone else. The delay, however, was for other reasons, and at teatime on Wednesday the agent phoned to say we could have it if we wished.

Patrick did not think much of this proposal, and very reluctantly agreed to have a look at it. The next morning we had to make a decision; someone else was interested, and anyway time was short. Patrick resisted taking it and wanted us to go to Middlesbrough — he had just received a reply from his mother, who was willing to have us temporarily. I asked desperately for guidance, then did what I felt best for my children — I signed for the flat. The lease had not yet been made out, and my signature covered only the rent for one month in advance. In view of this, Patrick decided it would suit him to come too.

After many last minute arrangements, on Friday we moved in. Teresa liked it, David did not; although he admitted it was still preferable to going to Middlesbrough. Anxiety had caught up with David and he was unwell for a fortnight with nothing specific. I allowed him to stay at home, and his school mercifully made no protest.

We lived at Larchfield for almost a month, during which time Patrick made no attempt to behave normally, staying out all hours of the night and also spending Sundays with his friends. His way, perhaps, of paying me back.

Nightly on his return he would tell me he couldn't endure me and did not wish to live with me any more. Sometimes he started amicably, but always it ended the same way. He would throw up my religious beliefs in a vitriolic fashion, and fall asleep as I lay crying. There were no books or mementoes around to vex him — all my belongings were locked away, and had been so since December. But nothing I could do made any difference.

One Sunday I tried to draw his attention to what he was doing to me — entreating him to stay at home as I felt so ill and distraught. When he refused I threw the contents of the refuse bin all over the clean kitchen floor, and smashed two saucers on the newly plastered wall, just missing his head. He took no notice and departed, leaving me to clear it up or go mad, whichever I chose. Such was his concern.

When the lease came through I dared not sign it, for I no longer had a job, having terminated it in expectation of going away — and Valerie's course was now finished and she had to leave us. I was afraid to commit myself legally to the necessary £10 per week without any income — Patrick having refused to contribute other than £3 weekly if we stayed on. I felt so indisposed it seemed more likely I would have a breakdown than find further employment . . . and the thought of a strange girl in the small, compact flat made me want to scream. Patrick was quite immoveable. His house would be ready sometime in August. He would therefore do nothing till then.

Wearily I wrote once more to Maud and stated my position, and once more she kindly agreed to take us in. I did not feel too sure about my decision, and David suddenly swayed the issue. He said he would like to go to Oxford and make a fresh start. Maybe we could settle there and begin a new life? His observations were saddeningly mature.

In Larchfield the vivid dreams commenced again, and some of these I knew to be precognitive. One in particular had the impact of immediacy. It began with a telephone ringing loudly and insistently. The call was for me, and Alison did her utmost to keep me from answering it. When I finally managed to lift the receiver she made such a noise I could scarcely catch the words of the speaker on the other end. Suddenly I grasped it was Inder. My vision opened and I saw him sitting on a hospital bed and peering intently at me. He spoke urgently, his voice rising strongly above Alison's — but in a strange language that made no sense. Occasional sentences broke through in English — he said Baba was dying and then recited a poem by Kabir. The words were jumbled; I could only distinguish a line beginning 'the night bird Chakor' . . . And all the time Alison shouted, "You shall *not* speak to him, you *shall not!*" as she struggled violently to take the receiver away from me.

Before leaving Cambridge I went once more to Alison's house. Her attitude again was such it was really more painful than staying away. Inder visited her regularly, and though there were no official meetings it was obvious things were much as they were before. I could discover nothing concerning him or his intentions; whether the book he had mentioned was under way, or what his visits to Alison signified. Nor why I was banned from seeing him but could still see Rose, Nell and herself . . . She told me of the destroyed letter, however, and when I asked if she had felt any pity for me in my plight at the time, she replied firmly, "No, Kate, I felt no pity for you at all." And that summed up most accurately our relationship.

Nell invited us to a birthday tea at her bungalow (not Inder) and this too was a misery. Alison and Rose were loftily patronising, and when I asked an innocuous question, the former asserted officiously that she was "forbidden" to discuss *anything* with *me*. It also slipped out in the course of conversation that certain instructions "from Inder" had been received by Alison which could not *under any circumstances* be revealed to myself. This put me completely in my place and raised many fresh queries as well — none of which could be asked, nor would have been answered, as I was well aware.

With these matters in mind, a few days later I wrote to Alison and told her I was currently writing a detailed account of our contact with Baba, and would she please ask Inder if I might send it to him when finished, via herself if he wished, as it concerned him intimately. I was asking this as, rightly or wrongly, I believed Baba wished me to make some use of the completed manuscript in an as yet unknown manner — and I did not feel I ought to proceed further without advice re possible deletions. I concluded with my apologies for intruding on their time.

I received an abrupt, indeed very rude reply which distressed me greatly. It said:

(a) you may not see Inder.
(b) nor may you send any communication to him via any source whatsoever.

Its effect was like a door slamming hard in my face.

Three days before we were due to leave for Oxford, Maud tried to defer our arrival as she had other people coming. It was now too late to undo our arrangements, and while I was trying to sort out this dilemma she wrote again to say a solution had been found. We could stay in a friend's unused house for several days until her visitors had gone.

During our last week at Larchfield I dreamt Inder came to me. He held me tightly in his arms and kissed me — then moved away again, holding his hands outstretched so that I could just touch the tips of his fingers. Wreaths of blue and violet light encircled his wrists in constant movement, glowing luminously — and I remember thinking, "Surely you *must* be a Master to be like this . . ." He laughed joyously as if reading my thoughts, and the colours swirled like tongues of flame along his arms. I said, "Why am I severed from you? Is there a reason?" and he replied, "Yes, there is a reason for this, which you may not know at present." Wistfully I asked, "Can't I ever see you again, then?" And he answered, "This is a standing order from Baba — no, you may not see me again . . ." but the last words were said on a different vibration, and I knew this even as I listened. They did not ring true.

Patrick drove us to Maud's Oxfordshire cottage on June 25th. A young Indian greeted us warmly (it was Jehangir) and told us Maud was waiting at Cowley, where we were to stay. The cottage looked inviting and I was sorry to leave it. I had not known that Jehangir was one of the guests, and the prospect of meeting him during the next few days was cheering.

But Cowley was dismal; the house bare and somehow frightening. Maud and two friends were already there and stayed just long enough to say hello. It was a daunting moment when they left. My head was swimming with strain and fatigue, and when Patrick too, prepared to depart, I felt like repacking and going back with him — but of course, there was now no home to go to, and he would be lodging at his pub.

It was like a ghastly dream. David was depressed, and even the cheerful Teresa complained of the 'darkness' in the house. Later we learned that it had been the scene of much disharmony and grief — for a young mother had left home taking her small children with her, and her husband attempted suicide and afterwards suffered a nervous breakdown, eventually having to leave as he could not bear the memories. All three of us registered the imprint of these sad events, and were much affected to say the least.

Two days after our arrival, Maud and her friend G. went to Earl's Court to attend the monthly meeting of the London group. I considered going with them despite my stringent finances, for Jehangir, who was himself *en route* there, offered the fare for us all. Yet I could not bring myself to take it, and after some persuasion he gave up, saying wryly, "If Baba *wants* you to go, a way will be found for you and you won't argue!" But I did not go, feeling sadly and deeply that it wasn't the right time.

Maud returned with a serious face. She announced bluntly and without any preamble that Inder had that day been taken by Adi to a *mental* hospital. It seemed he had recently arrived in London and became ill at once. Maud said he had constantly repeated Baba's name and in distress reiterated he was dead. As there was no-one to look after him and he had given up his lodgings, Adi had arranged for his hospitalisation.

I was deeply shocked. Jehangir was consoling and told me to try not to worry. He said Baba was looking after Inder, and he would probably be himself again in a few days time . . . but he did not, of course, regard him in any sense as I did. I wept miserably in the gloomy Cowley house that night, with Teresa asleep beside me. My world had really fallen to pieces now . . . though I could not convince myself that Inder was deranged, no matter what others thought or described.

Into my memory stole a vivid recollection from our early acquaintance. When in a humorous frame of mind he could clown fantastically, and laughing helplessly after a polished, impromptu performance, I had said he had missed his vocation and should have been an actor. He had beamed at me delightedly, casually lighting the inevitable cigarette before he rejoined, eyes smilingly fixed on mine — "I can be *anything*, Kate!" and I knew he could act any part to further the Master's work — and perhaps had even staged this brilliantly proficient display to imprint the fact on my mind.

After five days at Cowley we moved to Maud's cottage. It was much nicer there and she was very kind to us, encouraging us all to make ourselves at home. Jehangir had spent much time with me the previous weekend and was warmly cheering and understanding. He was also much concerned about my financial situation and sent me five pounds by post as soon as he got back to London, plus a long, aspirational letter. All my expostulations would not induce him to take the money back. It was "for the children" he said, to make things a little easier for them as they had been through so much. And in this way I accepted it, as he doubtless intended I should.

Patrick sent five pounds at the end of the week, and the briefest of notes. I had written a card to my parents and letters to each of my former friends and acquaintances, including Alison — and only Alison replied. My letter to her had communicated Maud's report, in case she hadn't heard this news, and in answer she said tersely that Inder was now out of hospital . . . she could not discuss his state or condition; and it was up to us to surrender to Baba and not be "distressed" by events that took place — this merely made it harder for ourselves and others. All perfectly true; but the way in which it was expressed, and the hardness and coldness of it all caused me much emotional pain. Alison knew what was going on, yet not a crumb would she give me to set my mind at rest.

On Saturday Patrick arrived unexpectedly, looking unwell, and behaving as aggressively as ever. He said he had come to see the children, then after a while suggested we talk privately — and for around two hours made the usual angry accusations before preparing to depart in a temper. His *grande exit* was ironically forestalled by the car, which refused to start, and eventually we had to telephone a garage to send a mechanic — who, to Patrick's chagrin, found nothing wrong save a slope in the road and started the car at once.

While we awaited the mechanic, Maud invited Patrick to supper and an overnight stay if he wished, making him very welcome. His temper cooled, and the tension between us relaxed. A little later he asked me out to the local inn to "talk sensibly together", which we did . . . but on our return, the atmosphere of Maud's quaint and ancient cottage with its pictures of Baba and the faint scent of incense, began to disturb him. This accumulated, and at midnight in a sudden smouldering rage he stormed outside and started the car — he would stay *here* no longer and "something definite must be done". I would have to choose between himself and Baba, he said furiously. I *could not have both*.

I stood disconsolately on the dark country road in my nightdress, unable to think constructively in the midst of continual bombardment. He called out that I should go inside before getting a chill; then without looking back, roared off into the night.

My second week at Maud's was really grim. Both mentally and physically I was right at the end of my strength, and at times I really thought I would break with the strain. Although outwardly normal, I lived in a strange and frightening limbo —

not belonging anywhere, either on earth or in heaven. It was a terrible feeling.

Late in the week a letter arrived for Maud from Alison, sent in reply to one of her own. It contained thinly veiled references to my personal lack of surrender, and feeling perplexed, she brought it straight to my room to show me. When I read it I broke down completely and cried in an abandonment of despair. It did something disintegrative to me quite impossible to describe. All the harshness, unkindness, cruel thoughts and ill-feeling that had lain on the periphery of my mental field, now found their point of entry and assailed my spirit with a weight of iron. Such was the psychological disruption, I feared I would suffer a total collapse, and begged Maud to look after Teresa and David for me if I became ill and was taken away from them.

I owe Maud much for her goodness to me at that time. She talked to me from the heart, pouring love upon me, comforting me and promising care of my children — encouraging me forward to the brighter pathway she was sure Baba had prepared for me. For that distrained and crucial hour she was mother and sister, councellor and friend, and I knew that Baba had willed it so for my salvation.

The day passed in a kind of blur, and gradually the grief lessened, and the crisis in my mind resolved itself into resignation. I drew a certain peace from the old, walled garden with its multitude of flowers and herbs. I remember particularly the white Chinese peonies with their subtle scent, and the dark red dutch roses exhaling fragrance as one walked by. The garden held a healing essence, and I drew deeply from it in my desperate need. It was as if nature herself reached out to me, and stilled the agony inside.

When I felt better I wrote a very long letter to Patrick, outlining once more all the things that had led to our disunity, reminding him of the long years I had cheerfully stayed at home every night, and recounting briefly the critical episodes in my life when my inner faculties had unfolded. I related again how I had been led to Baba, and tried to express the mode of my recognition — mentioning too the dreams and visions that had formed the basis of my conviction. I said our sole hope now of happiness together was for him to grant me the same freedom of thought and tolerance of expression that I gave to him — and to let me follow my intuitive pathway without continual persecution. If he was not prepared to do this, we should be better apart, both being young enough to rebuild our lives. I stressed that I cared deeply for him, and had grieved as much for his unhappiness as for my own — but I could not help what I was, nor alter it.

I thought this would be the end, and that Patrick, with his usual unreasoning misunderstanding, would say I had 'chosen' Baba. He came again the next Saturday, quiet and subdued, "to see the children". Maud was away, having gone to visit her daughter, and the children before long were occupied with their own pursuits in the garden. We were thus for a short while alone, and Patrick for once talked calmly and without antagonism. He said my letter had shaken him very much — he had been unable to work or eat on the day it arrived . . . but he had seen, suddenly, what he had done. He asked my forgiveness for his anger and said he knew it was he who was wrong. He had made life impossible for us . . . He would leave now, to get back before it was dark . . . he felt I would be happier on my own, and he would therefore set me free.

I looked at him, and saw the struggle in his face. Freedom for me would be a release — but how could I be free knowing his wretchedness? He did not understand his independence was vital to my own. The mother bird did not leave her fledgling until it could fly alone.

I asked him to stay for a meal at least; it was silly to go back without one . . . and as Maud was away, he could stay the night if he wished, without any awkwardness. Why not take this opportunity to rest and relax, and we could quietly discuss the future tomorrow? It had to be done sometime, and it would be much easier for us both to do so now, rather than putting it off.

He took little persuasion, and shortly afterwards was playing cricket with David and Teresa. He sat down to lunch looking much more at ease, and said earnestly again that he was sorry.

It was so painfully obvious he could not face life without us. That evening he asked me to come back to him, to "really and truly" make a fresh start. If I would only give him another chance he would never again be harsh with me, and I was completely free now to do as I pleased. I could have my pictures and my books; my friends could visit me — and he would even put the new house in our joint names . . .* He could arrange my immediate accommodation at the public house where he was living — they would welcome the children. Would I consider it?

As he spoke, the words of Baba's cable moved through my mind — 'adjust herself to circumstances confronting her, and bravely discharge her responsibilities . . .' Another circumstance confronted me, and as before, the way was indicated. I said I would tell him definitely within a few days.

I cannot define the sadness in my heart. He tried so hard that weekend, but as confidence grew, so his former attitudes reasserted; not violently as formerly, but very transparently overlaid.

All Maud's beds were single and I gave Patrick mine as the room was bright and comfortable, hers being somewhat austere. When eventually I crawled into her bed that night, wrapped in the handwoven blanket† she had given me, in an effort to comfort myself — I knew beyond doubt that Baba wished me to return. I lay absolutely still; utterly spent . . . exhausted to the very core. I could neither think, nor feel, cry, or move . . . and was quite empty save for the grief which had now burned so deep it was no longer a pain, but belonged to my soul. As I lay there scarcely breathing, a childish phrase rose ridiculously in my head. For a moment it seemed I heard bells ringing, then words swirled soundlessly in a swift mental flash — "Turn again, Whittington, Lord Mayor of London!"

The strange stillness continued long after Patrick left. Not the deep, inner stillness of spiritual peace; rather a 'burnt out', curiously resigned feeling — almost a resting in God in the exhaustion of extremity . . . Too fine to be called a sensation, it was nevertheless a mode of experience — akin to an indefinable, smokeless burning; eminently real. Attempts to describe this fall wide of the mark. There are no words in our vocabulary designed to delineate such states.

Maud's friend called to see me on Monday afternoon, having been asked to check that I was all right in her absence. I did not really wish to see anyone. It was an effort to speak, and I

* This was not done.
† made by, and belonging formerly to Mary Backett, one of Baba's earliest Western adherents.

simply desired to be left alone with my children. But Alys persisted; she literally forced me to talk to her, and I found to my surprise that it helped to consolidate my somewhat vague decision to rejoin Patrick. I had concerned myself solely with the spiritual aspects . . . now Alys drew my attention strongly to the more practical. I became aware that I was counselled through her, and by her firm and generous participation, was drawn back again into life.

On Tuesday we ventured to London. I had promised David and Teresa an outing of their choosing to give them something to look forward to during their bleakest days at Hurst Park Avenue. They chose a visit to the London Palladium, and the booking was made on the day in May when I first wrote to Maud. This much anticipated event was now upon us, and they had no suspicion of my trepidation. Still far from well, I was nervous of travelling and quite terrified of London on my own. I had booked an extra ticket at the time, despite the expense, in the hope that someone would come with us. Yet it proved an unexpectedly rewarding experience. We all liked central London and I felt oddly at home there — sitting in Berkeley Square in the sunshine as we ate lunchtime sandwiches, then later in Hanover Square when we fed the pigeons. I felt close to Baba all day, the first time in what seemed a very long while.

I found, alarmingly, that we could not get back to Maud's village that night, only to Oxford, and deliberated whether to travel on to Cambridge or to telephone Alys to see if she could help us. At length I phoned Alys, not able yet to face Patrick's pub — and she said of course we must come to her, and met us, near midnight, at the station in her car. Her genuine concern and consideration moved me very much.

The following day we returned to the cottage. I was very, very tired now, and thought gratefully of the beauty and peace of Maud's garden. On the doormat lay a letter from Jehangir. He had written me four long and heartwarming letters since his return to London, full of friendship, good humour and his own aspiration. This one was very brief — a note really. He had seen Inder, who was staying in the city, and had tried to tell him that I was at Maud's . . . but to his consternation and concern Inder would not discuss my situation, nor hear anything of me. Jehangir was so bewildered — he hoped I would understand his position and that he did not wish to involve himself further. He was leaving his present address for fresh accommodation the following day — would I please not write again.

I could scarcely believe it. He had been so kind, so understanding. Mercifully I felt nothing, and busied myself about the house automatically, unable to grasp the impact of repeated betrayal. I did not know what I had done to earn this continual ostracism, and tried to resign myself stoically to the loss of his much valued friendship.

I lift up this prayer to thee, O Lord:
accept me now in thy great love,
answer me with thy sure deliverance, O God.
Rescue me from the mire, do not let me sink;
let me be rescued from the muddy depths,
so that no flood may carry me away,
no abyss swallow me up,
no deep close over me.
Answer me, O Lord, in the goodness of thy unfailing love,
turn towards me in thy great affection.
I am thy servant, do not hide thy face from me.
Make haste to answer me, for I am in distress.
Come near to me and redeem me;
ransom me, for I have many enemies.

Thou knowest what reproaches I bear,
all my anguish is seen by thee.
Reproach has broken my heart,
my shame and my dishonour are past hope;
I looked for consolation and received none,
for comfort and did not find any.

*Psalm 69. The New English Bible. (c) 1970
by permission of Oxford and Cambridge University Presses.*

The next few days passed like a dream. Maud was still away, and I soaked up the quietness and peace in the old house and the rose-scented garden. Working or resting outside in the sunshine, the sheer beauty of my surroundings constantly penetrated my awareness. My depleted mechanism responded quickly to the healing inflow of natural energies generated in abundance by the profusion of plants and trees — and my burdened psyche was similarly eased via the essences released in the fragrance of flowers. All combined to loosen the tensions in me and then to actively resolve them. At first I dwelt in a state of emptiness and was neither happy nor unhappy — but soon there intermittently arose brief times of deep tranquility — and gradually the feeling of illness declined and a measure of strength and energy returned.

I found I was able to read again, and discovered a book on Maud's shelves by Vivekananda which contained a most illuminating chapter on Bhakti Yoga. It dawned on me as I read it that what had happened to me was by no means unknown, and in no sense unique. That this long ordeal with all its interior and exterior vicissitudes was part of a well authenticated developmental process still understood in the East. This knowledge was of itself restorative and blunted any residues of fear. Although I glimpsed only a fragment of the underlying design, I actually saw that a design *was there* and was thus content to leave for the moment its technicalities.

My many outgoing letters remained unanswered save for brief responses from Betty and Margaret. After three notes to Nell she finally replied, lecturing me severely in unconscious parody of Alison's utterances. It seemed she had forgotten there was anything good in me, and had rejudged me entirely on hearsay and assumption.

Maud returned on Friday bringing G. with her for the weekend, and expressed concern over my decision, as she felt (probably quite rightly) that the atmosphere of a public house would not be conducive to my present wellbeing. She said, too, with great kindness, that I must consider the cottage my home and if I wished to return I could do so. For this I was deeply grateful, and it was thus a little easier to leave.

Having accepted the thought of return, David was restless and fumed hourly with impatience — and perhaps the beginnings of boredom. He was looking much better; was suntanned and relaxed, and needed now his former activities and friends, and the same applied to Teresa. They had decided, on weighing things up, that Cambridge was, after all, 'home'.

I telephoned Patrick and told him I would come when he wished, providing he was still willing to be tolerant. He had now had several days to think about it, and said firmly he had not changed his mind and was looking forward to the future. That evening I sat late on the daisied lawn, listening to the ecstatic songs of the birds and reconciling myself reluctantly to bidding this refuge adieu. For some while I absorbed the sights and sounds of the verdant countryside, aware now and then, to my joy, that Baba was near. This solitary interlude revivified the lifeforce within me, causing the first faint and fragile stirrings of a renewed urge to live.

Patrick fetched us on Sunday and we drove back to Cambridge to our new lodgings. The landlord and his wife were extremely hospitable; made much of Teresa in particular, and eased our transition in every way possible. My son and daughter settled remarkably well, no doubt relieved to be within sight again of a stable home. Patrick could not move us fast enough to the almost finished house and we lived with our hosts for less than a fortnight. During this very short period he twice went back on his word, and I lay in bed quaking, dazed and disillusioned by the oh, so familiar vituperation, yet knowing the die was cast and I must go forward on the path I had taken.

Everything possible went wrong with the completion work — goods were not delivered, workmen failed to turn up, the plumbing sprang leaks, and chaos in general reigned. We still managed to move in, however, though it was not an easy task. The upper floor was finished but downstairs was an unprepossessing vista of concrete and plaster — doorless, cupboardless, paintless and floortileless. For five days we were without electricity, thanks to the electrician who forgot to send a card to the Electricity Board, and when at last it was connected, a fault was found — and up came the linoleum and floorboards on the landing *and* in the bathroom and Teresa's bedroom, where already our belongings were piled high. My nerves by this time were in shreds, a fact I strove constantly to conceal; but I was certainly 'earthed' and had come to grips with life again, and with time and patience order overcame chaos and our home was as before.

At the beginning of August Maud wrote to say she had received a letter from Mani, Baba's sister, which contained a message for me. It was a lengthy, warm and friendly letter, and the piece referred to was simply a sentence. This stated that I should "help Inder to obey Baba" and make no personal attempt to see him, as his own instructions were to have *no* contact with any members of the former Cambridge group. This curious assertion, which I did not understand at all, was my answer to a note written to Baba's secretary the day after I heard that Inder was in hospital, in which I offered any assistance permissable. The letter from India was dated July 15th, and had been delayed by the postal strike in England.

The night of its receipt I dreamt I was sitting in the passenger seat of a horse drawn carriage, waiting rather impatiently for the driver. I saw Baba walking to and fro, dealing with a pressing crowd of people. Suddenly he came towards me, placed a hand on the reins and said, very kindly, "Wait a little longer and *I Myself* will drive you."

I had been now in Cambridge for a month, and the house was virtually finished, the furniture out of store, and a mountain of cleaning behind me. I felt, all at once, a deep longing arise to see both Rose and Alison again and renew our past friendship. It was the same kind of feeling as that experienced in May when I had telephoned Alison after the closure of the group . . . a sense of sisterhood and affection that cancelled out all that was adverse between us. It occurred to me that they too might feel differently with Inder gone, and thus perhaps more willing to agree a reconciliation.

To assess this possibility I visited Nell, taking the chance of finding her at home, which she was. She was quite friendly though not at all as she used to be when I called, and it was very apparent she could not altogether approve of me now. The conflict between past friendship and present disapprobation was not easy for her to handle — we had known each other far too intimately. She disclosed magnanimously that Alison was feeling low and had cried over the weekend — yet did not appear to know why this was so — and my several questions concerning Inder were evaded. I had the distinct impression she knew quite well what went on, and was prepared to deliberately mislead me rather than risk revealing it.

A series of impulses stirred in my mind and I could not leave the matter alone. Two days later I called on Rose at her place of work, approaching her with considerable trepidation. She greeted me pleasantly and was exceedingly non-committal, saying she knew nothing, and could say nothing . . . though it was true Alison *had* been rather distressed — she had received some instructions from Inder she found difficult to fulfil . . . Rose felt if she had worked harder to attain Alison's status she might have been able to help her — it grieved her that through her own weaknesses, she must face certain things alone.

It was all maddeningly mysterious. I asked Rose if she thought Alison would object if I went to see her, but she could not presume to say — only to advise me to wait until Thursday, as she had gone to stay overnight with a friend. She did not know *where* she was going, or who the friend was — nevertheless she was looking after Avril. It seemed odd to me that she had not asked, as they were such friends. Surely this was carrying 'impersonal detachment' a little *too* far?

Travelling home on the bus, I suddenly knew where Alison was. She had gone to London to see Inder.

I telephoned Rose on Thursday to confirm Alison's willingness to meet me. She did not seem too sure. Hesitantly she said they would be at Cowper Road that evening and I could visit on the offchance if I wished. I mentioned I would bring the mementoes given me by Maud, including a wisp of Baba's hair. This evoked no comment, and I realised other things filled her mind of such pressing concern she could think of nothing else.

When I arrived that evening I found a note pinned on the door in Alison's handwriting. It said she had made a previous arrangement to go somewhere, and perhaps another time? Disappointed, I walked on to Rose's house. Paul opened the door and said she was out, he did not know where, but she wouldn't be long. He was curt and unfriendly and closed the door sharply. I knew then that wherever she was, it was with Alison, and returned home feeling mystified and snubbed.

Late that evening I phoned Rose to see what had happened. Paul answered and said she was still out, and he hoped I wasn't going to make a habit of phoning and visiting as he didn't want *me* in his house "weeping and wailing" — It was time I grew up and behaved like a woman — I needed a good slapping and he would tell my husband so too, when he saw him! The receiver slammed down without a goodbye. There seemed no end to it.

That night I dreamt I stood with Inder and Alison on London Bridge. She was crying and I tried to comfort her — she said she had been in difficulties for "three weeks" and could stand no more. Inder observed her in silence, his expression displeased. It was quite dark, and in the shadows I noticed a figure watching and listening, hovering indecisively — who appeared at last to come to a decision, turned on a heel and walked away. At the moment of turning I saw it was Rose. The scene then changed and we were in a small bare room that was vaguely familiar. Inder gave Alison a new bed and a quantity of clean sheets. I was given a small tablecentre and wondered why. He sat close to Alison and placed his arm round her shoulders, and as I looked she grew smaller and smaller until she was just a little child with a tearstained face.

For some obscure reason I felt impelled to see Alison however unwilling she might be, and went again to her home on Friday. Once more she was out, and I left a note to say I would come back on Saturday. This I did, to find another note on the door. It said the writer was sorry but she felt it better not to see me as I would only ask questions she could not answer, and however it may seem, this was not a personal vendetta against me. I left a message to say I had not come to ask questions, but in friendship. Where was her heart?

The whole thing was quite ridiculous, and at this point I fully intended to give up, not wanting to push myself upon Alison as she most obviously did not wish it. Yet constantly the impulse arose to see her, so powerfully and persistently that twice more I found myself outside her door, each time with the same result; and each time resolving firmly that I would leave well alone and not repeat my folly.

My arguments with myself proved useless. Again I was urgently impressed, and like a leaf borne on the wind I travelled across the city (on each occasion a little earlier) to find her just leaving home. She was plainly not pleased to see me — hesitated a moment as if debating whether to pause or not, then said uncertainly she would give me "five minutes", and we entered the small parlour that had housed so many meetings.

The five minutes became half an hour, during which time she told me, after much hedging, that Inder was now living with Nell. She had "brought him" from London the previous week and she and Rose were visiting him whenever possible, herself every day as he had asked her to personally look after him. She stressed she could say little about his illness or his private affairs — but he wasn't actually *ill* — just in a "strange state" requiring solitude and silence. Otherwise all was secret and she may tell me *nothing* — he had specifically forbidden it ... and if I had chanced to call on Nell, however innocently, he would have refused to see me. She revealed that she had visited him frequently in London, carried out every instruction, fulfilled every requirement. Even now, she was on her way to him ...

I asked if he had ever treated her as he did me. Her reply was no, he had been very, very kind. Outwardly I sat composed and made polite conversation — small and insignificant responses to each morsel of information given. Inwardly a deep wound opened in my heart, bleeding agonisingly and profusely.

I took the long route home on foot, trying to sort things out in my mind. Mani's letter was made senseless by the fact that Alison was caring for Inder, in Nell's home, and with Rose in attendance. She had not been fully informed of the situation when she wrote; there could be no other explanation, and I felt vexed that she should so mislead me, however mistakenly. That evening I sifted through my old correspondence, including diary entries and notes, many of them kept in the hope that things would change and thereby reveal their contents in a different light. These adverse trends had now become tangible facts and I had to accept them — so I burned Alison's letters, also Jehangir's and even the copy of Mani's ... and along with them much material that I afterwards wished I had kept.

After the grievous night that followed this meeting, I discerned an alteration in my condition. I found I had given up all expectation of reacceptance, and was committed wholly to an inner silence, or resignation — plus something more that I could not as yet define. I was unable to have what I most desired, and I ceased now to ask why; thus turmoil gave place to inward calm, and all struggling died away. It marked the end of another phase — a point of total eclipse wherein the lesser self was utterly extinguished. For some hidden reason this was the Master's will for me, and I yielded my blind human will to his. And in this climate, harsh and severe as it was, the seed of objectivity took root in the very core of my being.

On August 15th I wrote to Adi, Baba's secretary in India, telling him of my return to Cambridge and my continued efforts to sustain my marriage. I mentioned also my short talk with Alison and the conflicting data I had been given. I had the awareness that the letter could reopen the possibility of a direct communication from Baba.

A reply came quickly, indicating that Baba was pleased I had returned to my husband, and including Adi's advice to completely sever all connection with Inder and 'all Cambridge group activity', *and to link with the London group,* from whose secretary I would receive any general communications issued.

Patrick warmed immediately towards Baba as a result of this letter, and my perplexity and confusion I kept to myself. His view, as he firmly stated, was that Baba was trying to drum into me what he himself had told me all the time. Silently I tried to assess the undertones of this ambiguous information with its implied censure of Inder, conscious that somewhere along the line there was a vital factor I had either missed or misunderstood.

Again I dreamt vividly, and was sure the dream was precognitive. I lit a gas jet, and instead of one flame appearing it split into five. One of the five spluttered and smoked — first in wisps of grey, then in thick, black clouds. Quickly I picked up the jet and placed it outside, knowing it would soon explode. In the street an enemy army were in occupation, and their troops stood around in attitudes of aggression. Nell rapped agitatedly on the door and called out that Rose and Alison were having a disagreement. Then I saw Alison, who violently accused me of doing something *which I was not* — she was, in fact, *herself* doing what she accused me of, and did not appear to be aware of it.

Since my resettlement in Cambridge, Betty had visited me with increasing frequency, and followed closely whatever I could tell her. A friend of hers happened to live quite near to Nell's bungalow along the same road, and reported to Betty various comings and goings and the considered view that both Inder *and* Alison were in residence there — and Betty grew daily more concerned regarding the issues behind this puzzling situation. My letter from India accentuated this, and at my suggestion, the following Monday she went to see Rose — for as they had been the closest of friends in the past, this was seemingly the best and surest way to find out what she wished to know and set her mind at ease.

Rose was glad to see her and proved unexpectedly enlightening. She said Inder was "completely dependent" upon Alison, and appeared to be in an abnormal mental condition. He had cried and clung to her for "hours on end" believing Baba to be dead — but now he was calmer and "quite happy" as long as Alison ministered to him daily. He also observed complete silence, and communicated only on paper or by gesture when absolutely necessary.

This information, brought by Betty in a very disturbed frame of mind, produced a dual effect on me. It triggered off sheer torture, a fresh and acute intensification of the burning pain in the heart with all its accompanying hopeless longing . . . and my brief serenity was dispersed. Conversely, however, and *simultaneously* — my mind was alerted and worked with a quicksilver comprehension that retained its conclusions in latent form a hairsbreadth beneath the surface of consciousness . . . as if awaiting as yet unmanifest events before yielding them up.

In sleep that night, I was given a paper headed with my own photograph, which entitled me to a part-time and well paid position in a large store. The job was selling shoes. I took the paper to the supervisor, who ignored it, and said I lacked the necessary qualifications for employment. When I protested that my credentials were on the paper, she said she did not want me there anyway and had already given the job to another woman. I turned and saw that this was true — a hard-faced, well dressed woman was handling the shoes, which lay around in disorder, some in, some out of their boxes.

I awoke at this point, thinking unhappily that this surely

portended further exclusion — then drifted again into sleep . . . and dreamt I met Alison. Her demeanour was hostile; it was obvious she thought me less than the dust. Inder wanted *her,* she said; I was *out* of it all, and NOW *she had everything.* To my horror she held up a straitjacket and manacles, asserting loudly that Inder had *even given her power* to use them *on him* if she chose . . . The whole dream was utterly sickening.

The next morning, driven by an insistent impulse that would not be denied, I went to see her. She was at home, and invited me in as if quite pleased to see me. Her expression was pleasant and there was no trace at all of the feared hostility. She readily repeated all Rose had said the previous day, and was apparently well satisfied with life. Facing her, it was hard to believe there was anything amiss — it was *unarguable* that Baba had chosen Alison and cast me out, and I *must* accept it although I did not understand . . . Yet he had linked *me* with the London group *and not Alison* . . . It was all quite crazy.

I told her of the letter from Mani I found so perturbing. She looked mildly surprised, as if the contents were news to her. Even so, she didn't appear to regard it as of any significance, and her manner expressed such a total conviction of the rightness of her actions, I felt myself wilt. Coming home I experienced again the deep stillness which eased away the pain of my terrible loneliness.

A multitude of memories surfaced in my mind, and I turned them over, searching some clue to what was happening now. I recalled the vision Inder had spoken of last January . . . when he had "crossed his own grave" to reach Baba, who embraced him on the other side. I remembered asking if it meant that he would die soon, and he had replied that I should "think about it" and try to interpret it for myself.

I knew that Baba had undergone a strange state before attaining full cosmic consciousness, and most recorded biographies of Masters contain some reference to this constrained and often disoriented period before a Charge or Function is made operative. I wondered then if Inder had yet to come into the fullness of his own Masterhood . . . which would make sense of so many things at present unexplained. Or had simply transferred his consciousness to another plane in order that certain work should be done . . .

A further letter from Adi arrived the following day in

response to a second of my own. It reiterated that Baba wished me to have no contact at all with Inder and his 'group of foolish women' as they had *not* abided by his wishes, and had also disobeyed Baba's ORDER, cabled to them *direct,* to send Inder immediately home to India to be properly cared for by his father and family. It was a stern and exceedingly serious letter, and concluded with Baba's blessing and love to myself, Patrick and the children, and his expressed wish *that it be shown to Patrick.*

It took but few moments to grasp that this turned the situation round entirely, and whatever my own intuitive feelings, I must deal with the content as it stood. I gave the letter to Patrick, who read it warily, then said with some satisfaction how sensible it was and that he could even thank Baba for it. I suggested if he felt this way he should do just that — and to my amazement, after some consideration he actually wrote out a cable, saying simply, "Thankyou Baba. Patrick." He had no conception of the spiritual significance of what he had done.

Betty too, was shown the letter, and having given it some thought, she sent a cable as well, conveying her love. I also sent one. It acquiesced to what he required of me, and only he knew what it had cost me.

A reply arrived addressed to Patrick personally. It read:

'Contents of cables from you, Kate, Betty, made me happy. I send my love to you each. Meher Baba.'

There was now no doubt at all in my mind that my laborious journey with Patrick, with all its frustrations and heartaches, had been designed (in part) to bring him to this juncture; and that it contained profound inner meaning for both he and myself of which I was still only faintly conscious.

But this so important letter was also cause for much silent grief. It went against everything I knew esoterically, and its implication concerning Inder was completely unacceptable. However, there was obviously something not right somewhere, and as I naturally assumed that Alison was acting on legitimate instructions, the gist of which she had been forbidden to reveal to me, it could not fail to raise many queries in my mind. As I re-read Adi's sentences my intuition functioned with clarifying rapidity, and inwardly if not outwardly I understood the situation, and why such a communication had come my way.

That evening, Betty and I went to Nell's country bungalow,

and the following morning I sent a report of this visit to Adi in India.

My own involvement, indirectly activated, precipitated the dénouement of this strange and structured facet of the Master's work with us, and I later learned from Alison the whole story.

I knew already that the Cambridge group had been disbanded in May, and was eventually surprised to discover that no book had been embarked upon. The work given had involved the checking and correction of Maud's script, brought on Good Friday from Oxford, which was a collection of quotations from Baba's discourses and other sources intended for later publication.

Following the group's closure, the three concerned had been led into a series of events, in the course of which Inder showed signs of becoming ill — at first in London, where he sent for Alison and gave her the task of dealing with his affairs and finding him more suitable accommodation. She found this latter so problematical that she removed him to Nell's bungalow and continued her duties from there, aided by Nell and Rose.

Repeated communications from India had come to his London address, including the one mentioned by Mani to myself — but as Alison now dealt with all correspondence and believed, through remarks made by Inder, that they were from his father who wished by this means to make him return home, none were answered. Even cables signed Meher Baba and despatched direct from Ahmednagar were ignored, so sure was she that they were faked.

Inder at this point indrew, having first stated that he was a Master, then that he was 'Baba', and commenced a period of total silence. This he interspersed with scribbled comments that could certainly be construed the products of a disordered mind, reinforced by disoriented behaviour. Yet still Alison made no move to contact Baba, and neither Rose or Nell queried this.

My own part on that fateful evening consisted of enlightening them of their error by presenting the collection of authentic letters and cables received throughout my contact with Baba — all showing the same signatures and postal origins, and the more recent making the same statements as those sent to Inder. Incredibly, even this had no effect, and I met with enormous hostility — particularly from Alison. The following excerpts are taken from the report sent to Adi, perhaps illustrating more clearly the sequence of events.

'I have taken certain action both before and after receiving your letter which I feel I should tell you of, and would like to stress that I did these things willingly though without fully understanding why, and that to the best of my knowledge I could not do otherwise.

'On Monday Betty G. saw Rose S., who told her that Inder had been acutely distressed and appeared to be suffering from intermittent loss of memory, crying at one time because he believed Baba was dead and they were keeping it from him. Also for about four weeks now he has been observing silence and refusing to see anyone save Alison for more than a few minutes. Rose felt he was 'lost' and unaware of all that was happening to him, but said that of late he had been very happy in his indrawn state.

'The following morning I went to see Alison (this being the first time since my visit on returning from Oxford). She was friendly and quite communicative and obviously very content. I enquired about Inder's distress and his apparent lack of normal consciousness. She agreed this was so and said he was completely dependent upon her and she felt it to be Baba's Will that she should look after him. He had clung to her as Rose had said, and was now much happier in himself. *All* the prominent London people had been to see her except one, to whom she had spoken by telephone. Inder did not wish to see them and she had dealt with most of them in her own home. She said they had wanted to send him back to India and she did not feel this was right. She also said Inder's father had sent a number of letters and cables demanding his return. I asked if Baba still kept written contact with Inder, and she replied, "Not lately".

'The next day, Wednesday, your letter was received. I telephoned Rose S. and asked if she was aware of its contents. She said they had received communications from India and thought them to be fabrications of Inder's father using Baba's name to compel him to return. She was unwilling or unable to say more at that time.

'In the early evening, Betty G. accompanied me at her own request to Sawston. Alison and Nell forbade me entry to the house, but I told them I had received a letter from Baba which I felt they should see, and I also wished to be certain that Inder in particular knew of its contents. I entered the house without permission but nobody tried to prevent me. I did not attempt to break in upon Inder.

'Alison rushed off to speak with Inder and returned after some minutes to say he would not see me or receive any communication from me as this was forbidden by Baba. Alison and Rose read the letter but did not appear interested, or impressed, by its statements. Rose questioned its validity, even the signature, although I had three other letters with me all bearing the same. They said it was ridiculous to say either Inder or themselves had disobeyed Baba, and refused to accept that Baba could seriously mean what was written. They felt that as the letter had been sent to me it did not concern them, and stated openly they considered me disobedient, deluded, selfish, self-willed etc. Nell called me a traitor and threatened to strike me if I did not leave. She refused to look at the letter as she "received her instructions from Baba direct", (meaning interiorly).

'I requested the letter should be taken to Inder and that he should be told it was from Baba. Alison refused. Then I insisted that I should be allowed to speak with him, promising to stay only two minutes, but Alison barred the door with her body and would have used violence against me had I attempted to go near it, which I did not. She would not discuss Inder's affairs or correspondence, and showed considerable anger, possessiveness, arrogance and irrational thinking. She said I was out of all this and it was not my business. All three were prepared to remove me forcibly if I did not leave. Betty was frightened and continually implored me to go.

'In view of the above I concluded further discussion futile, and left immediately.

'As I walked past the front of the house, I looked through a chink in the curtains and saw Inder sitting crosslegged with a strange expression on his face. I called out to him that I had received a letter from India and could not believe what it said concerning him. I cannot describe his expression or the struggle on his face as he attempted to listen and normalise his consciousness, which was obviously deeply indrawn. He suddenly appeared annoyed by the disturbance and threw over the small table in front of him. Interiorly I registered his condition* and this caused me to leave at once.

'This morning I wrote the following letter to Alison and sent a copy to Rose and Nell, asking them to contact Baba in her stead if she refused.'

My letter informed Alison that I had seen and spoken to Inder, and that I now realised why I was not permitted to contact him physically, as *any* personal relationship with him at the moment could have disastrous consequences through no fault of his own.† It concluded:

'I entreat you to contact Baba to obtain precise instructions on his behalf as he no longer retains sufficient normal consciousness‡ to make directive decisions himself. If you do not do this, I fear you will shortly find yourselves in an untenable position from which Baba alone can extricate you.'

A reply to my letter arrived from Adi on September 28th, and conveyed that Baba knew my recent visit to Sawston was to "bring home to those concerned the seriousness of their continued disobedience; and that having been motivated with the intention of making them realise their error, you should now have no more to do with them."

In a rather different vein, Adi stated: 'It is inconceivable that these women can really believe that the instructions from Baba sent repeatedly from India were not genuine. It is not that they are fooling themselves, but trying to fool others into believing it. As they cannot bring themselves to obey an instruction that is displeasing to them personally, they are imagining a deep spiritual significance in their personal desire to keep Inder with them.

'Inder's father hopes to visit Cambridge shortly . . . and I

---

* What I registered was a state of such titanic indrawn intensity and power that any prolonged personal contact may well have caused me to lose mundane consciousness of my body, and thus my ability to live a normal domestic life. The unsheathed radiation generated by his condition would have proved overwhelming in my as yet unstabilised ultra-sensitive stage of development.

† Another reason for my severance from the group was the test set Alison, and also Rose. In fact the entire original group and all its contacts were tested on different levels and in different ways, as can be clearly traced with full possession of the facts.

‡ For detailed descriptions of seventh plane, God-merged, and other states, see Foreword and Chapter I of 'THE WAYFARERS' by William Donkin, with a second foreword by Meher Baba.

shall be sending with him individual letters to Inder, Mrs B., Mrs D., and Mrs S., warning them that if Inder does not return to India with his father, I will send out a Circular to all Baba's followers in the United Kingdom and elsewhere that they should not regard Inder and his group as having any association with Meher Baba's name and cause — a copy of the respective letter will also be given personally (by Inder's father) to Mr. S. and Mr. B.'

At the end of the letter was a request that it should be shown to Patrick and Betty. I remembered then what Inder had said about a Master sometimes leading his pupils deliberately in the wrong direction.

My reply to Adi was lengthy and again purely factual. The latter part read:

'I come now to the real point of my letter and trust Baba will not be displeased with me for apparently ignoring his wishes, for I went to see Rose this afternoon, she having said the least on my visit to Sawston and giving the impression that she was wavering in her mind as to the rightness of her present actions. She greeted me warmly, almost with relief, and was very disturbed by your letter, which I gave her. She said she had talked repeatedly to Alison about contacting Baba, and had known for the past ten days that she must cable him herself, even if Alison had to go on alone. She did, indeed, write out a cable whilst I was there, and I sincerely trust she sent it.

'I'm afraid Alison is facing a very difficult situation, as Inder's money has now run out, and without Rose's moral support she will be very lonely and doubtless frightened. If it is at all permissible, I would be grateful for the opportunity to help her if she becomes desperate enough to be willing to speak to me. Also Inder, for whom I will gladly do anything that Baba permits.'

Rose did send her cable. Two mornings later I received two letters, one from Rose, the other from Alison. The following quote is from Rose's.

'I passed your letter to Alison and she will let Nell have it to read, of course. You will know by now what action Alison has taken . . . her cable is much more precise and useful than mine — and will need an answer. There is no use attempting to describe how I feel now (quite humbled and empty of any direction . . .) one can only leave it all in Baba's hands. Love, Rose.'

Alison's letter read:

'Dear Kate,

Cable as follows has gone to India today.

'Impossible persuade Inder Baba genuinely wishes him return India. Situation beyond me. In spite appearances to contrary only wish do Baba's will. Humbly ask help. Please reply my address. Alison.'

Don't come and see me, but tell Betty and others, and please believe there has been, and is, no personal involvement with Inder. With love, Yours, Alison.'

Both letters I found moving, particularly so in view of the circumstances. It must have been very hard for them to send copies to me.

During this period I dreamed of Inder. He sat in a beautiful garden and I waited outside the gate that gave entry to it. I knew it was my turn to be with him, but to my disappointment I was again turned away and another took my place. I saw opening before me a short path I must take, aware dimly of the ocean in the background. At the end of the pathway stood Inder, waiting . . . and I knew he waited for me.

On Friday, another letter arrived from Alison. It said:

'Thanks for your letter. I enclose copy of a letter I sent yesterday to Adi K. Irani, and at the end you will see copy of cable I have just received from Baba. Perhaps I will come and see you one day. Tell Betty thanks for her love. Mine to you both. Alison.'

Her letter to Adi follows:

'Your letter of the 23rd to Kate Merton has been passed to me, and in view of some of the things you have said, and which are quite wrong interpretations of the situation at Sawston, I feel perhaps I had better put on record the true facts as far as I and the two ladies also concerned truly believe. The assumptions made in the second paragraph of your letter are entirely incorrect. Neither myself, Mrs S., nor Mrs D., have been trying to fool others or ourselves into believing anything, and neither have we *any* personal desire to keep Inder with us as you say. All through, we have acted in the sincere belief that we were doing what *Baba* wished, and all our actions and thoughts have been to this end.

'A few months ago Inder asked me if I knew of anyone who would be willing to look after him for a time; to give him rest and peace; and to look after his everyday needs, food, laundry etc. and who could be relied upon not to have him buried in a mental hospital at the slightest excuse. Inder has always seemed to me to be very close to Baba, and to have a true clarity of vision of what Baba's teachings really mean and what Baba IS, not because I have attributed Masterhood to him, but because I have felt that his surrender to Baba is of a quality which would in some way bring about a purity of thought and action which would express Truth. Therefore, when I was asked to help him I agreed. Please note I was *asked* not coerced in any way, and if I had said no Inder would have accepted this. Eventually it became evident that the only person who could have him was Mrs D., partly because her age precluded any possibility of scandal being brought on either Inder himself, or on Baba's name. So nine weeks ago today, Mrs D. and I brought Inder from London to Sawston. He has been looked after most selflessly by Mrs D. and is now much rested and far more composed than at first.

'To say that I have fully understood Inder's state of mind and actions during this period would be untrue, but I have sincerely felt that however it looked from the surface, the whole situation was in Baba's hands, and during the many hours I have sat with Inder in entire silence it has been Baba who has been in my mind and not Inder. I have never felt a personal desire to keep Inder with me, having always been aware that he is Baba's, and I have no claims on Inder in any way. All I have done has been done for Baba.

'Even if it seems unlikely to you as a person that my explanation is true, I can assure you that it is so, and in all humility I say that Baba, who knows all, knows I have written truly. We three ladies may have acted foolishly, but we have not acted from any personal motives whatever.

'To end I would also like to say that I believe that Inder himself is not deliberately and flagrantly disobeying Baba for his own ends, but that his actions stem from a deep conviction of what he believes, although I realise I have no right to claim anything on behalf of another person. I may of course be wrong, but I have felt that orthodox medical treatment for whatever condition he has been in, would have caused him great suffering, if not actual harm, and this is one reason that I have endeavoured to keep apparently well-meaning people from interfering. You will by now have received my telegram sent yesterday to Baba. Baba's Will be done. Sincerely yours. A.B.'

Added to this was a postscript by Rose:

'I feel that this is an absolutely true account of what has been carried out in the last nine weeks, and fully endorse all Alison's opinions. Rose S.'

Included with the letter was a copy of the cable Baba had sent to Alison in reply to her earlier plea for help:

'Inder's father coming Cambridge shortly. I want you to do your best to help him bring Inder to India. Meher Baba.'

On Saturday I received a cable, the contents of which appeared empty and rather pointless.

'Don't resume any contact with Inder. Advise Alison, Rose, Nell to cooperate and assist Inder's father bring Inder home to India. Meher Baba.' The date was October 3rd.

On October 5th came a letter from Adi, with copies of the cables sent to India by Alison and Rose, and also the return cables from Baba. These, Adi said, were for my information and records. Rose's cable was not the one written in my presence; for some reason she had altered it. It now commenced, 'Can no longer support Inder in any way.'

Baba's response to this was:

'I did not ask you to support Inder. Send Inder to India with his father who is coming Cambridge shortly. Meher Baba.'

The same day I sent off the following to Adi:

'On receipt of Baba's cable of the 3rd, I telephoned Rose and passed on the contents. She appeared to want to talk to me and suggested we meet the next evening, to which I agreed. She now realises that she acted blindly, and is very sorry about it. I saw her Sunday evening . . . she looks quite ill and says she feels at breaking point. I tried to persuade her to write to Baba, for he alone can help her now. She is afraid to do this as it is still too painful to put into words. There is no doubt she has been through a most harrowing time in her mind.

'Today I went to see Alison, taking the cable with me. There was no trace of the Alison who had behaved as described at Sawston, and she told me freely all that had happened since my severance from the group. At one point she suddenly broke

222

down and knelt at my feet with her head in my lap, crying as if her heart would break. She told me how afraid she had been and how she had known she was not doing the right things, but seemed powerless to help herself. She was broken and pitiful, like a little child, and I could only hold her in my arms and love her, knowing with gratitude there was now no barrier between us. I felt Baba's Presence with us in the room, and it seemed he used my arms to embrace her, and gave me the right words to say.

'Dear brother Adi, it does not seem right to bring out all that she said to me, for we are all such little people, cast in the same mould — and Baba alone knows the true contrition of the heart. Suffice it to say that Alison laid bare all the things she would have preferred not to say to me, and I knew there was some purpose behind it, for I dreamt it happened the previous night. Baba moves in mysterious and wonderful ways.

'Alison now knows that Inder was trying to awaken her to obedience, and that all that has happened has been to this end. Whatever difficulty she now faces . . . I do not think she will lose this understanding, so painfully earned.'

The next day another letter was received from Rose. She wrote:

'You'll see I have written — enclosed a copy . . . It is still not absolutely as it should be . . . I don't think I can get down far enough. Anyway it's gone now — I couldn't get it right last night but have typed it this morning and hope to dash out and get it posted express airmail. Can't write any more now. Love, Rose.'

The enclosed letter was most movingly written and I hesitate to include any part of it, as it came my way solely out of the exigences then current, and furthermore was written to Meher Baba. Yet I believe an extract is permissible, for it reveals that aspect of Rose that brought her to Baba in the first place, and which my recorded reactions and personal subjectivity may have sometimes obscured. So here is the first paragraph:

'Beloved, Merciful Father,

. . . I imagined that it was possible for me to surrender and to obey you. But you have taught me that I can do nothing of myself. Listening to others and following what they believed to be true was so wrong, and I lost my way and have been unable to act upon the promptings of my innermost heart. Each time I have questioned or doubted, *something* seemed to come between and I was unable to do anything . . . this has been such weakness — please, please forgive me.'

I went to see her that afternoon and found her much happier. She said she had begun to feel better as soon as she posted the letter. Adi's reply to myself came on Thursday, and said the contents of my letter had brought joy to him — also that he had received a letter from Alison and had sent her an answer that day — which she had been asked to show Rose, Nell and myself.

I felt she would come along as soon as possible, and about half way through the morning she arrived on the doorstep. I enquired rather anxiously if she was all right, and she said, as if surprised, "Oh yes, perfectly —" and when I read her letter I knew why.

It was kind and merciful, and very beautifully expressed — not in the least like any communication I had seen before. Her letter had made Baba happy, and he was pleased to hear of her desire to obey him. There was a gentle rebuke that in future they should try to follow instructions, and not their own judgements, for Baba knew all, and saw further than their limited vision. His directions were always for the benefit of those concerned, and much time could have been saved had they obeyed in the first place.

The rest was couched in the kindest of terms, as if there had simply been a misunderstanding. They were all three asked to do their best to help Inder's father when he arrived, for Baba wished Inder to be taken to Ahmednagar to receive his embrace. There was no severity or admonition — only gentleness and love.

Alison said she had written again on Tuesday, reporting that hourly since receipt of her cable, she had seen more clearly what had happened. She had also sent an apology to Inder's father for causing him unnecessary anxiety through not answering his letters, and apologies too, to various others.

When she had gone I felt quite empty. Even now I was still not permitted to see Inder — yet the others had free access to him and care of him despite all that had occurred. Patrick too, in his present mood would not have proved hostile to my saying goodbye, but even this pathetic wish was denied me. I found it hard to understand.

Hopefully I looked next morning for a letter which might grant the required permission — but none came, and I was obliged to accept, none would. Baba, for some inscrutable reason, did not want it that way.

Was it really all over? Had I misinterpreted so radically the symbolism of my dreams? Always, I had been aware that Inder's 'baby' could symbolise a book he would assist me telepathically to write; or the group itself, with which I had apparently been relinked, neither of these necessitating his presence.

But there were other indications, which I could not ignore, and which pointed the way to seeming impossibilities. What of the intuitive perceptions too subtle to factually record? Or the things he had said to me in the very beginning, which I did not then grasp, nor retain sufficiently well to quote with accuracy? Above all, the interior certainty in my heart that lay beneath despair and emptiness and resignation . . . that one day he would come for me, my most beloved Teacher and, in his own words, "It would all be all right in the end . . . and very beautiful."

Cambridge
October 10th
1964

APPENDIX

    My script concluded on the day on which I caught up with current events; and because I was still forbidden contact with Inder, my circumstances at once reverted to much their former condition. On the 23rd of October (as I was later informed) — Alison, having grown increasingly exasperated by the indrawn and non-communicative state of her charge, deduced him psychologically deranged and placed him in a mental hospital. *She now fully accepted that she had 'obeyed' Inder when she should not have done, instead of Baba — and he had maintained his silent intensity and absorption and did not respond when told of his father's portending visit. She tried repeatedly to impress him with this — and reaped the beginnings of anger.* Suddenly afraid, she consulted her doctor, and on his advice (and without his prior contact with the patient) removed herself and Nell from the bungalow and allowed the doctor and attendants to descend upon Inder without warning. They restrained and injected him, removed him forcibly to hospital, and subjected him at once to electrical treatment of the most barbaric kind — all without prior sanction from Meher Baba or his own father.*

    Mercifully, he made a speedy recovery and also emerged from whatever state he was in, returning alone to India exactly one month later, on November 23rd.

    Throughout the entire month Alison remained in charge of his affairs and visited him daily. Rose and Nell also saw him, though less frequently. I was not given permission to see him at all. No doubt through this I found myself still very much an outsider;

---

* a reaction consistent with an indrawn and God-merged state of this intensity, if interrupted.

and the attitudes of the others, no longer actively hostile, were decidedly cool . . . as if our brief renewal of friendship had been obscured by their continued freedom and my sustained restrictions, permitting a temporary backward slide into former patterns.

In my many hours of solitary reflection, I remembered with due consideration my sadly prophetic dream of the straitjacket and manacles, and the power invested by Inder in Alison to use them. A question I often asked myself was — need she have done so? Was the severe shock engendered in some way necessary for what he had to do? Did he used this means to gain access to an environment and its equipment where certain work for the future could thus be initiated? (bearing in mind Baba's own years of work with the psychically and psychologically disoriented, also the insane, in India)† . . . Or was there a choice? I did not know. But beyond doubt it caused him much suffering.

It was all too much for Rose, who several months later turned away and denounced Baba as a fraud, a man who "thought he was God", and Inder as a false teacher who had "taught them all the wrong things". Alison, however, unwaveringly held on to her convictions, though they have of necessity remained in the background of her life; and reverted by degrees to her former warm and loving self.

In December, I received a note from Adi with a curious message from Baba. He said I should now 'forget Inder Sain' and live a normal, worldly life. Shortly afterwards Alison had a letter from Inder containing details of his meeting with Baba. He had been told to "forget Kate Merton" and that he may "write three letters to Alison", of which this was the first. He thanked her most affectionately for her past care and companionship and stressed how much the latter had meant to him. Alison read it aloud to me in the New Year of 1965.

In January, too, she was asked, via Inder, to circulate a general message from Baba to all members of the former group, a task she promptly accomplished. In the course of this she recontacted Nigel, and as a direct result they were very soon reunited. They moved to Devon at the time of their reunion, and

† described in detail in 'The Wayfarers' by William Donkin.

for many years lived an active business and social life there, with Nigel again setting the tone of their activities.

Our friendship was fully restored in the course of time, mainly by letter, though we did meet occasionally — and the love and affection between us today is strong and real. We seldom reminisce, but in 1979 the matter of Inder arose from other issues, and by post Alison included the following among comments on the past, which I present for its relevance.

'One evening when Inder was leaving Cowper Road, he said to Rose and myself that we must always be alert to the danger of any one of Baba's people leading us astray. We must always judge for ourselves and if necessary consult Baba. "No matter who tells you something, do not follow without checking. Even if I am the one," or words very similar. I remember laughing at him and saying I couldn't imagine him leading us astray! Strange I did not recall this until long after all the happenings at Sawston and elsewhere.'

My contact with the London group commenced in January 1965 and opened a new world to me, into which both my children were drawn. It was a time of friendship, goodwill and total reacceptance. And in June of that year Inder returned to England and stayed once again at Nell's bungalow. Alison was now in Devon, and Rose had moved on to other things. My instructions had all been cancelled the previous April, and I thus saw him daily for several weeks, and my children visited him frequently.

It was a very strange interlude. I had hoped it would prove the beginning of all he had intimated, and was perplexed by the inner awareness that it could not be so — and after a month he was recalled to India for work elsewhere. During the time I spent with him, in some manner he veiled his light and I could not see him as before, though I was well aware that this was done intentionally. A few days before his departure he sat with me alone, quietly smoking, in Nell's small sittingroom — and suddenly I saw his light had been released and was irradiating his whole being. In silence we sat on opposite sides of the hearth, his face immobile and intent, his eyes fixed unblinkingly on mine. My consciousness expanded, and I re-experienced a former Peruvian contact with him, in which, as Teacher and pupil, we sat facing each other just as we did now. Through the media of his eyes he imparted to me a potent stream of information — which I regis-

tered as light so brilliant it temporarily dazzled me, leaving me slightly dazed. After perhaps an hour the impetus was withdrawn and he again indrew the visual luminosity, refusing to discuss what had occurred.

On our last afternoon together, having sadly gone to say goodbye — I asked if all the things he had once told me would ever now come to pass. He gazed at me steadily and replied, "When right time comes, Kate, when right time comes! You have to wait for others." Then he smiled suddenly and said, just as he had done at the very beginning, "Mature wine is best, Madam!"

After his return to India there was no further contact. He sent a letter of thanks to Nell for her hospitality, but neither letter or message to me. I heard by a roundabout route he had also written to a young woman patient (now discharged) from the adjoining ward to his own in his hospital days. A point well rubbed in and indicating that little had changed. Yet in dreams he communicated events of significance just as before; acting seemingly as an intermediary for Baba, who himself appeared prior to situations of a particularly powerful nature.*

In one dream, exceptionally lucid, I walked in bright sunlight with a long column of people towards an unknown destination, and Inder approached from further along the line and fell into step beside me. He looked me full in the face and said clearly, "It will all happen again, Kate", and the sunlight dimmed, and I saw the cyclic recurrence of events gone by.

And it did happen. The strangely intricate working I had already experienced, repeated again with the London group — with whom I now had many close friendships. The situation arose quite innocuously, and concerned the original m.s. of this account.

At the height of the delightful warmth and approbation found with these new relationships, came an offer for me to pioneer and supervise a new Centre — to be funded from a proposed joint business venture with a person held in the highest regard by the entire movement. This man had shown great interest in the original Cambridge group activities, and in my later efforts at continuance with quite new people (initially very successfully) —

---

* Or perhaps my mind created this division as a means of accurately translating degrees of consequence?

and also in me personally. He was convinced a mistaken view was held by certain of the staff in India, whom he felt had confused me with Alison, and he wished now to have this put right. So because of his position, and my own desire to clarify with absolute honesty what had occurred, I passed him my script before proceeding further. I recall even now his affectionate and warmly approving smile as he said benevolently that nothing it contained could make any difference . . . but I was later sent for, praised for my mystical perception of Baba, and advised, very firmly, to retract my statements concerning Inder . . . whom he, and all the London people, knew was "just an ordinary man". If I agreed (and he was quite sure that I would, as so much depended upon it) then all that had been planned could continue as arranged, and my "work for Baba" would be crowned with joy and success.

But I could not do this, and immediately said so; and this was reiterated when pressurised by others of similar status. At last in despair I despatched the offending manuscript by airmail direct to Baba, who sent me a card via Adi, to say he had "placed it aside, to be read or destroyed when he gave the instruction". In the meantime, other confrontations had occurred and my position was clearly untenable. Baba was again approached, this time by the truly charming man who had so recently sponsored me, and as a consequence, in January 1967 I was severed from the movement seemingly irrevocably — though not ostensibly by Baba . . . by two persons of consequence in India and my friend in England, whom he had authorised to deal with the situation as they thought best — without troubling him further in the matter.

We all have our little day of power; and to these good people whose integrity was beyond dispute (and whom I regarded highly), Inder was assuredly "just an ordinary man" . . . They remembered, too, the earlier furore in Cambridge, and the deluded young woman who had presumably been responsible for it all.

In fairness, they gave me a final opportunity to make amends — I was, after all, an absolutely dedicated follower of Baba — this was to agree that I would never again, in speech or writing, promote this completely erroneous misconception;* and when I

---

* I did not this time state that Inder was a Master but I would not agree that he was just an ordinary man, and said why. Nobody believed me.

could not give this promise, it was my name that was circulated, as punishment, amongst the whole of Baba's following in England, India and the U.S.A., thus expelling me in disgrace. The suffering thereby caused to me, and mine, was immense.

A month later, although my frantic letter and urgent cable† and been withheld from Baba, (as someone was kind enough to inform me), I sent a message combined with cabled birthday‡ wishes in the hope that it would inadvertantly be read out amongst the deluge of other greetings — so worded that it might escape notice by my erstwhile friends. And this is what must have happened, for Baba sent a telegraphed reply, by return, through one of the helpers, expressing His happiness at my surrender to Him Alone. And this, too, evoked no comment, and did not reopen the gates so firmly closed by those in authority.

Within a year of this traumatic event, my life made other links and moved into fresh channels of learning and experience.

In January 1969, Meher Baba died — a matter I knew of perceptively despite my exile, and I soon discovered that in certain ways he had beforehand ensured my continued connection with the teaching impetus. But that is another story, along with the many insights and perceptions that accompanied the whole of the foregoing.

Patrick and I separated intermittently from the spring of 1965 onwards, by the simple expedient of his total abandonment of me for months on end. My marriage finally concluded in 1968, and I afterwards applied for a divorce. In due time he was fortunate, and eventually remarried; also achieving distinction in his new career. He was given the things he had asked for so long ago, and I was deeply glad for him.

My mother, having cut me almost entirely from her life for seventeen years, read Baba's discourses when recovering from a stroke — and said, with grieved astonishment, "Why, he is just like Jesus . . ." Her remorse was tragic, though sadly too late to do what she wished to do — in this lifetime anyway.

As a closing thought, I recall my last glimpse of Inder in the July of 1965. We stood alone for a few minutes in Nell's front garden at the bottom of a cul-de-sac, myself reluctant to go, and

---

† Both telling Baba what had been done in his name.
‡ Baba's birthday was February 25th.

suppressing the tears that relentlessly stung my eyelids. I tried to kiss him goodbye — but he would not permit this, abruptly averting his face — and instead, took my hand. Sadly I thought even this last human gesture he had refused me . . . and now I realise why, as I also recognise other signs long buried.

For he cared for me too, in his humanity, in a way I dared not then believe. It was hard for him, as well as I — perhaps harder . . . to send me forth, on my own, to face all that he knew awaited me. Head high, and fighting back the tears, I walked away from him down the street, feeling his gaze on my back as he spurred me on . . .

And he watched me . . . right to the end . . .

Langton Green
Kent
July 1984